THE WORD IN STONE

THE WORD
IN STONE

The Role of Architecture
in the National Socialist Ideology

Robert R. Taylor

UNIVERSITY OF CALIFORNIA PRESS
BERKELEY, LOS ANGELES, LONDON

University of California Press
Berkeley and Los Angeles, California
University of California Press, Ltd.
London, England

For
Marjory and Angus
Taylor

Contents

Preface and Acknowledgments

As THIS study is based primarily on books about architecture, I owe a special debt of gratitude to Miss Sylvia Osterbind, Reference Librarian at Brock University and to her efficient assistants working on interlibrary loan. The staff of the West German Federal Archives in Koblenz were also helpful as were the librarians of the Rare Book Room at the Library of Congress in Washington, D.C. The Institute für Zeitgeschichte in Munich supplied me with very useful microfilmed material. Mr. Charles Thomas and Mr. James Trimble of the Still Photograph Division of the National Archives in Washington, and Mr. Jerry Kearns of the Prints and Photographs Division of the Library of Congress gave me invaluable assistance in seeking illustrations. Dr. Roland Klemig of the Bildarchiv in Berlin's Staatsbibliothek was also patient with my inquiries. The Audio-visual Department of Brock University, especially Mr. Wayne Windjack, quickly and correctly handled my requests for photoduplication. My typists, Mrs. Sally Pardy, Mrs. Jean Czop, Miss Lynne Teather, and my wife, Anne Taylor, did superior work, even under pressure.

Special thanks are owed to Herr Albert Speer, who unhesitatingly answered a host of queries and who shed an invaluable light on many problems. Herr Speer and Professor Gordon Craig, of Stanford University, read the original dissertation, upon which this book is based, and offered many useful, constructive criticisms. Frau Professor Gerdy Troost, although indisposed, was kind enough to answer several questions. Professor Gerald Feldman, of the University of California at Berkeley, offered many constructive suggestions. Professors Donald Goodspeed and Wesley Turner of Brock University's History Department read and commented helpfully on several chapters, and I was ably assisted in matters of translation by Professors Claude Owen, Herbert Schütz, and Donald McRae of the Brock German Department. My wife Anne offered continual moral support and believed throughout six years that eventually something interesting would emerge from my work.

Of course, I alone am responsible for any errors or misconceptions which may appear in the study, and, unless otherwise indicated in the footnotes or bibliography, for the translations.

Very little serious work has been done on the relationship between the National Socialist government of Germany and the arts. Art historians, when they deal with this problem, usually express only moral disapproval, which, justifiable though it may be, does not aid in understanding the phenomenon. Most other professional historians, interested in political, diplomatic, military, or socio-economic issues, nearly ignore the arts. Popularizers and journalists concentrate on the sensational elements of Nazi rule, and, if they mention the arts, stress only the effort at totalitarian control and the ensuing corruption of aesthetic values. The present study tries to fill a gap, but, of course, is only a tentative beginning. More precisely, it begins where Barbara Miller Lane concluded her "Architecture and Politics in Germany 1919–1945." Although it does not, in fact, go very far into "Nazi" architecture itself, it was her work which gave me the impetus to complete my own study and which also explained some of the origins of the view that there could be a peculiarly "German" architecture. I am also indebted to Anna Teut, who has edited a collection of excerpts from articles, speeches, letters, and books, *Architektur im Dritten Reich*, which was invaluable. For my part, I have studied right-wing nationalist, including *völkisch*, attitudes to architecture in the nineteen-thirties, as expressed in published, and, of course, state-approved, works. Much more investigation, however, needs to be done on National Socialist *Kunstpolitik*, particularly in such an area as the *Thing* theater. My own work will have succeeded if it inspires criticism and further research.

R. R. T.

List of Illustrations

CHAPTER ONE

The Significance of "National Socialist" Architecture

THE CONCEPT of genuinely "German," or "National Socialist," architecture, expressed in writings during the Third Reich, grew out of right-wing nationalist thought, much of which was permeated with *völkisch* ideas. Disillusioned by the Germany that emerged after the 1871 unification, radical nationalists sought even before 1914 to "purify" German culture and society of modern or foreign elements. Their movement flourished later in the Weimar Republic, until 1933 when it became state policy. However, it began long before the First World War.

Through the diplomacy and wars of the Prussian Chancellor Otto von Bismarck the German states were unified into a new Reich between 1866 and 1871. In the following forty-three years, this powerful new state enjoyed considerable economic prosperity as well as wide respect in Europe and the world. However, it was also prey to domestic tensions and was the object of foreign hostility. The sudden emergence of a new power in central Europe unnerved its neighbors, particularly after 1890, when Kaiser Wilhelm II placed himself in Bismarck's shoes and followed a more ambitious and more bellicose foreign policy. The Germans themselves reacted to foreign hostility by developing a sense of "encirclement" (*Einkreisung*). Further tension was created by the social revolution that was taking place. The rising numbers and potential power of the working classes frightened many of the bourgeoisie and upper classes. By 1912, the Social Democratic party, with its vocabulary of revolution, held 110 out of 397 seats in the Reichstag. Furthermore, the rapid industrialization of Germany after the eighteen-fifties with concurrent urbanization and growth of factory districts and slums upset people accustomed to a slower rhythm of life in small cities and quiet towns.

Thus, despite Germany's expanding economy and international power, many Germans experienced a sense of malaise. A new, fervent nationalism, unlike the earlier, more liberal, nationalist movement, developed. Right-wing nationalists opposed the socialists, in defence of order, respect for the Kaiser, and love of the traditional values of the Fatherland. They were suspicious of "foreign" Catholics and even of liberals, and soon became influenced by *völkisch* thought. Often the disciples of alienated intellectuals such as Julius Langbehn (1851–1907) and Paul de Lagarde (1827–1891),[1] the *völkisch* groups yearned for a romanticized past, before industrialization and liberal bourgeois or socialist values had profoundly altered Germany: they idealized the life of the German peasant, whom they imagined to have been — and still to be — racially "pure." The term, *völkisch*, which has no exact English equivalent, derives from *Volk*, "the people" or "the race," but also implies an otherworldly and eternal essence. The *völkisch* writers tried to protect and foster the *Volk*'s allegedly natural tendency to spiritual unity and their supposedly innate sense of communion with the "German" landscape. Xenophobic men like Lagarde wanted to eliminate Semitic and Roman, indeed all "Western," elements from German culture and to return to a

---

[1] On these two critics, as well as Arthur Moeller van den Bruck (1876–1924), see Fritz Stern, *Politics of Cultural Despair: A Study in the Rise of the Germanic Ideology*, Berkeley and Los Angeles, University of California Press, 1961. On anti-Semitism, see P. G. J. Pulzer, *Rise of Political Anti-Semitism in Germany and Austria*, New York, Wiley, 1966. This cultural criticism came mainly from the right of the political spectrum; the left, of course, had its own ideological concerns, often patriotic, but less racist.

pure "Germanic" way of life and religion. Before the First World War, *völkisch* thought had developed an attitude to the arts as well, maintaining that great works of art could emerge only from the German *Volk*; that is, from an organically linked "Aryan" or "Nordic" community (*Gemeinschaft*), racially "unpolluted" and with its roots in the "German" soil. Langbehn, for example, lamented what he thought was the decline of German culture, which he claimed was due to democracy, science, and modern urban life in general; his *Rembrandt als Erzieher* (1890) praised this "Nordic" genius, whose creativity was allegedly blood-based. In general, then, this was the "blood and soil" outlook.

Völkisch ideas penetrated the German educational system in the early nineteenth century.[2] Later, they emerged vividly in the Youth Movement, a nature-loving reaction of mainly middle class adolescents and young people against what they felt was the stultifying, artificial and materialist life of their parents in the last decade of the nineteenth century.[3] These youths, after they grew out of their hiking and camping expeditions to romantic areas of the German countryside became some of the teachers and professors who intensified *völkisch* influences in German schools. The *völkisch* attitude, meanwhile, also penetrated important right-wing nationalist groups such as the Conservative Party, the League of Landowners, and the Pan-German Association. Anti-Semitic groups were natural adherents of many *völkisch* views, and Wilhelm II's court chaplain, Adolf Stoecker (1835–1909), was both anti-Semitic and *völkisch* in many of his pronouncements in the highest, most respectable circles. Eventually, by 1914, the whole right wing of the German political spectrum was permeated by *völkisch* ideas.

Given their concern over Germany's social problems and lack of national unity, it was with an understandable relief and joy

[2] George Mosse, *Crisis of German Ideology: Intellectual Origins of the Third Reich*, New York, Grosset and Dunlap, 1964, pp. 1–10 and 149–203.

[3] Walter Z. Laqueur, *Young Germany: A History of the German Youth Movement*, New York, Basic Books, 1962, pp. 3–86.

that right-wing nationalist Germans began the patriotic defence
of their borders (for so it seemed to many) in 1914. In the elation
of August of that year, class differences and political rivalries
seemed buried in a *Burgfrieden* (civil peace or truce); the Kaiser
echoed the widespread feeling when he said that, for him, political parties were no longer important and that only "Germanness"
counted.[4]

This war, started with such high hopes, ended disastrously
for the Reich. By late 1918, not only was Germany defeated, but
the pillar of the old order, the monarchy, had been abolished,
and, even worse, the spectre of revolutionary violence appeared
throughout the Fatherland. This was a shock, especially to traditionally inclined Germans of the right. Of course, the "revolution"
of 1918 did not seriously change Germany's institutions, other
than the monarchy. The judiciary and the bureaucracy of the old
regime remained almost intact and still influential, and the Weimar Republic referred to itself officially as the *Reich* (empire).
The army, although reduced by the Versailles Treaty to 100,000
men, remained a reservoir of conservative and reactionary nationalism and was potentially strong. The cabinet and chancellor,
although theoretically the center of political power, deferred to
the interests of the army, and were unable to alter the attitudes
of judges and bureaucrats. Nevertheless, particularly to right-
wing nationalists, the democratic constitution was a kind of trea-
son and seemed to have been imposed by foreign enemies. In
fact, the new regime could do little to alleviate the tensions which,
decades earlier, had distressed cultural critics such as Lagarde
and which were now even more troublesome. Despite the repara-
tions exacted by the Versailles Treaty, Germany remained highly
industrialized, with urban centers, such as Berlin and Hamburg,
having populations over one million, and with a large socialist
proletariat. With the economic difficulties of the early twenties,

[4] *Reden des Kaisers: Ansprachen, Predigten und Trinksprüche Wilhelms II*,
report of the *Frankfurter Zeitung*, August 1, 1914, ed. by Ernst Johann, Munich,
Deutscher Taschenbuch Verlag, 1966, p. 125.

especially the inflation of 1923, which destroyed the savings of many of the bourgeoisie, the drab appearance of wartime German cities deteriorated even further as a symbol of the hard times into which Germans had fallen.[5] To many the culture of the twenties, moreover, seemed vulgar and decadent. Cinema, jazz, and *avant-garde* art as well as female emancipation were all disturbing; the visual violence of expressionist painters such as Emil Nolde (1867–1956) and Karl Schmidt-Rottluff (1884–) all too well reflected this turbulent era. On the political scene, the Social Democrats, representing many of the workers, were often in power, albeit in coalitions, and their radical cousins, the Communists, formed a German party in 1919, which won sixty-two seats (out of 472) in the elections of May 1924. Yet many Germans could remember the "good old days" before the war, and some remembered the time before the working classes and materialism seemed to have become a threat to traditional German values. Contemporary urban life, symbolized by smoke-belching factories and by the humiliating Treaty of Versailles, was repulsive to millions of nationalist Germans, and they looked for a way to return to a political and social status quo that in fact may never have existed.

Völkisch and radical nationalists found some hope after the war in the old Conservative party; if *völkisch* elements did not actually control its leadership, they nevertheless determined its public image and helped to spread and to make respectable *völkisch* views in the new republic. Significantly, the party changed its name to *Deutschnationale Volkspartei*. Hitler's *Nationalsozialistische Deutsche Arbeiterpartei* increasingly supported a *völkisch* attitude, too, as did several other groups, such as the long-established Pan-Germans and the newer *Stahlhelm*, the veteran's organization. Right-wing publishing houses, such as Diederichs and Callwey, were the literary voices of nationalist and *völkisch* writ-

---

[5] During the war, for example, copper roofing was often removed for military use. Wartime drabness in Berlin was noted by Hans Peter Hanssen, *Dairy of a Dying Empire*, Bloomington, Indiana, Indiana University Press, 1955, pp. 131 and 278.

ers. By 1933, therefore, the radical rightist ideology was a firmly established part of the German political scene.

In the nineteenth century, *völkisch* critics were not much concerned with architecture, although by the turn of the century, they had influenced Paul Schultze-Naumburg (1869–1949), an architect and writer. It was after 1918 that these enthusiasts turned their guns on modern architecture, in defence of tradition and "German" building. In the twenties, some progressive German architects proclaimed that only a stark, geometrical style of building was suitable for the twentieth century. Gathered mainly around Walter Gropius (1883–1969) and his *Bauhaus* school, they rejected the heavy styles of decoration and the historical imitation of the later nineteenth century. (See illustration no. 1). They felt that since the neo-classical architect Karl Friedrich Schinkel (1781–1841), German — and indeed European — architects had gone astray, trying only to imitate the building styles of the past and ignoring the qualities of new building materials such as steel, glass, and concrete, as well as the new problems of a mass society, such as the need for cheap housing. The neo-Gothic of the Munich City Hall (1888–1908) or the neo-baroque of the Berlin Protestant Cathedral (1894–1905) (see illustrations nos. 5 and 11) were regarded as creative dead ends, inexpressive of the mood of the industrial age, which needed an objective (*sachlich*) or functional style to express its character. Moreover, a simple, efficient style was better suited to the inexpensive construction of proletarian apartments. This movement was not born during the Weimar period, for Gropius had begun designing factories with glass walls (such as the Fagus shoe factory at Alfeld) before 1911, when other European architects had also begun to reject historical imitation. (This drive had led, in part, to the *art nouveau* or *Jugendstil* form of decoration and to a revival of neo-classicism.) However, after 1919, *avant-garde* architecture became more acceptable; commissions, particularly from city governments, were granted to Gropius and Mies van der Rohe (1886–1970); the city council of Frankfurt, for example, commissioned the modernist Ernst May (1886–) to design several large housing developments (*Siedlungen*).

Of course, what bothered some nationalist Germans about the new architecture was simply its newness. It was different. Coming at a time of diplomatic and military disaster for the nation and at a time of economic tribulations for individuals, "objectivity" offended wide strata of the general public. Moreover, many of the new architects, such as Bruno Taut (1880–1938) had idealistic visions of a new social order; or like Ernst May, had no hesitation about working in the Soviet Union; or like Gropius, had vague socialist sympathies. Therefore, not only were the new flat roofs called ugly and impractical, and the glass walls cold and inhuman, but modern architecture became associated with the revolution which (even after 1919) was felt to threaten Germany and with all the misfortunes which had overwhelmed the Fatherland since 1918. Right-wing nationalist Germans and their radical *völkisch* allies wanted buildings recalling more stable times and somehow expressing specifically "German" values, which the blank façades and stark lines of the *Bauhaus* style did not.

In the early thirties, there was a conjunction of these two discontents: the general dislike of Germany's political and economic situation and the specific dislike of *avante-garde* architecture, as a symbol of that situation.[6] The National Socialist party, with its ramshackle, often contradictory, but very nationalist ideology, seemed capable of solving contemporary national problems, including even architectural problems. The Nazis promised to

[6] The political reaction to *avant-garde* architecture is well described by Barbara Miller Lane, *Architecture and Politics in Germany: 1918–45*, Cambridge, Mass., Harvard University Press, 1968, especially chapters 3, 5, and 6. The title of this work is not completely accurate, since it deals in greatest depth with the period 1918–1933. On the work of Walter Gropius and the *Bauhaus* see Hans M. Wingler, *Das Bauhaus 1919–1933: Weimar, Dessau, Berlin, und die Nachfolge in Chicago seit 1937*, Bramsche, Rasch, 1968. Of course, conservative Germans were not the only Europeans to reject *avant-garde* architecture. See Anthony Jackson's *The Politics of Architecture: A History of Modern Architecture in Britain*, Toronto, University of Toronto Press, 1970.

rescue Germany from her lamentable economic, social, military, and cultural position. The Nazi "philosopher," Alfred Rosenberg (1893–1946) came out strongly against some destructive aspects of modern urban life, and promised that, along with a return to more suitable "German" standards of dress and behavior for women and less "foreign" influence in the arts, a new style of building – a "German" style – would develop. The vast majority of architects still favored traditional styles at this time and many were strongly nationalist. The economic troubles of the Weimar period had led some into unemployment. Hence it was natural that they should gladly accept commissions from the new Nazi government after 1933 and that like-minded writers on architecture should publish books and articles on the new "German" building. By 1939, radical "Bolshevik" architecture seemed to have been defeated, and new structures appeared in German cities and in the countryside which seemed to express time-honored "German" values. So noticeable was the monumental type of new Nazi-approved architecture that many foreigners talked about these as "Nazi" architecture, or the "Nazi" style. For many Germans, however, these structures were not specifically "Nazi" (or the products of a dictated party line), although they were obviously built under the aegis of the government of the Third Reich. The important thing for right-wing nationalists was that the party seemed to have done something in many fields, including architecture, to exclude foreign or socialist influences, and to buttress a way of life which they held to be genuinely German.

The use of the word "ideology" here is not meant to imply a hard and fast set of doctrines which can easily be labelled "National Socialist"; however, the Germany of the Third Reich saw an awkward confluence of strands of nationalist thought, political as well as esthetic, which had long prevailed in disparate spheres. These themes appear in official pronouncement as well as in private declarations of ideals, goals, and values. In general, the approved commentators were right-wing nationalists; many were totally or partially *völkisch* in inspiration. As for those who truly believed in what seemed to be the party's ideology, this is a theme too complex for this study. Perhaps for some of the party leaders, such as Goebbels and Hitler, the ideology was merely a tool for the attainment and holding of power. However, some men, such as Alfred Rosenberg, seemed to sincerely want to tie some of the strands together in a system — a difficult task, since many of these ideas were contradictory. For other men, such as Albert Speer (1905–), the intense nationalism of the ideology, not its anti-Semitism or any other specifically political element, was the decisive factor; in his case, one element of the ideology was accepted; another, ignored. The appeal of the "Leader" himself was also important, for Speer and many others. For the mass of the people — and for political individuals who rose from the mass to declare their support for the regime — the ideology was neither a creed nor a smokescreen. Most architects or writers on architecture mentioned in this study thought that, in fighting *avant-garde* architecture, or in fostering a "German" style, they were saving the Fatherland from "Bolshevism." For them, participation in a nationalist movement (*Bewegung*) was more important than learning any Nazi catechism.

The government's building program was impressive. However, whether such structures as the monumental Zeppelin Field in Nuremberg incorporate specifically "German" values is another matter. The leading German architect of the thirties, Albert Speer believes that there was no such thing as a "Nazi" style, and holds that the Nazi ideology had little to do with the appearance of the tribune of his Zeppelin Field, because its neo-classical lines derive from an earlier period and a wider, European movement.[7] On the other hand, the commentators (some writing before 1933) thought that such a "Nationalist Socialist" style, expressing "German" and nationalist concepts definitely did exist, and hoped that it could fully reflect the spiritual revolution that had allegedly

[7] Interview with Albert Speer, June 13, 1968, in Heidelberg-Schlierbach.

occurred in Germany. In fact, Speer and these writers are both
partially correct. The contemporary attitude to architecture was
eclectic; a "German" or "Nazi" quality was expressed through different styles of varying backgrounds. As will be shown, this in-
choate theory of architecture influenced much of the building in
the Hitler period, as well as the copious writing on new buildings.

Considering the great number of books on architecture in the
Third Reich, one might assume that much was the cynical propaganda of a totalitarian regime and that the official view of architecture resulted from a need to impress the masses. But the government's attitude was not new or revolutionary. There was indeed no one unified "Nazi style," and the many styles and views of
style had their roots before 1933, even before 1914. Moreover,
most of the writing on architecture in the thirties had some popular appeal insofar as it reflected nationalism. In this regard, the
idea of "community" (Gemeinschaft), to be expressed in vast
meeting places and in Thing theaters (outdoor amphitheaters) is
an important part of the contemporary attitude. This nationalist
view of architecture was by and large sincerely held, and was not
a façade. Most of Hitler's architects and writers believed in their
work.

In the nationalist literature on good "German" architecture,
particularly in comments on the new Chancellery in Berlin, völkisch and right-wing nationalist views merged, as they often did
even before 1933. Yet a difference between the two forms of fervent nationalism is also evident, for not all right-wing nationalists
were totally völkisch in outlook. Hitler, who commissioned the
Chancellery, did not use explicitly völkisch terms in describing it.
Although publicly he passed for a nationalist, he was, of course,
most concerned with self-glorification through impressive buildings. Speer, the nationalist architect who designed it, was concerned to produce a neo-classical structure which might reflect
glory on Germany. Many other nationalist writers and architects
who commented on it stressed its "Prussian" or "German" quali-

ties; that is, its "clear" lines and "orderly" layout, using a vocabulary bordering on the *völkisch*. Others, thoroughly imbued with the "blood and soil" ideology, reveled in the fact that "German" stones from the "German" earth, in "German" tones of beige or brown were used. This shading of right-wing nationalist expression is found in most of the architecture books and articles approved for publication in the Third Reich.

Lack of one typical "Nazi" style was no sign of an indifferent attitude to building. What was built, and how, was of supreme importance to both Nazi political leaders and to sympathetic writers on culture. Of course, architecture had a special impor-tance to the politicians, who, like most totalitarian leaders, sought to influence all aspects of human life.[8] But they were supported by many nationalist commentators who believed that the leadership could influence what Germans planned and built as a means of developing the bonds of the German community. Because these commentators viewed particular styles as representative of other ideologies, they tried to combat Germany's political enemies by denouncing undesirable styles.[9] Yet their approach was more than merely negative. They wanted to build. Especially in the new representative (or official) buildings, the fact of the German revolution was to be made apparent everywhere.

Moreover, not only major cities, but small villages as well, were to express the achievement and the nature of the German people. The very face of the land was to be transformed. It was not enough to limit "Marxist" or "liberal" architecture. The new buildings must proclaim to the world and to the unconverted German that the era of the "thousand-year Reich" had dawned. Obviously, then, in seeking to influence the foreign visitor with its overpowering representative edifices, the Third Reich was didactic and theatrical. This was even more true for the domestic audi-

---

[8] This viewpoint is thoroughly developed by Helmut Lehmann-Haupt in his *Art under a Dictatorship*, New York, Oxford University Press, 1954.

[9] On the Nazi attitude to Marxism and to "Bolshevik" architecture, see Lane, *Architecture and Politics*.

ence, the *Volk*. Architects were encouraged to make the living masses themselves a part of the great theater in which National Socialist truths were proclaimed and taught. In the Nuremberg celebrations, on the many parade squares, and above all in the *Thing* places, architecture and *Volk* were to merge in a spiritual communion of all "Aryans," living and dead, above and within the soil which bred them.

Despite the lack of a single unified style, therefore, one idea united most of the important new buildings of the time. Each was supposed to express or teach the idea of "community." The half-timbered cottages were to do so implicitly, suggesting the "good old days" when Germans lived close to the nourishing soil. The stadiums and amphitheaters were to do so explicitly, not only in their triumphant statement of the German community's power, but through the ceremonies which took place within their walls. The message was always present, whether in the imposing colonnade of Zeppelin Field, or in the quieter mood of a settlement of thatched-roof homes. All were to speak of the importance to the German of his racial community, and to the world of the power of that race.[10] This didactic architecture, then, had an important role to play in proclaiming the National Socialist ideology.

There are recurrent motifs which, in large representative structures, characterize architecture of the Third Reich. These buildings have neo-classical colonnades (of columns or, more often, pillars), severe porticoes, horizontal lines and a rectilinear appearance emphasized by heavy cornices and rows of thickly-framed windows. The traditional elaboration of columns with bases or capitals was simplified and the quality of the stone itself was stressed. Both these trends suggest that the "Nazi" architects were aware of the *avant-garde* drive for simplicity and for stress on the texture of building materials. *Führer* balconies for speech

[10] Unity of style was not considered essential by Werner Rittich, a Nazi writer on "German" architecture. See his *Architektur und Bauplastik der Gegenwart*, 3rd ed., Berlin, Rembrandt, 1938, p. 164. Rittich assisted Robert Scholz after 1936 as editor of *Die völkische Kunst*, a racist journal, becoming sole editor himself.

making are common. In general, a heavy neo-classicism was the most obvious characteristic of the monumental style of the Third Reich.

The Nazi regime also stimulated building in traditional rural or medieval styles. This *völkisch* trend was marked by different styles for different areas of Germany, since architects sought to build with local and natural materials: stone and brick were preferred to concrete. Sloping roofs and hand-carved fixtures, such as traditional, wooden horses' heads on the ends of roofs were common. Older structures were to be preserved and all new buildings in the countryside were to be in the indigenous German style.[11]

Symbolism, graphic art, and hortatory inscriptions were prominent in all forms of Nazi-approved architecture. The eagle with the wreathed swastika, heroic friezes, and free-standing sculpture were common. Often mottoes or quotations from *Mein Kampf* or Hitler's speeches were placed over doorways or carved into walls.[12] The Nazi message was conveyed in friezes which extolled labor, motherhood, the agrarian life, and other values. Muscular nudes, symbolic of military and political strength, guarded the entrance to the Berlin Chancellery. Alexander von Senger, who was especially concerned with the "Bolshevik menace," noted that as Communist architects hated the "ornamental-creative" in architecture, the Nazi movement should therefore revive it and develop the "mythic-symbolic-magic" powers of

[11] This was not a new concern in Germany; see, for example, Albrecht Haupt, *Die älteste Kunst: Insbesondere die Baukunst der Germanen von den Völkerwanderungen bis zu Karl den Grossen* Leipzig, Degener, 1909, pp. 155–156. (Haupt was an architect and a historian.) It is obviously not always political or nationalistic to wish to preserve older buildings in characteristic styles. Reconstruction of prehistoric villages, or preservation of medieval houses, was not necessarily *völkisch* or "Nazi" in inspiration. However, in the thirties, this concern for German historical architecture was often xenophobic.

[12] An inscription at the Vogelsang *Ordensburg* addressed the Nazi trainees: "You are the nation's torchbearers; you carry the light of the spirit forward into battle." Rittich, *Architektur und Bauplastik*, p. 33.

architecture.[13] The swastika was the most recurrent of these symbols, often appearing in the wreath grasped by the German eagle's talons, but sometimes stylized into a geometric pattern, as on the ceiling of the porch of the House of German Art in Munich. (See illustration no. 79.) The oak leaf in wreaths or branches, was another recurrent symbol used in patterns; the oak tree itself was often part of architectural planning and landscaping, as on the Nuremberg Party Rally Grounds, where it symbolized "German" strength rooted in the "German" earth. Indeed, for Hitler, as for many others, buildings themselves were symbols. "We are erecting," he said, "the shrines and symbols of a new and noble culture."[14]

In short, these buildings were supposed to appeal to German right-wing nationalism. Their style and symbols reflected a desire to affirm the values and to buttress the strength of a closely knit racial community. The government literally built on this concept. Fortunately for the government, many were willing to believe that Germany had been revived by an ideology that was traditional and nationalist, not revolutionary. Its edifices were therefore supposed to be the expression, as Hitler said, of "the Word in stone."[15]

[13] Alexander von Senger, "Der Baubolschewismus und seine Verkoppelungen mit Wirtschaft und Politik," *Nationalsozialistische Monatshefte*, V (1934), 497ff. Rosenberg also stressed the importance of symbols in building. See *Portrait eines Menschheitsverbrechers: Nach den hinterlassenen Memoiren des ehemaligen Reichsministers*, ed. by Serge Land and Ernst von Scheck, St. Gallen, Zollikofer, 1947, pp. 276–77.

[14] Hermann Rauschning, *Hitler Speaks: A Series of Political Conversations with Adolf Hitler on His Real Aims*, London, Thornton Butterworth, 1939, p. 262. On Hitler's understanding of how symbols and flags could serve to hold together a community, see Karlheinz Schmeer, *Das Regie des öffentlichen Leben im dritten Reich, Munich*, Pohl, 1956, pp. 13–14.

[15] For this speech at the German Architecture and Crafts Exhibition in Munich, January 22, 1938, see Max Domarus, ed., *Adolf Hitler: Reden und Proklamationen 1932–45*, Munich, Süddeutscher Verlag, 1965, p. 778. (Hereafter cited as Domarus, *Reden*.) See also N.H. Baynes, ed., *Speeches of Adolf Hitler*, New York, Fertig, 1969, I, 602. (Hereafter cited as Baynes, *Speeches*.) Here Hitler was probably plagiarizing from descriptions of Gothic cathedrals, whose sculptured walls and stained glass windows were supposed to communicate the "Word" of God.

CHAPTER TWO

Adolf Hitler and Architecture

ADOLF HITLER, a frustrated artist-architect, inspired the multifarious National Socialist ideology, amalgamating various of his own discontents with those of postwar Germans. Needless to say, his ideas on architecture also played an influential role in the Third Reich, so that many writers maintained that particular buildings were the expression of the *Führer's* ideas, and architects often declared that they were executing Hitler's will. About the design for the German pavilion at the 1937 Paris Exhibition, Albert Speer wrote, "We are realizing the ideas of the *Führer.*"[1] Contemporary writings on architecture often reflected Hitler's concepts, prejudices, and tastes, and writers created an image of Hitler as a great builder of the state, of the party, and of German cities. The talents of statesman and architect were apparently united in his genius. His plans and his ideas were praised. His earliest sketches were reproduced and admired.[2] He was the ex-

[1] Heinrich Hoffmann, ed., *Deutschland in Paris: Ein Bilderbuch von Heinrich Hoffmann*, Munich, Heinrich Hoffmann Verlag, 1937, p. 5. (Hoffmann was Hitler's photographer.)

[2] Some of Hitler's sketches and paintings were published during the Third Reich. See Adolf Hitler, *Sieben Aquarelle*, Munich, Eher, 1938. (These were all done during the First World War, four of the seven being of ruined buildings in Belgium.) Others have been reprinted in Heinrich Hoffman, *Hitler was my Friend*, London, Burke, 1955, p. 80; David Roxan and Ken Wanstall, *Jackdaw of Linz: The Story of Hitler's Art Thefts*, London, Cassell, 1964, p. 18ff; Albert Zoller, *Hitler Privat: Erlebnisbericht seiner Geheimsekretärin*, Düsseldorf, Droste, 1949, plate facing page 32.

pert to be cited in architectural matters. Hitler did have some talent for architecture and he agreed with many Germans in condemning modern art and architecture. Because so many Germans shared his reactionary and nationalist views, one can assume that there was much faith — misplaced, of course — in his abilities.

Hitler was a creative genius, wrote one Nazi.[3] His brilliance was supposedly evident on both politics and the arts. A writer in the *Völkischer Beobachter* believed that Hitler's political accomplishments had their origins in his artistic temperament.[4] Another commentator maintained that Hitler, "the architect, born and trained," shamed the Vienna Academy of Fine Arts which had rejected him for lack of talent.[5] It was Hitler's architectural bent, rather than his skill as a painter, which was praised most highly, and often with the note that the *Führer* was a man of the people, "an unknown soldier of the Great War," who became the "master builder of the Third Reich," and who possessed a "quite special and prominent architectural gift."[6] Many architects themselves as well as writers on architecture continued in this vein. For one architect, Rudolf Wolters, Hitler was the "supreme builder."[7] Because he possessed allegedly great gifts, he was customarily cited on matters of art and architecture. In *Die Stadt*, Werner Lindner

[3] Hans Severus Ziegler, *Wende und Weg: Kulturpolitische Reden und Aufsätze*, Weimar, Fritz Fink, 1937, pp. 3–4, (Ziegler was special advisor to the Nazi Minister of the Interior in Thuringia, 1930–1931; after 1934 he supervised the German National Theatre in Weimar.) Ziegler still thought highly of Hitler's artistic and architectural abilities in 1964. (Ziegler, *Adolf Hitler aus dem Erleben dargestellt*, Göttingen, Schütz, 1964, pp. 49–50 and 100–101.)

[4] Robert Scholz, "Kunst als Grundlage politischer Schöpferkraft," *Völkischer Beobachter*, Munich edition, April 24, 1936, front page; this article concerns Hitler's watercolors.

[5] Hermann Nasse, in *Die neue Literatur*, Heft 12 (1936), p. 736.

[6] Hermann Nasse, "Zum Geleit," preface, to Hitler's *Sieben Aquarelle*, p. 2.

[7] Wolters, *Albert Speer*, Oldenbourg, Stalling, 1943, p. 16. Another Nazi writer stated that "without the high cultural attitude of the Leader, there would have been no success in stopping the destruction of architectural Bolshevism and the barren leveling of its technoid madness." (Hans Kiener, "Germanische Tektonik," *Kunst im dritten Reich*, 1937, Vol. I, cited in Anna Teut, *Architektur im dritten Reich*, Berlin, Ullstein, 1967, p. 186. Kiener taught art history in Munich.)

and Erich Böckler's analysis of the decline of German city life and culture, Hitler's discussion in *Mein Kampf* of the same problem was cited; Wolters quoted from this source and from one of Hitler's speeches in his *Vom Beruf des Baumeisters*.[8] Furthermore, he was often presented graphically as the master builder; the frontispiece to Wolters' book on Albert Speer is a photograph of Hitler and Speer together poring over architectural plans.[9] (Of course, Hitler enjoyed having himself described as an artist and architect; some of these comments must have been centrally dictated or inspired by a desire to flatter.)

An examination of Hitler's youth shows that he had no training in architecture, but did possess some natural talent. The story of his youthful ambitions and disappointments is well known. In school, he was successful at sketching, and therefore decided to become an artist.[10] However, he graduated from the lower *Realschule* with a poor record, and never attended an upper Realschule; he was thus unlikely to gain entrance to any school of art or architecture in Austria. Yet, he had a slight hope for acceptance, because some fine-arts academies and architecture schools occasionally made exceptions for applicants with obvious talents.[11] Perhaps with this in mind, he allegedly studied

[8] Werner Lindner and Erich Böckler, *Die Stadt: Ihre Pflege und Gestaltung* Munich, Callwey, 1939, pp. 13–15. (Lindner wrote for the *Deutscher Heimatbund*; Böckler was an architect.) Rudolf Wolters, *Vom Beruf des Baumeisters*, Berlin, Volk und Reich, 1944, p. 45.

[9] Wolters, *Albert Speer*, The official Munich art exhibition of 1939 contained a large painting of Hitler as a sculptor-architect. (Described in Lehmann-Haupt, *Art*, p. 49.)

[10] On Hitler's public school education, see Bradley F. Smith, *Adolf Hitler: His Family, Childhood and Youth*, Stanford, Hoover Institution, 1967, pp. 55–100. On his youthful love of art, see *ibid.*, pp. 109–150; *Mein Kampf* (trans. by Ralph Manheim, Boston, Houghton Mifflin, 1962, p. 17; August Kubizek, *The Young Hitler I Knew*, translated by E. V. Anderson, Boston, Houghton Mifflin, 1955, pp. 82–84; Franz Jetzinger, *Hitlers Jugend: Phantasien, Lügen — und die Wahrheit*, Wien, Europa, 1956, p. 105; Konrad Heiden, *Der Fuehrer: Hitler's Rise to Power*, Boston, Houghton Mifflin, 1944, p. 49.

[11] Several of his contemporaries (Peter Behrens, Bruno Paul, Hermann Giessler, and Paul Schultze-Naumburg) became architects without formal training. If Hitler had known this, it might have given him hope.

drawing at a private art school in Munich during tht fall of 1905,[12] but he failed the written examination and the test drawing for the Vienna Academy of Fine Arts in 1907. He reapplied in 1908 and was again rejected. Nevertheless, the rector of the Academy praised his potential gift for architecture; "It was incomprehensible to him," Hitler claimed, "that I had never attended an architectural school or received any other training in architecture."[13] The young man was shocked that he had been refused, but took heart from the rector's recommendations: "In a few days," he said, "I myself knew that I should some day become an architect."[14] Although without a better academic background, he could not enter the Technical Academy, Hitler does not seem to have been thoroughly cast down; he would teach himself.

After he settled in Vienna, Hitler decided to try to find work with Heilmann und Littmann (a firm of architects) "as a designer,"[15] and therefore had to train himself with this goal in mind. Here, he had some success. Although his attitude was dilettantish and although he rarely finished plans he began, he did become familiar with the major buildings of the Austrian capital and, through reading, with those of other major European cities.

In architecture, Hitler lacked originality. Just as he rarely tried to paint an original picture, usually copying photographs or other paintings, so his critical opinions were rarely his own. His opinion of the Vienna Opera House, as overloaded with gold and silk, was the common modern opinion.[16] In this one regard he was

[12] Heiden reports this (*Der Fuehrer*, p. 51), but Smith doubts the truth of the story, and concludes, "If this is true, the experiment lasted only a few months." (*Adolf Hitler*, p. 100).

[13] *Mein Kampf*, p. 20.

[14] *Ibid.*

[15] Adolf Hitler, *Hitler's Secret Conversations 1941–45*, New York, Signet, 1961, pp. 117–118 (October 29, 1941). Hereafter cited as *S.C.*

[16] Hitler, says Kubizek, thought that the interior of the opera was "not very stirring. If the exterior is mighty majesty, which gives the building the seriousness of an artistic monument, the inside, though commanding admiration, does not impress one with its dignity." (Kubizek, *The Young Hitler*, p. 104.)

abreast of *avant-garde* views. But nowhere does he indicate that the Austrian architectural innovators of the period, Adolf Loos, Otto Wagner, or Josef Maria Olbrich, affected him in any way.[17] At times his own taste in interior decoration suggests that he may have been influenced by the ideals of the *Deutscher Werkbund*, founded in Munich in 1907, which sought greater simplicity in architecture and furniture, in contrast to the overdecorated and overstuffed styles of the late nineteenth century. But this was as far into the twentieth century as the *Führer's* taste developed.

In *Mein Kampf*, Hitler described himself as a potential architect who decided to sacrifice his chosen career to his patriotic duty. As noted above, his followers, after 1933, praised him as the master builder. Paradoxically, Hitler did not usually refer to himself as an architect, but rather as a painter. His rent contract of 1929 describes him as an "artist and writer";[18] moreover, he told Sir Neville Henderson in September 1939 that, when the Polish problem subsided, he would become, not an architect, but an artist.[19] Although in Vienna he sometimes called himself a student, in his youth he never tried to pass as an architect.[20] By the time he reached adulthood, he probably had come to fear that it was too late for him to succeed in that profession.

Despite his failure to gain professional training in Vienna, Hitler's taste was greatly influenced by the city's architecture. He describes in *Mein Kampf* the effect of a visit to the neo-baroque Museum of Fine Arts (1871–1891) when he was fifteen years old; "the purpose of my trip was to study the picture gallery . . . but

[17] According to Speer, the spacious conception of city planning in an Otto Wagner book is one possible influence on Hitler's views. (Probably *Einige Skizzen, Projekte, und ausgeführte Bauwerke von Otto Wagner, Architekt*, Vienna, A. Schroll, 1905.) Because Wagner was one of the most famous prewar Viennese architects, it is quite possible, as Speer suggests, that Hitler was influenced by reading this work. (Correspondence with Albert Speer, December 14, 1968.)

[18] Jetzinger, *Hitlers Jugend*, p. 157.

[19] Joseph Wulf, ed., *Die bildenden Künste im Dritten Reich*, Gütersloh, Sigbert Mohn, 1964, p. 6.

[20] See Teut, *Architektur*, p. 12.

I had eyes for scarcely anything but the museum itself."[21] (See illustration no. 3) The other major buildings of the city also fascinated him. "For hours I could stand in front of the Opera, for hours I could gaze at the Parliament, the whole Ring boulevard seemed to me an enchantment out of the 'Thousand and One Nights.'" Vienna as a whole was a "fair city."[22] The postcards which he sent home to Linz from Vienna were of the Karlskirche (1716–1737), the Parliament (1873–1883), and the Opera (1861– 1869). Later when he himself was producing postcards and sketches, the Parliament, the Burgtheater (1874–1888), and other landmarks were his favorite subjects. Judging from his comments, Hitler's favorite architect seems to have been Theophilus von Hansen (1803–1883). The Parliament, with its tall marble pillars and walls of black and white marble, the colonnaded Exchange (1877) and the Academy (1872–1876) itself with its Renaissance neo-classicism were all works of Hansen. Hitler liked what connoted past and present grandeur. The neo-baroque and neo-Renaissance remained his favorite styles until the thirties.

Hitler may also have been aware that Vienna's buildings were part of Habsburg propaganda. Significantly, the declining Empire put on its grandest show in the last fifty years of its existence. Hitler's eclectic reading could have included Gottfried von Semper's Uber Baustyle (1869), in which the Viennese architect maintained that monumental architecture served those in power, and helped to direct and control the "apathetic, restless masses."[23] If he did read von Semper, it is possible that he remembered this

[21] Mein Kampf, p. 19. The building was designed by Gottfried von Semper (1803–1879) and Karl von Hasenauer (1833–1894). On Viennese architecture of this time, see William A. Jenks, Vienna and the Young Hitler, New York, Columbia University Press, 1960.

[22] Mein Kampf, p. 19. Twenty years later, the exterior effect of the French Renaissance Opera House of Eduard Van der Null (1812–1868) and August von Siccardsburg (1813–1868), built 1861–1869, had not waned. "The Vienna opera house," said Hitler in 1942, "so marvellously beautiful, puts the Paris Opera in the shade." S.C., p. 212 (January 13, 1942).

[23] A speech given in Zurich, cited in Teut, Architektur, p. 179. Besides designing the Museum of Fine Arts, Semper had also worked on the new Hofburg.

advice later when he inaugurated the Third Reich's monumental building program.

Considering Hitler's youthful enchantment with Vienna and the extent to which its prevailing architectural styles stamped his own taste, it is at first difficult to see why he said, in 1942, that he had "never succumbed to the magic of Vienna." Nevertheless, some explanation is found in his added remark that he had always "been adamantly true to [his] German sentiments."[24] Vienna, for all its impressiveness, was a multi-racial city, a cosmopolitan metropolis, and as such Hitler hated it. It was a haven for Marxism and social democracy, for Jews and Slavs. His experiences here caused him to loathe big cities for the rest of his days; this dislike — as well as his love of monumental architecture — is another product of his Vienna years.[25] (Later, the "blood-and-soil" Nazis, with their bucolic propaganda, took heart from Hitler's anti-urbanism.)

Otto Dietrich, the Reich press chief, declares that "there were scarcely any works on architecture which Hitler had not read, and no new publication which he did not immediately want to read."[26] This claim is exaggerated, but, from what he did choose to read, Hitler learned and retained a great deal. He continually astonished people by his knowledge of the architectural details of buildings that he had never personally visited. He seemed familiar with the palace of Versailles (1624–1682) and spoke of the roof construction "as though he himself had had a hand in the glazing."[27] Hitler's secretary reports that he could discourse on a "staggering number of details in the building style of churches,

[24] S.C., pp. 630–631 (September 1, 1942).
[25] According to von Schirach, "Hitler never loved Vienna. He hated its people. I believe that he had a liking for the city because he appreciated the architectural design of the buildings on the Ring." (International Military Tribunal, *Trial of the Major War Criminals before the International Military Tribunal, Nuremberg, 14 November 1945 – 1 October 1946*, Nuremberg, XIV (1947–1949), 429.) Hereafter cited as I.M.T. *Trial.*
[26] Otto Dietrich, *Zwölf Jahre mit Hitler*, Munich, Isar, 1955, p. 174.
[27] Hans Frank, cited in Lehmann-Haupt, *Art*, p. 254, note 10.

abbeys, and castles,"[28] and he was proud of being more familiar
with the architectural sights of foreign countries than were experts of those lands. For example, in 1940 he visited the Opera
House in Paris (finished in 1875) and asked to be shown a particular oval room; when told that no such room existed, he indicated a particular door as being the entrance to it. The room had
been divided into many smaller rooms long before, but Hitler
knew by heart the original plans.[29] Occasionally, his interest in
architecture overcame his interest in art. In 1934, when visiting
an art exhibition in the Crown Prince's Palace (1687; rebuilt in
1732) in Berlin, he took little notice of the paintings but commented repeatedly on the Arsenal (1694–1706), the Neue Wache
(1816–1818), and the Opera House (1741–1743), which were to
be seen from the windows of the gallery.[30] He would often bring
architecture into his conversation, producing paper and pencil,
and sketching buildings. Ernst Hanfstaengl reports that on one
occasion, he produced in ten minutes sketches of the Paris Opera
(completed 1875), Notre Dame (1163–1250), and the Eiffel
Tower (1889).[31] This was in 1928, before Hitler had ever been to
the French capital. Even in March 1945 when his Reich had nearly
collapsed, he was studying models for his planned expansion of
Linz, his home town.[32]

Ziegler, Nazi supervisor of the German National Theater,
wrote that "the Führer and Reich chancellor once confessed (in
his deep modesty, which continually amazes us) that he really
felt he knew something about architecture."[33] What in fact, did

[28] Zoller, Hitler Privat, p. 37.
[29] On this extraordinary knowledge of the details of buildings which he had
never seen see Percy Ernst Schramm, "Erläuterungen zum Inhalt," introduction in
Henry Picker, Hitlers Tischgespräche im Führerhauptquartier 1941–42, Stuttgart,
Seewald, 1963, p. 58; hereafter cited as Tischgespräche. See also Arno Breker,
Paris, Hitler et moi, Paris, Presses de la cité, 1970, pp. 94–113; a description of
Hitler's visit to Paris in 1940, accompanied by Breker and Speer.
[30] Described in Paul Otto Rave, Kunstdiktatur im Dritten Reich, Hamburg,
Verlag Gebrüder Mann, 1949, p. 41.
[31] Ernst Hanfstaengl, Unheard Witness. New York, Lippincott, 1957, p. 150.
[32] Zoller, Hitler Privat, p. 57.
[33] Ziegler, Wende und Weg, p. 18.

he know? Despite the many instances of broad knowledge cited above, his appreciation was more visual than technical. He remembered what he had seen, in reality or in pictures, what had been described by others, and what he had read.[34] But he cared little for the technical side of building. To be sure, according to his own account, he worked in Vienna as a construction laborer;[35] hence he may have acquired some practical knowledge of building construction. But his zeal remained that of the amateur sketcher of imposing monuments. He cared more for the impression a building made, than for how it was erected.

However superficial his interest may have been, it did not wane with time. Apparently he read about architecture while in Landsberg prison, 1924–1925. In 1941, he claimed that he always looked at pictures in architecture books before going to bed.[36] In 1945 his private library contained sixteen books on art, thirteen of which concerned architecture or city planning.[37] Toward the end of his life, he maintained that, had the First World War not interrupted his career, he would have probably become the leading architect of Germany.[38]

It is doubtful that he could have ever become a successful architect either by teaching himself or even by taking the proper training. Speer has said that he could indeed have become a competent, although not a brilliant, architect.[39] On the other hand, Anna Teut finds his powers of judgment limited and sees a lack

[34] His work was neat and showed good draftsmanship. See, for example, the *Aquarelle*.
[35] *Mein Kampf*, p. 39. However, Alan Bullock does not believe this to be true. (*Hitler: A Study in Tyranny*, New York, Harper and Row, 1962, pp. 32–33.)
[36] *S.C.*, p. 82 (October 13–14, 1941).
[37] These are listed in Lehmann-Haupt, *Art*, p. 50, note. 8.
[38] *Tischgespräche*, p. 323 (May 10, 1942).
[39] Cited in G. M. Gilbert, *Nuremberg Diary*, New York, Farrar Strauss, 1947, p. 308. Speer believes that if a rich citizen of Vienna or Munich had commissioned him to design a villa before 1914, Europe would have been spared the Third Reich ("Die Bürde werde ich nicht mehr los," *Spiegel*, XX:46, November 7, 1966, 50). He expressed similar ideas to me (Correspondence, March 9, 1969) and in his *Erinnerungen* (Berlin, Ullstein, 1969, p. 93); *Inside the Third Reich* (translated by Richard and Clara Winston, New York, Macmillan, 1970, p. 79).

of ability to conceive and carry out an idea.[40] This seems to be the most valid estimate of the man's abilities. Even had he obtained the necessary marks in high school or been admitted to an architecture school, he did not possess the determination to finish a building plan, or even formal training. He would probably have been unwilling to submit for long to those aspects of an architect's education which he disliked. For example, he hated mathematics.[41] Thus Hitler remained a dilettante in architecture. His natural drive for self-expression found its outlet in politics, not in art or architecture. Perhaps, his decision to become a politician [42] was based partially on a realistic assessment of his chances as a student architect.

Yet his plans and projects reveal something of both his mind and what was to come in the Third Reich. The postcards he painted in Vienna represent the pompous edifices which he loved. This interest in the monumental can be traced back even further, to his Linz days. At that time, reports his friend Kubizek, the seventeen-year-old Hitler showed him detailed designs, some of a new bridge over the Danube, others of an expansion of the local museum, some for a large subterranean railway station.[43] Kubizek and Hitler explored the medieval Lichtenhag ruins on the Pöstlingberg, a hill across the river from their native Linz; Hitler measured the old walls and entered the figures in the sketchbook that he always carried. He then completed a sketch of the original castle, with moat, drawbridge, pinnacles and turrets.[44] The impressive staircase at the baroque monastery of St. Florian (1686–1750), also near Linz, fascinated him too. Particularly large buildings designed to serve — and to impress — the masses, such as

[40] Teut, Architektur, p. 12.
[41] Heiden, Der Fuehrer, p. 49. In the first semester of his last year at school, he received an "unsatisfactory" in mathematics.
[42] Mein Kampf, p. 206.
[43] Kubizek, The Young Hitler, p. 19. Later, he tried to have such a station built in Munich. (See Chapter XI.)
[44] Ibid., p. 24.

a projected theater in Linz, appealed to him.[45] (He later called this sort of building "community" architecture.) His plans for a rebuilt Linz reveal the same concern for the monumental in architecture. In his own designs, public buildings — such as a concert hall he sketched at age eighteen — are predominant, always in traditional pompous styles. At this time he loved the Italian Renaissance (as in the Vienna Academy of Fine Arts); only much later in his life, and only temporarily, did he reject this and the baroque for a simpler neo-classicism. Even before he had permanently left his home town, Hitler was concerned with the style of public buildings and that style was almost always monumental. There was little sign of an interest in public housing or the dwellings of the workers.

His other opinions on Linz are also significant. He particularly liked the town square, a rectangular open space laid out in 1260 near the Danube River, with impressive patrician homes, the town hall (1658–59), and the Trinity Column (1717–1723). Hitler felt that the two buildings on the river side of the square blocked the view of river and hills. He planned to move them apart, allowing an unobstructed view of a new widened bridge and the Pöstlingberg beyond.[46] This appealed to his love of space. The town hall, admittedly an unimpressive building, he disliked, believing it to be unworthy of a town like Linz. The castle (seat of Emperor Frederick III, 1489–1495) would be restored to its original appearance as in a Merian print and would become a museum of local history. Linz's own museum (built in neo-baroque style in 1892) he approved, but planned to enlarge. Its 110-meter-long marble frieze depicting events in Austrian history he would extend, along with the museum itself, into the adjoining convent garden, so that it would become the biggest frieze in Europe, 220 meters long.[47] After 1862, Linz began to build a neo-Gothic cathedral. Although it was to become the largest church in Austria,

[45] Ibid., pp. 260–261.
[46] This was achieved in 1943–1944.
[47] Kubizek, The Young Hitler, p. 88.

Hitler hated its Gothic style and the fact that its spire was only
135 meters high, compared to the 136 meters of Vienna's St.
Stephen's.

He planned also to remove the railway station, which he
thought was too near the town center, into the open country, and
run the tracks underground. The space gained in this way would
be used as a public park.[48] Here Hitler revealed not a concern for
the people's health, but a hatred of the unpleasant visual aspects
of technological development. Yet all the resources of modern
technology would be needed to construct his bridge in the hills
near Linz; this structure, 500 meters long and 90 meters high, was
to span the Danube and would probably be the most impressive
bridge in the world. Another new bridge, in the city of Linz would
also be built over the Danube with the aim of impressing the
viewer; the iron bridge of 1872 would be torn down and a new
bridge constructed, proportioned so that the visitor approaching
it from the town square would believe he was seeing, not a bridge,
but a broad avenue.[49]

Highly impressed as he was with Vienna in 1907–1913, the
young Hitler planned to remodel it too. The old *Hofburg* (16th
to 18th centuries) (the Habsburg palace) built of brick must be
demolished; Hitler admired the plans for a new palace and for
another wing matching the one built in 1881–1913 and facing it,
enclosing the *Heldenplatz* (Heroes' Square) (19th century) (see
illustration no. 4). The *Burgtor* (1821–1824) would remain and
two more triumphal arches would unite the square and the museums across the Ringstrasse into one complex. The old court
stables (also of brick) would be demolished and replaced by a
monumental building equal in size to the Hofburg and linked to
it by two other arches.[50] The fact that the Heldenplatz was an
ideal place for mass meetings did not escape Hitler; even in the

[48] *Ibid.*, p. 89.
[49] *Ibid.*, pp. 96–97. Actually built in the Third Reich.
[50] *Ibid.*, pp. 257–258.

unrebuilt square today, the spectator still receives a monumental impression from nearly every angle.

If brick was inadequate, so was plaster an inferior building material. Beautiful façades, which might conceal a flaw in the general plan, were also anathema to young Hitler. Kubizek declares that construction aimed at mere visual effect was bluff to Hitler.[51] It was not the visual effect that annoyed Hitler; it was the likelihood of hidden weakness, the lack of inner strength on the builder's part. He made an apt parallel between such deception and the crumbling edifice of Habsburg power.[52]

What of the social aspect of city reform? Kubizek reports that, in his Vienna years, Hitler began to plan for the working classes, and that he became aware of the need for healthy and suitable housing for the masses. He visited the working class districts, and studied the housing and living conditions of the proletarians there. Feeling that the worker's minimum needs included light, air, gardens, and playgrounds, he planned small units, four-family two-storeyed houses. According to Kubizek, Hitler once spent four nights exploring the tenements of Vienna and trying to estimate the land available for relieving the city's congestion. Furthermore, Hitler seems to have believed the worker should be able to commute quickly from his home to his place of employment; hence a string of railroad stations would be scattered over the whole city, connected with the urban center and catering to specific districts, and offering fast communications.[53] Even if Hit-

[51] Ibid., p. 164.

[52] Mein Kampf, p. 123.

[53] Kubizek, The Young Hitler, pp. 167–170. This scheme became part of his later plans for Berlin. Speer stresses Hitler's lack of interest in public housing. (Correspondence, March 9, 1969; see also his Erinnerungen, pp. 92–93, or Inside, p. 79.) Hitler made a rare reference to public housing in discussing his plans for Linz in 1942, possibly under Speer's influence, the latter being much more interested in this area. (Tischgespräche, p. 298 [April 26, 1942].) Lehmann-Haupt believes that Hitler was interested in "the practical side of building and in low-cost housing" (Art p. 51), citing as evidence the presence of three books in the "Hitler Library" on these matters. Again, Speer's influence may be seen here, but it is doubtful that Hitler was seriously concerned.

ler really cared for the workers' dwellings at this time, he had lost the interest by 1933. At least, during the Third Reich, monumental buildings took precedence over small private dwellings. In the Vienna period (1907–1913), he was probably concerned only with the outward appearance of the city and with preventing a Marxist revolution. For Hitler, "community" architecture never meant building to meet the social needs of the community.

Hitler's interest in building did not end when he left Vienna in 1913, nor in 1914 when he became a soldier. He sketched and painted water colors (almost always of architectural subjects) during the war;[54] in the twenties, when he began to work full time for the National Socialist German Workers' party, his plans became more grandiose and increasingly ideological in intent. In Landsberg prison, while dictating Mein Kampf and looking ahead to victory, he designed a triumphal arch, which was later incorporated into Speer's plans for Berlin. After the successful Nuremberg rallies of 1927 and 1928, he began to sketch plans for a permanent center for rallies. In the early thirties, before he became chancellor, he often spent afternoons with his new friend and favorite architect, Paul Ludwig Troost, looking over plans for monumental buildings in the latter's studio. Apparently by 1933 Hitler knew what he wanted built in the Third Reich: "The Führer," wrote Goebbels in that year, "has all his plans finished."[55] He took a deep interest in rebuilding Munich and Berlin and suggested ideas to Speer, who was in charge. To the end of his life, he not only sketched, but enjoyed contemplating the architecture in his Hall of Models in Berlin. On these occasions, he seems to have completely relaxed.[56] In May 1945, his bedroom in the bunker beneath the Chancellery's ruins contained a set of German architectural magazines. There may be a direct relationship between the frustrated architect's desire to remodel the face of cities

[54] See the Aquarelle, and the NSDAP Hauptarchiv microfilms (Hoover Institute, reels IA, 2, and 3.)

[55] Cited in Heiden, Der Fuehrer, p. 437.

[56] Speer, Erinnerungen, pp. 147–148; Inside, pp. 132–133.

and the *Führer's* drive to political power. His sketchbook in the early twenties contained, on the same pages, drawings of monumental buildings and of battleships.[57] For whatever psychological reasons, Hitler wanted the power to change his environment As he told Heinrich Hoffman, when asked why he did not become an architect, "I decided to become the master builder of the Third Reich."[58] This facetious remark contains a germ of truth. As *Führer*, he moved individuals, crowds, and armies almost at will, just as he had previously hoped to move marble and iron in great structures. Both his architectural plans and his political leadership satisfied his craving for power. One might say that the sense of space in his sketches and plans corresponds to the apparently unlimited vistas he faced when in control of most of Europe in the spring of 1941.

Hitler's love of architecture, superseded by his drive for political power, may have been dilettantish in nature, but it was intense. He liked to be described as an architect and to be photographed with architects. He respected, admired, and envied men he considered good artists.[59] He thought of architecture as an art, and although he worked closely with the architects to whom he gave commissions, he allowed the chosen few a remarkable freedom. His relations with Speer are significant in this regard. Not only did Hitler rarely intervene in the plans of his leading architect, but he treated him with unusual respect, refused to allow him to enlist, and concerned himself with the well being of Speer's family.[60] When Speer, as minister of armament and war production, contravened Hitler's "scorched earth" orders in 1945, he was forgiven. Speer quotes him as saying, "If you were not my archi-

[57] Speer, *Erinnerungen*, p. 54; *Inside*, p. 41.
[58] Heinrich Hoffmann, *Hitler was my Friend*, p. 184.
[59] He believed that an artist should sit in the Reichstag, and therefore made Speer replace a member who had left in 1941. (I.M.T., *Trial*, XVI (June 19, 1946), 431.)
[60] According to Speer, he "radiated a great amiability, and was very concerned about me and my family." (*Spiegel*, Nr. 46 (November 7, 1966), p. 48. See also his *Erinnerungen*, pp. 44, 68, 93, and 182; *Inside*, pp. 31, 55, 79, and 167.)

tect, I would have to take the steps necessary in these cases."[61] To the end, Hitler retained this respect for architects. Thus architecture was to develop within relatively free bounds in the totalitarian Third Reich. Hitler's influence, as will be seen, was both pervasive and limited.

In its policy towards painting and sculpture, his government persecuted, rejected, and coordinated, yet offered little that was new or far-reaching to replace jettisoned ideas. But in architecture a more constructive program evolved, largely because of Hitler's own view of the role of building in the community. Architecture was for him the highest form of art. Through its buildings, a creative civilization expressed its values. Its monumental architecture was more impressive to foreigners or to later generations than any other form of spiritual or cultural achievement; with almost religious emphasis, Hitler said, "it is the Word in stone."[62] Therefore, German architectural monuments in the Third Reich would be witnesses to the reawakening of the German spirit in the twentieth century.[63] The designer of the Parthenon (447–432 B.C.) expressed the noblest thoughts of the ancient Athenians; Hitler hoped that providence would grant the Germans a similar great master "who . . . shall immortalize [our ideals] in stone."[64] Centuries later, the stones would still speak to new generations of German greatness. Hitler believed that one could learn from architecture whether a civilization was in decline or in ascendancy.

[61] Speer, Erinnerungen, p. 457; Inside, p. 451. Lehmann-Haupt exaggerates in stating that Hitler "wanted to reserve for himself complete control of everything" in architectural matters. (Art, p. 54.) Even in his monumental plans, Hitler could take advice from a select few.

[62] Domarus, Reden, p. 778. (Speech at the German Architecture and Crafts Exhibition in Munich, January 22, 1938.) See also Baynes, Speeches, p. 602. For Hitler, architecture was "the noblest of all the arts." (Rauschning, Hitler Speaks, p. 262.

[63] Domarus, Reden, pp. 1218–1219 (speech at the German Architecture and Crafts Exhibition, Munich, July 16, 1939); Baynes, Speeches, p. 608.

[64] Baynes, Speeches, p. 575 (September 11, 1935). Note that often Baynes does not quote the same passages as does Domarus, although both may include extracts from the speech; hence the occasional reference to Baynes alone or to Domarus alone.

Habsburg Austria was a good example: ". . . in the field of cultural or artistic affairs," said Hitler, "the Austrian state showed all the symptoms of degeneration. . . . This was most true in the field of architecture."[65] A nation's architecture revealed whether it had any living ideas. Hitler found the Tudor Gothic Houses of Parliament (1837–1857) in London the perfect expression of English civilization. On the other hand, when Hansen designed the Parliament in Vienna he had nothing to use as decoration, but "borrowings from antiquity." Whereas the English building was a national hall of fame with a style appropriate to the nation's traditions, the Viennese parliament sported busts of Roman and Greek statesmen, merely embellishing "this opera house of western democracy." Hitler noted: "In symbolic irony, the quadrigae fly from one another in all four directions above the two houses, in this way giving the best external expression of the activities that went on inside the building."[66] Of course these ideas contradict his favorable opinion of Viennese architecture. Although many of Hitler's views are indeed logically incompatible, in this particular case, he would probably hold that the multiracial Habsburg Empire was merely using this ideal architecture as a façade.[67]

In comparison, good "German" architecture would have both a therapeutic and a propaganda function. "I am convinced," said Hitler, "that art, since it forms the most uncorrupted, the most immediate reflection of the people's soul, exercises unconsciously by far the greatest direct influence upon the masses of the people."[68] Of the power of building, Hitler declared that everyone was influenced by the buildings in which work and recreation took

[65] *Mein Kampf*, p. 123.
[66] *Ibid.* p. 75.
[67] Hitler approved of borrowing from other ages and styles if there was direct racial affinity, which was lacking in cosmopolitan Vienna. (Speech at the Party Congress, September 1933, cited in Teut, *Architektur*, p. 91.)
[68] Domarus, *Reden*, p. 528 (Speech on Art, September 11, 1935); Baynes, *Speeches*, p. 574.

place.[69] Architecture, then, could be used to improve the spiritual and psychological condition of the German people. Appropriately designed buildings would help the German community to rid itself of its inferiority complex,[70] and would inspire patriotism. In 1935, Hitler declared that architecture which embodied the values of a people helped them to keep their faith in their own future.[71] In stimulating community spirit, the architecture of the Third Reich would give people a strong sense of unity and a "limitless self-confidence."[72]

Hitler's buildings would be designed for the use of the Volk, with a view to improving the life of the whole community. The theme of community life (the national racial community, the local community, and the labor unit) is repeatedly stressed in Hitler's speeches and in the writings of others. Public buildings must be large and impressive and must imply that the life of the people as a whole was superior to individual lives. Hitler claimed to believe that, if "community buildings" were to give confidence to the race, they must be much more imposing than those erected by "capitalist interest."[73] A building created by the whole people must worthily represent those who commissioned it — the Volk.[74] Public buildings were more important than private ones, because seeing great "community" buildings reminded people of their natural unity and led to mutual aid.[75] Nevertheless, no "Marxist" intention is implied here; while the sense of community would be

[69] Rauschning, Hitler Speaks, p. 262.

[70] Baynes, Speeches, p. 603 (November 21, 1937).

[71] Domarus, Reden, p. 528 (speech on Art, September 11, 1935); Baynes, Speeches, p. 572.

[72] Domarus, Reden, p. 719 (speech on Art, September 7, 1937): Baynes, Speeches, p. 594. It has been suggested that Hitler's desire for a symbolic, didactic architecture may have been created by the avant-garde mood of architects in the early twenties; men such as Bruno Taut believed that buildings could exude the spirit of a radical new society. (Lehmann-Haupt, Art, pp. 107–108; and John Elderfield, "Total and Totalitarian Art," Studio International [April 1970], p. 154.) Given Hitler's great interest in architecture, it is conceivable that he was at least aware of this movement.

[73] Domarus, Reden, p. 528 (Speech on Art, September 11, 1935).

[74] Baynes, Speeches, p. 581 (Speech on Art, September 11, 1935).

[75] Ibid., p. 576.

heightened, "the individual capacity for achievement" would be also improved.[76] In both ways the nation's moral strength would be increased; the *Volk* would be convinced of their higher mission and would be ready for self-sacrifice.

Hitler's model here was the Roman Catholic Church. "The mysticism of Christianity," he said, created buildings with a "mysterious gloom which made men more ready to submit to the renunciation of self."[77] Hitler was deeply impressed by the organization, ritual, and architecture of the church. In writing of the spell which an orator can weave over an audience, he said, "The same purpose is served by the artificial and yet mysterious twilight in Catholic churches."[78] He might have envied the powerful influence which the church exerted on the masses, for on one occasion he declared that "the concluding meeting in Nürnberg must be exactly as solemnly and ceremonially performed as a service of the Catholic Church."[79] But whereas Nazi buildings should reflect the devout spirit of the movement, there was no place for mysticism in them. Nazism was cool-headed and realistic, said Hitler, adding that it mirrored scientific knowledge. It was not a religious cult. He noted that the Nazi party had "no religious retreats" and "no rooms for worship" with "the mystical gloom of a cathedral," but "halls for the *Volk*," "areas for sports," and playing fields, all brightly lit.[80]

Not only did public architecture express the community's values and teach new generations what those values were, but it had a role to play in foreign policy. Architecture was one of Hitler's weapons in Germany's political battles. "My acts," he declared, "are always based upon a political mode of thinking. If

[76] *Ibid.*, p. 577.
[77] *Ibid.*, p. 599; Domarus, *Reden*, p. 893. See also Adolf Hitler, *Reden des Führers am Parteitag Grossdeutschland 1938*, Munich 1939, p. 35. (September 6, 1938.)
[78] *Mein Kampf*, p. 475.
[79] Zoller, *Hitler Privat*, p. 193.
[80] Baynes, *Speeches*, p. 396 (September 6, 1938); Domarus, *Reden*, pp. 893–894; also Hitler, *Reden*, p. 40.

Vienna expressed the desire to build a monument two hundred meters high, it would find no support from me. Vienna is beautiful, but I have no reason to go on adding to its beauties."[81] Besides, it was still too Slavic for Hitler. In the German Reich, pure "German" architecture would outshine that of any other race. In this competition, the architect was a "fighter."[82] It was this desire to astonish and overwhelm foreigners, which prompted him to build the new Chancellery and the Reich Sport Field in Berlin.

What sort of building was a "community" building? Hitler believed that the Colosseum (A.D. 72–80), St. Peter's basilica (1503–1667), and the castle of San Angelo in Rome (136–139 A.D.) were the "product of a collective effort."[83] How this was so, Hitler never clearly explains. Apparently they were "community" structures because they were landmarks and the populace was proud of them. They were used by the community and they embodied powers which controlled the community. In short, to Hitler, any structure which was imposing and had some governmental function was community architecture. Hitler's architecture would not take the form of hospitals, public housing, or völkisch cottages, but of monumental edifices which symbolized "that common mental attitude, that common view of life, which govern the present age."[84]

Although some Germans might still be poverty stricken, Hitler was determined that great monuments would be built; besides, a healthy race, however poor, should not be stopped from expressing itself,[85] and a great people naturally produce great architecture. Hitler saw Germany threatened in the twentieth century and therefore certain measures were to be taken in order to help

---

[81] S.C., p. 104 (October 21–22, 1941).

[82] Domarus, Reden, p. 719 (September 7, 1937); Baynes, Speeches, p. 594.

[83] S.C., p. 40 (July 21–22, 1941); Tischgespräche, p. 34.

[84] Baynes, Speeches, p. 599 (September 6, 1938); obviously, Hitler's use of the term "community" differs from that common in the twenties. Yet some architects, maintains Wolters, were led to believe that Nazi "community" architecture implied a program of homes for the poor. (See Wolters, "Versuch einer Rechtfertigung," in Teut, Architektur, pp. 368–372.)

[85] Baynes, Speeches, p. 571 (September 11, 1935).

the *Volk* develop the architecture latent within itself. "Some measure of culture and beauty shall penetrate into even the humblest of our towns . . . ," declared Hitler and he was going to assist this process.[86] It was a time of revolutionary change and "those who are responsible for the shaping of nations in the sphere of politics or world view must endeavour to direct the peoples' artistic forces."[87] Some form of government intervention and control was necessary.

According to Hitler's ostensible faith in the people's creativity, no petty intellectual critic would be allowed to denigrate monuments which the *Volk* (and its government) would build. In a speech at the German Architecture and Crafts Exhibition in Munich in 1938, Hitler declared that the models exhibited were to be built regardless of the critics' views.[88] The critics ignored the fact that the German people knew instinctively and spontaneously what type of building was suitable to them and to their environment. Their great architecture would reduce the "small carping critic" to silence.[89]

Although Hitler declared that the spontaneous emergence of great architecture was imperilled by the conditions of the time, yet state leadership was bound to assist its growth and bureaucratic methods were to be avoided. It often seemed that the *Führer* had no faith in men with official accreditation or training. His conversations reveal an anti-intellectualism, probably rooted in those days in Vienna when the Academy of Fine Arts had rejected him. "It's all wrong," he said, "that a man's whole life should depend on a diploma that he either receives or doesn't at the age of seventeen."[90] As for the academies, they stifled genius. Self-taught architects, on the other hand, rising out of the common people

[86] S.C., p. 425 (May 1, 1942); *Tischgespräche*, p. 304.
[87] Baynes, *Speeches*, p. 607 (July 16, 1939).
[88] December 10, 1938; cited in Lehmann-Haupt, *Art*, p. 54. This remark was irrelevant because all traditional art criticism was forbidden by a law of November 27, 1936.
[89] Baynes, *Speeches*, p. 583 (September 11, 1935); Domarus, *Reden*, p. 528.
[90] S.C., p. 117 (October 29, 1941); see also p. 508 (June 30, 1942). Despite this viewpoint, Speer and Troost both had thorough qualifications.

(like Hitler), carried in them the will of the race. Their designs expressed the style which would best represent the people. They needed no formal instruction. These men would be allowed to build in the Third Reich.

This picture of an enlightened leadership carefully guiding and defending the spontaneous creativity of an artistically fertile race might be considered propaganda, but it is closer to Nazi practice than at first apparent. Hitler's dominance in the field of architecture was remarkably mild. The Reich Chamber of Culture imposed some restrictions,[91] to be sure, but enough architects were willing to build in Nazi-approved styles; Hitler was not the dictator in architecture that he was in politics.

Hitler's foremost aim for Nazi architecture was that the *Volk* must be able to express and glorify itself. To accomplish this, "community" buildings would be built to stand for eternity, witnesses to the German people's archievements and character. Hitler had two fixed ideas on their style: monumentality, and a general neo-classicism. All "community" buildings should be large and commodious, or at least should give the impression of monumentality. "The eyes of the children must be weaned from the niggardly, and trained on the grandiose," said Hitler.[92] For example, he approved of Hermann Giessler's remodeling of Schloss Klesheim (1700–1709) near Salzburg, for it corresponded closely to his own ideas of spaciousness. In Hitler's words, the architect had left "vast spaces between the portals and staircase and between the staircase and the entrance to the reception halls." This accorded with his view that architects should plan on "broad and spacious lines."[93] He derided the Protestant cathedral in Berlin (1905) for its limited seating capacity, and criticized the building of a theater with only 1200 seats in a city of 150,000 inhabitants.[94]

---

[91] These restrictions were "informal," according to Hildegard Brenner. See her chapter, "Aufbau der informalen Kontrollen," *Kunstpolitik*, pp. 87–130.

[92] *S.C.*, p. 426 (May 1, 1942); *Tischgespräche*, p. 304.

[93] *S.C.*, p. 425 (May 1, 1942); *Tischgespräche*, p. 304.

[94] Domarus, *Reden*, pp. 983–984 (December 10, 1938). Hitler does not specify which theater he means.

As for his taste for classical design, Hitler did not always prefer the stark form which developed in the Third Reich. Originally his taste was more baroque, revealing the influence of Vienna. The twentieth-century neo-Greek movement developed before 1914, but Hitler seems to have missed its strong influence as a youth. Speer maintains that Troost, in the years 1930 to 1934, weaned the *Führer* away from baroque to a purer ("Doric") neoclassicism.[95] Possibly Alfred Rosenberg's praise for the "Aryan" Greek of antiquity (in *Der Mythus des 20. Jahrhunderts*, first published in 1930) affected Hitler, although he rejected many of Rosenberg's other ideas. It is also possible that he read Moeller van den Bruck's book, *Der preussische Stil* (published first during the First World War and reprinted often later), which praised the neo-classical work of Schinkel and Gilly for its political qualities.[96] After Troost's death in 1934, Speer became Hitler's favorite architect, not only because he was ready to build monumentally, but also because he was in the neo-classical movement.[67] In the later plans for Berlin, which he approved in the early forties, the baroque reappears, suggesting that Hitler never outgrew the experiences and taste of his youth.

It would be wrong to infer from Hitler's temporary preference for a stark neo-classicism that only such a style was permitted in the Third Reich. In 1933, Hitler declared that whatever the past had to offer, Germans should freely use and develop further.[98] While blind imitation of the past, he admitted, could be senseless,[99] yet tolerance toward the great monuments of other ages

[95] Speer, *Erinnerungen*, p. 54; *Inside*, p. 41.

[96] Prussian architecture of the late eighteenth century was described herein as primitive and manly, a soldier style; in its monumentality and spaciousness, it expressed the political outlook of Prussian leaders. (Moeller van den Bruck, *Der preussische Stil*, 5th ed., Breslau, Korn, 1931.)

[97] Lehmann-Haupt shows that three books in Hitler's private library stress the mutual interaction of classical antiquity and Germanic culture. (*Art*, p. 50, note 8.)

[98] Adolf Hitler, *Die deutsche Kunst als stolzeste Verteidigung des deutschen Volkes: Rede, gehalten auf der Kulturtagung des Parteitages 1933*, Munich, 1934, p. 12 (September 1, 1933).

[99] Baynes, *Speeches*, p. 581 (September 11, 1935).

was a "supreme law."[100] From this equivocation, it should not be surprising that Hitler was often vague in his public speeches on architecture. He could praise objectivity (*Sachlichkeit*), the catchword of the leading German architects of the twenties.[101] At the same time, he lauded the use of natural building materials, and the development and preservation of crafts such as woodwork in architecture.[102] But although he praised neo-classicism, this style did not become the party line. It influenced the monumental public, party, and government ("community") buildings of the period; but much more was built which was neither monumental nor neo-classical in design.[103] In all likelihood, his equivocation was due to his desire not to alienate those architects who would be necessary to Germany's technological growth. At the same time, if nonmonumental buildings were allowed to be erected in a modern "functional" style in the thirties, this was probably because Hitler had little time for architecture that did not fit his interest in "community" building. Speer maintains, moreover, that when factories were built of glass and steel (in the *Bauhaus* manner), Hitler was not distressed, for he believed that a factory should not resemble a state building.[104]

Hitler stated that the best styles of the past might be imitated in the Third Reich; what he considered worthy of copying suggests what he hoped Nazi Germany would build. Because he apparently believed that the Greeks and the Germans were linked racially, it seemed natural that the Germans in their ascendancy should build in a variation of the classical style. He believed that an architect could return to those elements of form which in the past were invented by a race similar to his own.[105] At Nuremberg in 1933, he said that,

[100] *Ibid.*, p. 596 (September 7, 1937).
[101] *Ibid.*, p. 579 (September 11, 1935).
[102] *Ibid.*, p. 580 (September 11, 1935).
[103] See Barbara Miller Lane, *Architecture and Politics*, Chapter 8.
[104] Correspondence with Speer, March 9, 1969. On factories built in the Third Reich, see Teut, *Architektur*, pp. 234–249; or Lane, *Architecture and Politics*, p. 204.
[105] Baynes, *Speeches*, p. 581 (September 11, 1935).

it is . . . no wonder that each politically heroic age in its art immediately seeks bridges to a not less heroic past. The Greeks and the Romans suddenly become very near, because all their roots lie in a founding race, and therefore, the immortal accomplishments of the ancient peoples have an attractive influence on their racially related descendants. Therefore, since it is better to imitate something good, than to produce something new but bad, the surviving intuitive creations of these peoples can today doubtless fulfill their educative and leading mission through style.[106]

Greece and Rome, therefore, he saw as racially linked and as being the cradle of all true ("Aryan") culture.

Hitler never visited Athens, but he loved its ancient buildings, especially the Parthenon. He felt that the Greeks had combined functionalism with clarity, two qualities which the Germans could appreciate because they also understood them instinctively. He particularly liked the sloping roof of the Parthenon. All "Nordic" peoples, he felt, built this sort of roof — not a flat roof — to meet the vital needs of climate.

However, if Greece impressed Hitler with its racial affinities to Germany, ancient Rome impressed him with its monumentality. His visit to the Italian capital in 1938 had a great impact on him. He stopped at the Pantheon (27 B.C.), which he considered the most perfect of all buildings, and sent his retinue away, so that he could enjoy it better alone. He also wanted to be alone in the Colosseum (A.D. 72–80), and was fascinated by the huge ruins of the Baths of Caracalla (early 3rd century A.D.)[107] The size of these ruins was undoubtedly their most appealing feature,

[106] Hitler, *Die deutsche Kunst*, p. 11 (September 1, 1933).

[107] Percy Ernst Schramm. "Adolf Hitler: Anatomie eines Diktators," *Spiegel*, Nr. 7 (1964), p. 42. In 1941 Hitler said, "We can be glad the Parthenon is still standing upright, the Roman Pantheon and the other temples. It matters little that the forms of worship that were practised there no longer mean anything to us. It is truly regrettable that so little is left of these temples." *S.C.*, p. 141 (November 11, 1941); *Tischgespräche*, p. 151. It is no coincidence that the half-finished *Kongresshalle* in Nuremberg today looks like the ruined Roman Colosseum. Moreover, the Pantheon probably influenced Hitler's own design for a *Volk* hall in Berlin. (See his sketch in Speer, *Erinnerungen*, following p. 160; *Inside*, following p. 286. There is another sketch in Reel 3, Folder 64, Film 1004 of the NSDAP Hauptarchiv, Microfilm Collection.)

but they were also an example of "community" building. Of ancient Rome he said, "The first place was not taken by the villas and palaces of individual citizens, but by the temples and baths, the stadiums, circuses, aqueducts, basilicas, etc., of the state, hence of the whole people." By comparison, in contemporary Germany, hotels and "the department stores of a few Jews" were most prominent.[108] In the future, the Germans would have to build as the Romans had done.

Hitler's opinions on medieval architecture are ambivalent. On the one hand, ignoring the fact that the architects of the Hohenstaufen Reich did not build in the same way as the ancient "Aryans," Hitler praised German cathedrals. "Amongst us, the only witness of our greatness in the Middle Ages are the cathedrals . . . [If they disappeared] what a void, and how greatly the world would be impoverished!" He saw in them products of a closely knit communal life, structures which totally dominated the bourgeois homes around their base. Despite his praise for "the loveliness"[109] of the cathedrals, he lamented the supremacy of the clergy in this period, and he had no real appreciation for either the Romanesque or the Gothic style. The typical Gothic cathedral was too "Asiatic" in appearance,[110] overdecorated and gloomy. Only the Strasbourg cathedral (1015–1505) pleased him, because here there was a strong sense of space. (See illustration no. 6.) Accordingly, he planned to make this church into a hall of fame for the German unknown soldier after the Second World War. As a nationalist, then, Hitler was proud of the architectural accomplishments of the German medieval community, but he disliked the very concept of a great house of Christian worship.[111]

[108] *Mein Kampf*, p. 265.

[109] *S.C.*, p. 141 (November 11, 1941); *Tischgespräche*, p. 151.

[110] "The *Führer*," wrote Alfred Rosenberg, "does not like the Gothic." (*Das politische Tagebuch aus den Jahren 1934, 1935, und 1939*, Munich, Deutscher Taschenbuch Verlag, 1964, p. 149.) (Hereafter cited as *Tagebuch*.)

[111] The cathedral of Quedlinburg (completed in 1129) was seized by the S.S. in 1938, in order to convert it into a national shrine in honor of King Henry I. (See Willi Schulze and Lotte Zumpe, "Der Quedlinburger Dom als Kultstätte der SS," *Jahrbuch für Wirtschaftsgeschichte*, IV (1966), 215–234.)

"Of course," said Hitler, "the Renaissance was the dawn of a new age, Aryan man's rediscovery of himself."[112] Yet he usually had little to say about this period. He praised St. Peter's basilica in Rome as an imposing product of a collective will. He studied the Palazzo Pitti in Florence (1548–1764) and knew the details of its proportions. He rhapsodized on "the magic of Florence and Rome, of Ravenna, Siena, Perugia! Tuscany and Umbria [are] lovely." The smallest palace in Florence or Rome was worth more than all of Windsor Castle (1180–1528).[113] Despite its neo-classicism, the Italian Renaissance was probably also too closely linked in his mind with the Catholic Church. The German people, moreover, had not produced many monuments in this period. Perhaps the Tuscan Renaissance style of the Viennese Academy of Fine Arts had rendered him indifferent to this historical period. At any rate, this particular architectural period received little notice from Hitler, except in his conversations in the early forties, after his 1938 visit to Italy. He was much more emphatic about the virtues of the baroque.

In an ironic mood, Hitler remarked in 1941 that the Germans should be grateful to the Jesuits, who brought them a "light, airy, bright architecture" and who restored to them "the world of the senses."[114] The baroque movement banished the gloom from German churches and produced magnificent structures in Vienna, Dresden, and Würzburg. Hitler had praise for Versailles and, of course, for the neo-baroque of the nineteenth century in Vienna and in Bavaria. Nazi theorists felt otherwise about the neo-baroque and Hitler himself moved later towards a starker neo-classicism; but the baroque, original or imitation, was his first love. Buildings in this style were often imposing and large and usually represented a supreme power; this was what drew Hitler to them.

[112] S.C., p. 40 (July 21–22, 1941); Tischgespräche, p. 134.
[113] In 1938 Hitler visited Florence and was shown many of its palaces and museums. He came away pronouncing Florence the city of his dreams. (Elizabeth Wiskemann, Rome-Berlin Axis: A Study of the Relations between Mussolini and Hitler, London, Collins, 1966, p. 138.)
[114] S.C., p. 38 (July 21–22, 1941); Tischgespräche, p. 133.

Dietrich reports that, in the early years of the movement, Hitler enjoyed excursions to Herrenchiemsee (1878–1885) and Neuschwanstein (1869–1886), Bavarian palaces built in neo-baroque and medieval styles (respectively) by King Ludwig II, and that he felt great sympathy for the mad king who had built in these historical styles.[115] Although Hitler was impressed by nineteenth-century imitations, many contemporary architecture experts condemned the whole historicist movement, relating it to the ugly sprawl of industrial cities. Hitler was again ambiguous here. Although he did not often criticize historical imitation found in late nineteenth-century public buildings, he often lamented that, in the same period, smoke-belching factories and crowded tenements had destroyed the beauty of German cities. Modern towns such as Vienna, were "masses of apartments and tenements, and nothing more."[116] They had no community centers, no symbols of community life. This desolation was due to the degrading influence of liberalism, cosmopolitanism, and the Jews.[117] The liberal concern with law and constitutionalism was exemplified for Hitler by the Palace of Justice (completed in 1883) in Brussels which he found "typical of the epoch of liberalism, a cyclops which dominates the whole town." "Fancy having the Law Courts, of all things, as the dominating feature of a place!"[118] The Law Courts Building was not a community structure in the Hitlerian sense. Such a structure could never be the expression of the collective will of a dynamic *Volk*.

Nineteenth-century German governments had not spent enough on architecture, said Hitler; nor had they built in a style

[115] Dietrich, *Zwölf Jahre*, p. 174.

[116] *Mein Kampf*, p. 263. It is interesting to find similar passages in Gropius' work: "Since my early youth, I have been acutely aware of the chaotic ugliness of our modern man-made environment when compared to the unity and beauty of old pre-industrial towns"; in *Scope of Total Architecture*, New York, Harper and Row, 1954 (Volume 3 of World Perspectives, ed. by Ruth Nanda Anshen), p. xiii.

[117] *Mein Kampf*, pp. 263–266.

[118] *S.C.*, p. 651 (June 13, 1943).

expressive of the great race they governed. The capitalist mentality had made rulers too much aware of costs, and thus unwilling to express great ideals. But for Hitler, grandiosity and spaciousness were so important that cost should be no obstacle. "I wish to be a builder," he announced in 1941: "The means I shall set in operation to this end will far surpass those that were necessary for the conduct of this war."[119]

In the twentieth century Hitler saw the spread of the same capitalist, liberal mentality. Whereas the architecture of the twenties was a manifestation of the "private capitalistic business life,"[120] the intellectual architects of the *Bauhaus* indulged in mere sophistries, producing structures remote from the needs of the *Volk*. Yet in all of Hitler's pronouncements, there is no sustained or repeated condemnation of *avante-garde* architecture. There is little denunciation in *Mein Kampf*; this was written before the nationwide *völkisch* attack on flat roofs and glass walls began in the later twenties. Even after 1930, Hitler refrained. For example, in his speech in September 1933 at the party congress, he praised *Zweckmässigkeit* (functionalism), but differentiated it from *Sachlichkeit* (objectivity), the slogan of the intellectuals of the *Bauhaus*. This speech is typical of his later pronouncements on the modern movement. The most important criterion, he said, was a "functionalism filled with crystal clarity." This had nothing to do with "that so-called functionalism which cannot understand that the human being does not want to exchange harmonious beauty with animalistic primitivism."[121] However, in the same speech, he said it was ridiculous to reject the "knowledge and experience" of later generations just because earlier ones had discovered profound truths.[122] Accordingly, he praised the use of steel, iron, glass, and concrete in building, and said that modern technology forced men to find new ways of building. Even ma-

[119] S.C., p. 104 (October 21–22, 1941).

[120] Domarus, *Reden*, p. 528 (September 11, 1935); Baynes, *Speeches*, p. 583.

[121] Hitler, *Die deutsche Kunst*, p. 10 (September 1, 1933).

[122] *Ibid.*, p. 11 (September 1, 1933).

chines could exude "more of the Greek spirit . . . than many a badly conceived edifice."[123] For Hitler, a "functional" building would use every means to fulfill the purpose (function) for which it was constructed. In short, if a building's function were to impress the masses with a patriotic message, then all means or any style that worked could be used. (He believed, of course, that monumental neo-classicism was most practical in these circumstances.)

Although many Nazis associated the *avant-garde* with the Jews.[124] Hitler rarely made this connection. In 1935 he declared that the Jews never had an architectural style of their own.[125] But he was apparently not interested in associating Le Corbusier or the *Bauhaus* style with a Jewish plot.

This indifferent attitude continued throughout his rule. Still, he had to have an opinion on modern architecture and because many modern German architects were concerned with functionalism, accordingly, in the aforementioned 1935 speech he redefined functionalism and again vaguely. All great buildings were practical or "functional" in some way. Yet this functionalism did not necessarily exclude art or beauty, as some of the more experimental modern ideas seemed to do; each building could serve its purpose and therefore be practical, but it must also be beautiful.[126] He again implied that the style of a monumental building, although important, was not as vital as the degree to which it impressed the viewer. Thus his moderation and "practicality" were rooted in a basic cynicism.

After spending his youth in Linz and Vienna, Hitler lived much of the rest of his life in Munich and in Berlin, an experience which led him to conclude that the German city was in a state of

[123] *Ibid.*, p. 13 (September 1, 1933).
[124] For this attitude see the writings, for example, of Bettina Feistel-Rohmeder, *Im Terror des Kunstbolschewismus*, Karlsruhe, Müller, 1938. (This is a collection of her articles which originally appeared in the *völkisch* "Deutsche Kunstkorrespondenz," a syndicated column of the twenties.)
[125] Baynes, *Speeches*, p. 577 (September 11, 1935).
[126] *Ibid.*, pp. 579–580 (September 11, 1935).

decline. In the nineteenth century, it began to lose its character as a cultural site and to degenerate into a mere human settlement. The proletarian lacked attachment to the town he lived in because it was only his accidental stopping place and nothing more. Around 1815, German cities were small and possessed some culture. When Munich had only 60,000 inhabitants, it was one of the first of German art centers. By the twentieth century, nearly every factory town had reached this size, but few were cultural centers. As the population increased, even large cities grew poorer in art, and at the same time lost any physical or spiritual cohesion. Few German cities possessed monuments or symbols dominating the skyline, giving "unity" to the city, or reflecting the greatness and wealth of the town. The ancient principle of giving first place to public works ("community buildings") had been lost. Government spent too little on state buildings.[127] Nothing was built to last forever, but only to satisfy the needs of the moment. The result was that the urban dweller felt no sense of belonging to a community.[128]

As an example of nineteenth-century governmental irresponsibility, Hitler singled out the Berlin Reichstag building (built after 1884 by Paul Wallot, 1841–1912). He lamented that, whereas the imperial government spent sixty million marks on a battleship, it spent only half this sum on what should have been "the first magnificent building of the Reich, intended to stand for eternity." In this petty sum, Hitler claimed to see parliamentary stupidity symbolized. "When the question of interior furnishings came up for decision, the exalted house voted against the use of stone and ordered the walls trimmed with plaster."[129] Granite and marble would have been more suitable, Hitler thought. However, he still valued the monumental Reichstag, and, when Speer later

[127] If Germany did not begin to build great buildings now, Hitler believed that the capacity of German craftsmen would slowly die out. (Baynes, *Speeches*, p. 581; September 11, 1935.) *Inside*, p. 151.)
[128] *Mein Kampf*, pp. 263–264.
[129] *Ibid.*, p. 266.

suggested tearing it down, he refused to consider the idea, wanting rather to incorporate it into the imposing new Adolf Hitler Platz near Berlin's *Volk* hall.[130]

Hitler did not think highly of the capital of his Reich. In 1941, he declared that the British bombers would do no great harm if they destroyed Berlin.[131] Although he did not see it as a true capital, Berlin still had a future: "It is my unalterable will and determination," he said, "to provide Berlin with those streets, buildings, and public squares which will make it appear for all time fit and worthy to be the capital of the German Reich."[132] This "millenial city" would be the "true center of Europe, a capital that for everybody shall be *the* capital."[133] As a world capital, it could compare only with Babylon or Rome. Indeed, it would eclipse its "only rival," Rome, because it would be built on such a scale that St. Peter's and its square would seem "like toys in comparison." Foreign visitors to the Chancellery would arrive along wide avenues dominated by the triumphal arch, the pantheon of the army, the square of the people, "things to take your breath away."[134] As for the ordinary German, he should try to visit this mecca at least once in his lifetime.[135]

Because Berlin's traditions were military, Hitler doubted that the city could ever become a metropolis of the arts. Munich was different. Not only did Hitler love the Bavarian capital because of its place in his own life and career, but he admired its architecture, "this wonderful marriage of primordial power and fine artistic mood."[136] He found the baroque Wittlesbach *Residenz* (seventeenth to nineteenth centuries) "miraculous" and the Palace of

[130] Speer, *Errinnerungen*, p. 166; *Inside* p. 151.

[131] *S.C.*, p. 40 (July 21–22, 1941); *Tischgespräche*, p. 134. For a Nazi view of urban problems, see also Hans F. K. Günther, *Die Verstädterung*, Leipzig, Teubner, 1938.

[132] Baynes, *Speeches*, p. 600–601 (November 27, 1937).

[133] *S.C.*, p. 67 (September 25, 1941).

[134] *S.C.*, p. 103 (October 21–22, 1941).

[135] *S.C.*, p. 550 (July 22, 1942).

[136] He wrote ". . . I am more attached to this city than to any other spot of earth in this world." (*Mein Kampf*, p. 127).

Justice (1887–1897) "perhaps the most beautiful example of the baroque of recent times."[137] He was impressed by the Königsplatz (buildings erected 1816–1862) and the neo-classical buildings of Leo von Klenze (1784–1864), too. Needless to say, Munich, center of the party's initial successes, was the first German city to be remodeled after 1933.

Hitler hated the large city, yet, paradoxically, he planned to build urban centers overpowering in their magnificence. Again, both feelings seem to stem from his youth in Vienna. What he disliked about the Austrian metropolis was the socialism of the proletariat and the racial intermingling inevitable in a large city: what he liked about Vienna was its representative splendor. The cities of the Third Reich would also be as impressive as Habsburg Vienna, but they would be purged of impure racial elements and the disturbing manifestations of Marxism.

As for the rest of Europe, Hitler was familiar with most of the larger cities, even though he had not visited them. The other Danubian capital, Budapest, exerted a fascination for him. There was no German city to compare with it, "the most beautiful town in the world."[138] He had praise for the Houses of Parliament (1885–1902), the citadel, the cathedral and the bridges over the river. Vienna lacked the same setting and its buildings were smaller in scale than those in Budapest. Why this praise for a capital of an inferior race? Hitler was careful to note that the major buildings of Budapest were designed by German architects.[139] Nevertheless, Budapest remained a non-German city, and if any monuments were added to Vienna in the Third Reich they would be built "only to infuriate the Hungarians."[140] Obviously, Hitler regarded architecture as a political weapon.

[137] S.C., p. 651 (June 13, 1943). These comments show that Hitler never completely lost his original love of baroque.
[138] S.C., p. 621 (August 28, 1941).
[139] At least one of the leading Budapest architects in the nineteenth century was of German descent; Emmerich von Steindl (1839–1902) planned the neo-Gothic parliament.
[140] S.C., p. 423 (April 28, 1942).

Farther east in Europe, most architecture ceased to have any
value for Hitler. Even when he admitted the existence of beauties
here, he saw rotten foundations. He had no hesitation about
"wiping out Kiev, Moscow, or St. Petersburg."[141] Moscow, for
example, would be looted and then would disappear from the
face of the earth. Leningrad (St. Petersburg), too, although "in-
comparably more beautiful than Moscow,"[142] was doomed to
decay. He seems to have assumed that the siege after 1941 would
succeed in destroying Leningrad. He had similar views about
Warsaw, although Prague would be saved, because of the German
origins of its architectural landmarks.

The only other European cities about which Hitler expressed
any deep feelings were Rome and Paris. The Italian capital "cap-
tivated" him on his 1938 visit.[143] St. Peter's and its square impressed him. As for Paris, which he visited as conqueror in 1940,
it could not compare with Rome. Only the monumental and nationalistic Arch of Triumph (1806–1836) was more impressive to
him than Rome's architecture. Even Vienna was superior to Paris
in taste and magnificence. The Eiffel Tower (1889) and the
Champs Elysées (begun in 1667) were notable, but the buildings
and streets near them lacked unity.[144] Yet, not wanting to destroy
Paris, he was glad the city was not bombed in 1940, for there was
something to be learned there. He said that he had sent all the
Berlin architects to Paris to seek inspiration for their own city's
improvement. The "sober grandeur" of the Madeleine (1806–
1828) and the "deep impression" made by the dome of Les In-
valides (1690–1691) (respectively, neo-classical and baroque in
style) were to be models for Berlin's new monuments.[145] However,

[141] S.C., p. 94 (October 17–18, 1941).
[142] S.C., p. 35 (July 5–6, 1941).
[143] S.C., p. 267 (January 31, 1942).
[144] S.C., p. 73 (October 1, 1941). Breker reports that Hitler was impressed
with the Place de la Concorde and with the exterior of the neo-baroque opera ("the
most beautiful theater in the world!"), (Breker, Paris, Hitler et moi, pp. 101, 102–
106). On this tour, see also Speer, Erinnerungen, pp. 186–187; Inside, pp. 171–172.
[145] S.C., p. 118 (October 29, 1941); this did not prevent him from ordering
the destruction of Paris in 1944.

he reflected modern critical opinion in calling the Sacré Coeur basilica (begun in 1876) "appalling" and in finding the interior of the Paris Opera "overloaded."[146] He was disappointed, too, with the Panthéon's (1764–1781) interior, which he felt was crowded with too much sculpture.[147] It is to be expected that Hitler would not be enthusiastic about the architectural achievements of this "inferior" people; yet it is also to be expected that those monuments he approved were large and in the classical mode.

Despite his interest in German and other European capitals, Hitler's predominant concern in city replanning was for his home town, Linz, on the Danube in Upper Austria, which was to be completely revamped and would become the art center of Europe.[148] The "Linz Project" suggested the way the new Germany would look.

Hitler never forgot his youthful plans for this city.[149] After the 1938 Anschluss, he toured Linz and decided that the time was ripe for realization of his plans. He set up a Baukanzlei (building office) there under his personal direction, and put the architect Roderich Fick in charge of the overall plan.[150] Fascinated by the prospect of surpassing Vienna and Budapest — and Paris — he was still working on the Führerauftrag Linz as late as 1944.[151] The re-

[146] S.C., p. 118. Nevertheless, Breker maintains that he found the Madeleine too "academic." (Paris, Hitler et moi, p. 102.)

[147] S.C., pp. 118 (October 29, 1941). He preferred the opera houses of Vienna and Dresden. (S.C., p. 650 [June 13, 1943].) However, Speer (who accompanied him in Paris) reports that at the time he was "enthusiastic about the neo-baroque interior, but later became ashamed to admit to such an opinion." (Correspondence with Speer, March 9, 1969; see also Speer's Erinnerungen, pp. 186–187; Inside, p. 171. This explains the enthusiasm in note 143.)

[148] Linz; Stadt am Strom, edited by Linz, Osterreich in Wort und Bild, Bauer, 1962 (no pagination), and Speer, Erinnerungen, pp. 112–113; Inside, p. 99.

[149] See Kubizek, The Young Hitler, pp. 89–97. Kubizek maintains that the plans which Hitler drew up while still a boy in Linz are identical with the town-planning scheme that was inaugurated there after 1938. (The Young Hitler, p. 86.)

[150] Dissatisfied with Fick's work, Hitler later replaced him with the Munich architect Hermann Giessler.

[151] Martin Bormann noted that on August 18, 1944, shortly after the assassination attempt of that summer, at Hitler's headquarters the architects Speer and Gies-

construction of Linz was not merely a sentimental dream of Hitler, but another political tool.

Linz was to expand to three or four times its normal size. Trade would be attracted from Vienna bringing along laborers, who would work in the new Hermann Goering Steel Works. This would help ease Vienna's housing and congestion problems. Compared with the former Austrian capital, Linz would be "purely German," and would surpass Budapest in its beauty. Its magnificence would prove that the artistic sense of the Germans was not inferior to that of the Magyars.[152]

Probably with Budapest as his model, Hitler would exploit Linz's river location. The bank of the Danube was to be "built up in a magnificent fashion," with private homes, "models of their kind."[153] But typically, Hitler was more concerned with "community" buildings. The new Linz would have a central avenue at each end of which were two large squares, a pattern found in his plans for other cities. Around this core was to be built the cultural centers, which would make Linz the Paris of the German-speaking world. Along the *Prachtstrasse* (ceremonial avenue) were to be two theaters, a concert hall, a theater restaurant and cafe, and a trade school. At the north end of the avenue was to be the larger square, dominated by three structures: the opera house, a museum, and a library. Also on the square was to be the buildings of the Hitler Center: the Bruckner Hall, an operetta theater, art gallery, and a cinema. Behind the Center was to be the air-raid shelter (a practical fixture found in much of Hitler's planning). At the southern end of this mall was to be the railway station, flanked by the railway offices and the post office. These were all "community" buildings, constructed to serve, represent, and impress the *Volk*.

The art gallery here was probably Hitler's favorite project.

sler, visited the *Führer*: "Giessler is bound to divert the Fuehrer somewhat with his plans for Linz." (Martin Bormann, *The Bormann Letters*, translated by R. H. Stevens, London, Weidenfeld and Nicolson, 1954, p. 81.)

[152] S.C., pp. 421–422 (April 28, 1941).

[153] S.C., p. 422 (April 28, 1942).

It was to contain the largest and most comprehensive painting collection in Europe, with the best examples of Rembrandt and other masters. Its neo-classical façade would include a colonnade 150 meters long. Roderich Fick, who designed several other Linz buildings, drew up the first plans for this *Führermuseum*. The Linz Library would contain more than 250,000 books and manuscripts. There would also be one museum for sculpture and one for furniture, tapestries, and rare coins. On the Pöstlingberg outside the city would be built an observatory surmounted by a dome, containing a planetarium. Troost's stark style would govern its design as well as the interior decoration. The façade would be "of quite classical purity," said Hitler, and the pediment would bear the words, "The heavens proclaim the glory of the everlasting."[154] As for the new Danube Hotel, designed by Fick, it would be Italian Renaissance in design. Linz would also be able to boast of an olympic stadium, a *Wehrmacht* headquarters, and that suspension bridge which Hitler had planned as a youth. Finally, in Linz, Hitler would be buried, in a crypt beneath a tower.

The plans for Linz remained in the project state with one or two exceptions. The bridge over the Danube was rebuilt, widened so that it does indeed appear more like an avenue than a bridge, just as Hitler wished. Two large buildings flank the entrance from this avenue-bridge to the city square. These do not, however, block the view from the square across the Danube toward the hills. This reconstruction was carried out from 1939 to 1944 as Hitler had planned before 1914. However, because of the war, little else was undertaken.

This, then, was the new Linz. The plans show Hitler's penchant for the neo-classical style. What is more important, they show his concern for "community" architecture, and for the political use of architecture — in this case, to surpass the French, the Viennese, and the Magyars. The plans for Linz, especially the

[154] S.C., p. 312 (February 20, 1942). The words are from a poem by C. F. Gellert (1715–1760), "Die Ehre Gottes aus der Natur."

long, wide avenue and the two large squares, were echoed in plans for other German cities.

Hitler's own residences do not reveal much about his taste or plans for Germany. (Of the Berlin Chancellery more will be said later.) In Munich, Hitler lived in several different flats before 1933; one, a large apartment on Prinzregentenstrasse, an expensive district. His retreat on the Obersalzberg near Berchtesgaden in southern Bavaria may, however, be a more significant residence. Here, in the natural grandeur of the Alps, far away from the "decadent" metropolis, Hitler had two buildings constructed in the local style, at once modest and pompous, blending with their surroundings and still impressive to visitors: the *Berghof* and the "Eagle's Nest." (See illustration no. 31.) However, neither of these can be called "community" buildings except as they had a representative function. Their impressiveness, of course, was due as much to their geographical location as to their style. They were built with local, natural materials, in the style of Bavarian chalets, and thus conformed to Hitler's traditional taste. In this way, too, they could be considered part of the *völkisch* architecture movement which the ideology reflected. Unique as they were, they do not seem to play any large role in the National Socialist architecture program.

Hitler did not care much about the local styles of domestic buildings (peasant cottages or rural villas)[155] and was out of sympathy with men like Paul Schultze-Naumburg (1869–1949), director of the State Academy in Weimar, who tried to influence the party this way; he did not discourage these people, however, and this attitude is typical of his role in the building program. He rarely intervened directly in the program and never tried to enforce one style for all new building in Germany. He approved large, neo-classical or baroque buildings for "community" projects.

[155] Hitler was pleased that the Berghof did not clash with its surroundings. "We've succeeded in maintaining a unity of style," he said, noting that Alpine chalets should not be built in urban areas, but only in districts where a pentroof was necessary. (*S.C.*, p. 641 [September 4, 1942].)

But beyond these, his influence on style was slight. His concern for "community" architecture, of course, was shared by his followers (although many understood the term in a more social context), and his awareness that the army and air force as well as German industry would need new buildings was shared by leaders in these fields. Despite his love of architecture, except for monumental building, he rarely made his influence directly felt.

Ziegler noted in 1937 that Hitler was careful not to pronounce judgment on the many architectural and monumental plans which he conceived himself; nor would he pronounce on others.[156] This behavior is also described by Speer, to whom Hitler would submit his ideas and plans; when the professional architect made corrections, Hitler would usually approve. Serious disagreements between Speer and Hitler were rare before the former became armaments minister in 1942.[157] It seems, furthermore, that Hitler's respect for Troost was that of a pupil for a revered master.[158] In the field of architecture, at least, the *Führer* was willing to bow to professional opinion.

To be sure, there are some instances of Hitler's intervention in architectural matters. He was careful to see that the new Congress Hall at Nuremberg should be built of natural stone and not of concrete. His preferences determined the winner in the contest for a new Reich bank in 1933. He disapproved of the 1934 Houses of Work contest with the result that it was abandoned. In 1940 he contravened the jury's decision in the contest for plans of a new "National Socialist university." These examples, however, seem to be exceptions to the rule.

Hitler's views on architecture were more important for what he favored than for what he opposed. City planning on a grand

---

[156] Cited in Joseph Wulf, ed., *Die bildenden Künste im Dritten Reich: Eine Dokumentation*, Gütersloh, Sigbert Mohn, 1963, p. 132.

[157] Interview with Albert Speer, Heidelberg, June 13, 1968.

[158] Speer, *Erinnerungen*, p. 52; *Inside*, p. 39. Hitler wanted 3000 seats in the new Munich opera house, but gave up the plan when experts told him it was impossible. (Karl Arndt, "Das Wort aus Stein," *Filmdokumente zur Zeitgeschichte*, Göttingen, Institut für den wissenschaftlichen Film, 1965, p. 21.) As is well known, Hitler rarely valued professional opinion in any other field.

scale and large monumental buildings were his penchants. In these fields, he gathered around him men who could execute his dreams. Troost, Speer, Giessler, and Todt he admired because they could think on a grand scale as he did. He gave them relative freedom because of his respect for tradition-oriented creative talent and because they shared his dreams. Details were unimportant if the overall concept could be realized.

Hitler never came out emphatically for or against modernism, but, as was often his practice, he compromised and avoided a dogmatic stand. When the *Bauhaus* debate raged, he was busy fighting the party's political battles; he never lost interest in architecture, but at this time when there was little hope that his architectural ideas could be realized, he concentrated on achieving political victory first. This practical concern with the attainment of power (later, over Europe) continued to dominate any concern he may have had for the subtleties of architectural theory. Throughout the twelve years he was in power, Hitler's outlook remained more pragmatic than critical. He wanted to build; his style was usually neo-classical and his scale always grand. It did not bother him that the Reich Chamber of the Arts included "undesirable" moderns as Mies van der Rohe, or that some of the Air Ministry's buildings were in a style only slightly removed from that of the most radical of the *Bauhaus* designs. He was not interested in public housing, health facilities, or factory designs. He was indifferent to their style.

While he did care deeply about producing his own answer to Habsburg Vienna or imperial Rome, it could never be maintained that power-hungry Hitler loved architecture because he admired beauty of form or functionalism or the impressive work of human — or of German — hands. His "community" architecture was designed to control a community. In the end, buildings were only tools for his wielding of authority. In 1945, he was prepared to destroy every German palace, cathedral, castle, stadium and theater in his attitude of "scorched earth." The tools had not worked well. They could be discarded.

CHAPTER THREE

Ideologues and Architects

OF THE many men who served the "master builder," there are perhaps four who deserve close examination for their influence on architecture. Given the official positions of Alfred Rosenberg, Joseph Goebbels, Paul Ludwig Troost, and Albert Speer, their ideas on architecture are of interest.

Alfred Rosenberg (1893–1946) supplied Hitler with some philosophical basis for his architectural as well as for his racial theories. He was the leading *völkisch* ideologue of the Nazi movement and had fixed opinions on many subjects, including architecture. Although some of his views were ignored or used only as propaganda by Nazi leaders, he did influence Nazi architecture in two ways. He helped to direct Hitler's taste toward "Doric" classicism, and he inspired many *völkisch* architects.[1]

Rosenberg, a Baltic German, studied architecture at the Technical University in Riga, Estonia, and at St. Petersburg, and graduated in 1917 from the University of Moscow. It may have been Rosenberg's architectural background which made his ideas appealing to Hitler, whose own early life was similar but less successful. When Rosenberg came to Munich in 1919, he made a living for a while by selling sketches of medieval Baltic cities,

---

[1] Brenner has shown that, in his *Kultur* speech of September 1933, Hitler used many Rosenbergian terms and phrases. *Kunstpolitik*, p. 70. On the other hand, Hitler ridiculed Rosenberg's ideas on religion. *S.C.*, p. 400 (April 11, 1942). Here, as elsewhere, Hitler probably used only what was expedient.

such as Reval. In the Bavarian capital, Rosenberg also met that
political and artistic ferment which confronted budding politicians
like Hitler, as well as architects such as Troost. In 1921 he joined
the Nazi party, becoming editor of the party's journal, the *Völkischer Beobachter*.[2]

Trying to defend "pure" German culture from alien and Communist influence, he founded in 1928 his *Kampfbund für deutsche
Kultur* and its voice, the *Deutsche Kulturwacht*.[3] In 1930 Rosenberg published his most important work, *Der Mythus des 20.
Jahrhunderts*, and in 1934, *Revolution in der bildenden Kunst*, a
pamphlet. During the Third Reich, he edited *Kunstkammer*, a periodical issued in 1935–1936 by the Chamber of Art,[4] as well as the
same office's monthly *Mitteilungsblatt*. From 1937 to 1944, he
helped edit *Die Kunst im dritten Reich*,[5] a lavish review of the
arts, During the war, he headed an organization for collecting
European art treasures (some of which were to go to the Linz
collection). His role, therefore, was potentially crucial in determining the attitude of the party and government to art and architecture.

However, Rosenberg had no official position of real power
from which he could control the arts; he clashed seriously with
the Minister of Propaganda Joseph Goebbels on party policy, and
even disagreed with Hitler on important points. Consequently,
his influence on building was to be indirect. If he influenced Hitler, it was only before 1933. Although he did influence the *völkisch*
schools, after 1933 he and the *völkisch* architects were largely
ignored by Hitler. Yet his ideas were similar to those of lesser

[2] For an account of his career, see J. C. Fest's *Das Gesicht des Dritten
Reiches*, Munich, Piper, 1963, pp. 225–240.
[3] Not until 1934 did the *Kampfbund* become a branch of the party, indica-
tive of Hitler's lack of interest in *völkisch* groups. In 1934 the *Kampfbund* took
the name "National Socialist *Kultur* Society" (NS-*Kulturgemeinde*), and regularly
published *Die völkische Kunst*. Its *völkisch* views now had apparent party approval,
but, of course, it could also be more effectively supervised, as a branch of the
party.
[4] The Chamber of Art was founded in 1933.
[5] After 1940 it was called *Die Kunst im Deutschen Reich*.

writers and architects. Moreover, he expressed himself more often and more coherently than Hitler, and, although his views were not totally absorbed into acceptable theory, they hint at how some aspects of Nazi architecture theory were to evolve.

Rosenberg's concept of racial affinity between the ancient Greeks and the Germans affirmed what Hitler had apparently learned from Moeller van den Bruck and others. Both the Greeks and the Germans had a deep consciousness of their "Nordic" racial roots, said Rosenberg. The ancient Greeks, in fact, were "brothers of the Germans who came to maturity earlier."[6] Proof of the link between the two groups was found in the types of houses they built. The "Nordic" ancestors of the ancient Greeks migrated from the valley of the Danube, bringing with them a post-and-lintel type of construction and a rectilinear ground plan.[7] The Greeks later brought this form to perfection in their stone temples, an "expression of their racial awareness" and a "protest against Asia." The form of the temple expressed also the "Nordic" sense of space (*Raum*).[8] Although the patriarchal Germanic tribes migrated to Italy, too, their sense of form did not blossom as freely there, because a struggle developed between the post-lintel construction and the Etruscan round-arch form. The latter form, which, according to Rosenberg, was "un-Aryan" and belonged to the matriarchal society of the Etruscans, unfortunately triumphed in Italy and reappeared later in the central (or circular) type of church plan (versus the basilica, or rectilinear plan). These architectural forms, the circular plan and the round arch, had always been foreign to the Germans, said Rosenberg.

[6] Alfred Rosenberg, *Revolution in der bildenden Kunst*, Munich, Eher, 1934, pp. 10–11. (Hereafter cited as *Revolution*.)

[7] Rosenberg showed that the stone houses of prehistoric Brandenburg had the same type of ground plan as Greek buildings, thus allegedly proving "Aryan" kinship. (*Der Mythus des 20. Jahrhunderts: eine Wertung der seelisch-geistigen Gestaltenkämpfe unserer Zeit*, Munich, Hoheneichen, 1936, p. 383.) Hereafter cited as *Mythus*.)

[8] *Mythus*, p. 352. See also *Revolution*, p. 11, and *Mythus*, p. 383.

The circular form limits the view on all sides. It is directionless; it is, in plan, at the same time free on all sides; in the deepest sense of the three-dimensional, a round building cannot communicate a real sense of space, no matter how strong the artist's hand which formed it.[9]

It is typical of the Nazi building program that Rosenberg's strictures on the effeminate round arch did not prevent its recurrence in the new architecture, such as in the Nuremberg Congress Hall. Rosenberg himself seems inconsistent. He praised the German Romanesque cathedrals which exhibit "the highest Germanic masculinity"[10] Here round arches were not considered alien or feminine, but a part of masculine, "Nordic" solidity and reserve.

"Spiritual attitude" determined the quality of architecture. The "Nordic" soul possessed elements of masculinity and strength which "Nordic" architecture should express.[11] Romanesque and Gothic churches did this well; indeed, "The German cathedrals were not built by Catholics . . . they are the creation of the German race."[12] The "tragedy of the Middle Ages"[13] was that the southern alien church distorted and suppressed the striving of the "Nordic" soul for full expression.

Thus the Gothic style proved to be a dead end for the German will to expression, said Rosenberg. Whereas the rejuvenated life strength of the medieval "Nordics," disciplined and energetic, was struggling towards freedom, the final form of most Gothic cathedrals represented a repression of this genuine force of will seeking its goal.[14] Ultimately the vertical Gothic form became ecstatic and hysterical. Only in certain cathedrals, such as Strasbourg, did the German sense of space prevail, for "here the heavy columns do not

[9] *Mythus*, p. 384. Rosenberg describes how during his youth in Riga he planned a crematorium with a series of round arches. Apparently he later discovered the "un-Germanness" of this style. (*Portrait eines Menschheitsverbrechers*, p. 34.
[10] *Revolution*, p. 7.
[11] *Ibid.*, p. 4.
[12] Alfred Rosenberg, *Tagebuch*, p. 247.
[13] The phrase is a chapter heading in the *Mythus*, pp. 70ff.
[14] *Revolution*, p. 7.

block the view through space."[15] Hence for Rosenberg this sort of building represented not only Catholicism, but also "refined Germanness." Such ideas significantly occur again in Hitler's speeches and conversations, often linked to his distaste for the Catholic Church. When Hitler declared that a great people could not be prevented from building monuments to themselves, he might have been recalling the section in the *Mythus* on the *aesthetische Wille*.[16] Here Rosenberg described how the "Nordic" soul had continually sought to express itself, to find an "embodiment of [its] highest spiritual potency with eternally new means in eternally new forms."[17] This "European life pulse"[18] throbbed most strongly in three periods; the Gothic, the baroque, and the neo-classical age of Goethe and Schinkel.[19] The "life pulse" would beat again for a fourth time in Hitler's Reich.

Although he approved of neo-classicism, Rosenberg had not much to say about the style of architects Friedrich Gilly (1772–1800), Karl Friedrich Schinkel (1781–1841), or Leo von Klenze (1794–1864). As for the latter half of the nineteenth century, he shared the *völkisch* view that it was a period of moral and artistic decline, a time of "ideological chaos." "With pity and shame," he wrote, "a modern architect looks down on the Friedrichstrasse in Berlin, or at the Munich City Hall."[20] It would be Germany's "eternal shame" that her metropolises contained this "pseudo-architecture," these "Moorish railway stations," these "pompous monuments."[21] The time had come to cease imitating foreign styles — if only because the German people were "tired of building

---

[15] *Tagebuch*, p. 149. This recalls Hitler's praise for Strasbourg.

[16] *Mythus*, pp. 404ff.

[17] *Ibid.*, pp. 376–377. This reference to new forms and new means did not imply that Rosenberg favored the new forms and means of the *Bauhaus*.

[18] *Ibid.*, p. 367.

[19] *Ibid.*, p. 377.

[20] *Ibid.*, p. 386. Friedrichstrasse was the nineteenth-century business section of Berlin. The Munich City Hall, designed by Hauberisser in neo-Gothic, was built in the late nineteenth century. (See illustration no. 11.)

[21] *Revolution*, p. 6.

warehouses and bank palaces."[22] Believing that a new architecture must be found, Rosenberg shared the discontent which
also motivated Gropius, Le Corbusier, and other architectural
innovators. His solution to the problem, however, was very different from theirs.

Although Rosenberg did not sympathize with the turn-of-the-
century movement in decoration, *art nouveau*, he saw it and its
German equivalent, *Jugendstil*, as efforts to break away from imitation.[23] This process, however, ended during the First World War,
when the "ecstatic" lines of the *Jugendstil* conveyed a "poisoning"
of the will. Rosenberg felt that the mind of the German people
was confused; the *Volk* could produce only purely intellectualized
schemes, such as those of the *Bauhaus*. For him, the false and
sterile architecture of Gropius and his followers, which represented the nadir of this misguided search for a new style, was impractical and soon antiquated. Twentieth-century culture had
thus disintegrated and lost contact with the best traditions of
German architecture. Modern building was symbolic of a mass
society wherein atomized individuals had lost all sense of identity
and community.

Rosenberg's views of New York skyscrapers are interesting.
Across the Atlantic was emerging a "new rhythm in stone,"[24]
truly functional, an expression of the "Nordic" spirit struggling
again to emerge. The Americans, however, had made too many
mistakes in creating Manhattan. For Rosenberg these skycrapers
were decorated in a dishonest Renaissance or baroque manner;
they were also built too closely together, without an inner standard of value or an organic relationship. Yet this phenomenon
challenged Europeans to find different but suitable answers to
their own architectural problems. Rosenberg found Fritz Höger's
(1877–1949) Chile House in Hamburg (1920–23) a healthy re-

[22] *Mythus*, p. 617.
[23] *Revolution*, p. 13.
[24] *Mythus*, p. 380.

action, as were the plans of Wilhelm Kreis (1873–1955) for tall buildings of a German type.[25]

What did Rosenberg expect of genuinely German building? Having studied architecture himself and being aware of current trends, he felt justified in calling architecture "the first art which is on the way to becoming honest again."[26] The German "feeling for life" was reawakening, breaking through the old lies about the internationality of art, proving again that art was always a creation of "the blood" and that the art of one race could only be understood by that race itself.[27] In 1934 when he wrote *Revolution in der bildenden Kunst,* this feeling was not yet strong enough for a "monumental" expression. Nevertheless, said Rosenberg, that expression would eventually be as heroic as the words of the Horst Wessel song. It would be neither intellectualist (*Bauhaus*) nor ecstatic (expressionist).[28] In 1930 he said that the new architecture would not try to escape the realities of this life but would "honor the soil, give it shape, and inform it with spirit."[29] In the finite, the Germans would see a symbol of the eternal, and suffuse material strength with spiritual values. Always Rosenberg came back to the material and the earthly. In 1934 he wrote that the German race had a "healthy feeling for nature"; Germanic man listened to the laws of nature and had learned to live in harmony

[25] *Ibid.,* p. 381 footnote. The *Chilehaus* was built of red brick. Aside from the semimilitary towers of the *Ordensburgen,* the Berlin *Maifeld,* or the Nuremberg *Märzfeld,* no functional skyscrapers were built in the Third Reich. However, Rosenberg's idea for a new university (*Hohe Schule der NSDAP,* described below, Chapter X) did include sketches for a monolithic tower twelve storeys high. A photograph of a model of this symmetrically designed building is in Teut, *Architektur,* p. 211. See p. 197 of the same volume for a sketch of the planned center for the *Oberkommando des Wehrmachts* (OKW or General Staff) in Berlin, which also contained a tower (see also below, Chapter VII). On Kreis' towers (usually each twenty storeys high), see Hans Stephan, *Wilhelm Kreis,* Oldenburg, Stalling, 1944, pp. 46–48. (Stephan was an advisor to Speer in the latter's capacity as general building inspector for Berlin.)

[26] *Mythus,* p. 386.

[27] *Ibid.,* p. 120.

[28] *Revolution,* p. 13.

[29] *Mythus,* p. 386.

with these laws. Therefore the new architecture would be earth-bound, but would also express the qualities of the "German soul." [30]

Thus Rosenberg tried to amalgamate *völkisch* views of architecture, which were originally concerned with rural or small-scale building, and the nationalist desire for imposing monumental structures. He believed that "Aryan" spiritual traits were best represented through monumental buildings, which, in his diary, he described as "a community's ideas in stone." The new *Gau* houses, the *Ordensburgen* (political training schools), the *Volk* halls, the planned Nazi university would show that the Germans of the Third Reich thought well of themselves and of their ideology, just as did the Christians in their age. In *Der Mythus*, Rosenberg showed how this new architecture would express the strength of the German race and its renaissance:

> For monumental buildings, our age must pile building block upon building block; for water towers, we need powerful closed forms; for corn silos, simple gigantic masses. Our factories must lie heavily on the earth. . . . Buildings of a large factory which formerly were strewn accidently draw together organically in an inner community. . . . Hotels will rid themselves of their phony decoration. . . . In new rhythms, a resounding song of iron and stone will be sung.[31]

Mass, weight, unity — this was for Rosenberg an excellent description of Germany's new architecture. For him, symmetry of architectural form was also important in monumental buildings. A large building would have its horizontal lines stressed and extended into two complementary wings, flanking a heavy massive tower. To avoid the mistakes of New York, these towers should not be built too closely together, or they would lose their effect. In this way, the German architect could express his "blood-based" sense of space and order.[32]

[30] *Revolution*, pp. 8–9.

[31] *Mythus*, p. 379.

[32] *Mythus*, pp. 380–381. The planned *Hohe Schule* or university of the party was designed this way.

From Rosenberg's writing, Hitler may have derived his concept of "community" architecture, although both men may have plagiarized — and distorted — the term as it was used by *avant garde*, socially concerned architects of the twenties. It seems likely as well that, by linking post-lintel, Greek construction with the "Aryan" background of the Germans, Rosenberg strengthened Hitler's own predilection for the monumental and the neo-classical, and provided philosophical and "scientific" rationalizations for what Hitler wanted to build. Secondly, his stress on racial purity gave support to the less successful *völkisch* movement. Yet, his works did not set any tone determining the building program of the Third Reich. They merely provided the ideological rationalization for the monumental "community" structures. Just as Troost and Speer provided the form, so Rosenberg provided some of the ideological content for these buildings. During the Third Reich, Rosenberg's role actually diminished, a phenomenon shown best in his conflict with Goebbels.[33]

The propaganda minister and head of the Chamber of Culture, unlike Rosenberg, seems to have had few deep convictions on architecture. Goebbels influenced the Nazi architecture program even less. His comments on architecture are few and far between; whereas Rosenberg adhered to the *völkisch* "blood and soil" idea, Goebbels does not seem to have even used it much in his propaganda machine.[34] He never supported monumental neo-classicism; neither did he support the *völkisch* architects. Under his influence, *avante-garde* architecture (and art) might have been given fuller freedom. His initial appreciation of the painting of the German expressionists might have been the reason why the more *avant-garde* architects were not actively persecuted, but rather ig-

---

[33] A rare citation of Rosenberg in a contemporary work on architecture is in Erich Böckler, *Landschaftsgemäss bauen? Eine Antwort durch Wort und Bild,* Munich, Callwey, 1943, p. 34 (a note on the supposedly innate German feeling for nature).

[34] Except briefly, 1934–1937, when he supported the *Thing* movement. However, this was not out of ideological conviction. (See Chapter IX.)

nored.[35] Of all the Nazi leaders, he was the most open to modern developments in all the arts.

As early as 1933, Goebbels declared his opposition to Rosenberg and the *Kampfbund*. His Reich Culture Chamber, set up in 1933, with himself as president, was to be a rival organization of the *Kampfbund* until the latter's demise in 1935.[36] Although Goebbels was cool to the "blood and soil" outlook, and was not (at first) publicly an opponent of modern architecture, he did not in the end support the modern style of building. Perhaps, concerned only that the Third Reich should not appear reactionary, he followed a pragmatic policy similar to that stated in Hitler's appeal to essential technicians and architects.[37]

The propaganda minister was not without interest in architecture. In his part of the Berlin bunker was found a set of illus-

[35] Speer, *Erinnerungen*, p. 41; *Inside*, p. 27; see also Brenner, *Kunstpolitik*, pp. 78–82.

[36] The Goebbels-Rosenberg conflict is well described in Lane, *Architecture and Politics*, pp. 175–184, and in Brenner, *Kunstpolitik*, pp. 63–86. The Reich Ministry for Propaganda and Enlightenment of the People (*Volksaufklärung*) was headed by Goebbels, while the fine arts section was supervised by Dr. Franz Hofmann. Another part of this ministry and a corporative branch of the German Labor Front was the Reich Culture Chamber, founded on September 22, 1933. President of this chamber was Goebbels and head of its Chamber of Fine Arts was at first an architect, Eugen Hönig, and later a painter, Adolf Ziegler. In each *Gau* or district, there were culture supervisors, who cooperated with the Propaganda Ministry and its local leaders. On the Presidential Council of the Culture Chamber sat the head of the Weimar National Theater, Ziegler, Speer, and Hönig, among others. The Third Division of this chamber was concerned with architecture, landscape gardening, and interior decoration (see Brenner, *Kunstpolitik*, pp. 243 and 247 for a diagrammatic representation). The League of German Architects was incorporated into the Culture Chamber and membership of all practising architects was mandatory.

[37] With regard to Goebbels' convictions on architecture, Speer believes that the propaganda minister had "wider horizons" than many other Nazi leaders and would have been more open in his support of modern trends had not Hitler come out against them. (Correspondence, August 13, 1969.) Nevertheless he authorized the campaign against abstract and expressionist painting, that culminated in the Munich exhibition of "degenerate art" in 1937. With Goebbels, as with Hitler, convictions on specific trends in art and architecture were probably less important than power itself.

trated books on opera-house architecture.[38] Agreeing with Hitler
and Rosenberg on the importance of building (and possibly influenced by the dispute over *avant-garde* building in the Weimar
period) he said that "architecture is the symbol of the life of the
state."[39] His ministry was housed in the former Leopold Palace
(1737) on the Wilhelmsplatz in Berlin, opposite the Chancellery.
It had been remodelled by Schinkel in 1828, and Goebbels apparently liked its appearance,[40] but found it impossible to work in it,
at least in its 1933 condition. Accordingly, he had the interior
renovated, tearing out old plaster and wooden panels. His comments on this procedure reflect a modern view of interior decoration: "I must have around me clarity, cleanliness, and pure, distinct lines. Twilight is repugnant to me."[41] One might assume
that like Hitler, Goebbels may have been influenced by the modern movement towards architectural simplicity. But these words
were written for his propaganda "diary," and the rest of his notes
in this volume show only a superficial concern for suitable party
buildings.[42] His lack of interest in a subject as important as architecture annoyed Rosenberg and his colleagues, such as Schultze-
Naumburg, who were violently opposed to any suggestion of
laxity toward "Bolshevik" architecture; still, Goebbels' view obedi-
ently imitated that of his leader.

[38] H. R. Trevor-Roper, *Last Days of Hitler*, New York, Macmillan, 1947, p.
57, note 16.

[39] A speech of 1934 cited in Teut, *Architektur*, p. 289.

[40] Curt Riess, *Joseph Goebbels: A Biography*, New York, Ballantine, 1960,
p. 91.

[41] Joseph Goebbels, *Vom Kaiserhof zur Reichskanzlei: Eine historische Darstellung in Tagebuchblättern*, Munich, Eher, 1934, p. 279. "My new rooms," he
added later, "correspond to my taste, sun, air, light; here one can work." *Vom
Kaiserhof*, p. 286.

[42] In October 1932 he attended the opening of Speer's new *Gauhaus* on the
Voss-Strasse in Berlin and noted vaguely that he found "everything well appointed" and "in good order," "a worthy office for the great movement." (*Vom
Kaiserhof*, pp. 181–182.) In a speech of May 1933 he indicated his approval of
the new Italian (Fascist) architecture — also starkly neo-classical — and called it
"impressive," but he never seems to have publicly gone beyond these generalities.
(Cited in Brenner, *Kunstpolitik*, p. 80.)

In 1934 Hitler openly gave his support to Goebbels' more pragmatic stance, without, however, approving the propaganda minister's private flirtation with modern painting.[43] He fobbed off Rosenberg with honorary posts and avoided a strong line on architecture. By 1939 when Hitler could see around him the monumental buildings which he considered the finest form of architecture, Germany's building program satisfied him. To actually persecute the exponents of modern architecture might be politically unwise; moreover, he was simply not interested in the implications of *völkisch* thought. Rosenberg, therefore, was made head of the foreign policy bureau of the party, later "custodian of the entire intellectual and spiritual training and education of the party," and eventually commissioner of the occupied eastern territories. Meanwhile, the Culture Chamber took over the architectural concerns of the Fighting League.

Goebbels proceeded to follow a middle-of-the road approach. When the Decree on Architectural Form of 1937 required architects to plan buildings which would "express the proper architectural views,"[44] these views were clarified neither by Goebbels, his Propaganda Ministry, the Culture Chamber, nor Hitler himself. Consequently a unified style was never emphatically decreed by party or government in the Third Reich. There is a further paradox; the men who designed some of the most impressive "community" neo-classical monuments — Troost and Speer — were not outspoken Nazi ideologues, nor were they propagandists in the sense Goebbels was. They were Nazis, to be sure, but considered themselves part of the European neo-classical movement.

As soon as he came to power, Hitler chose Troost,[45] an acquaintance of several years, to begin remodeling the face of Germany. Troost, active as an architect in Munich before 1933 and a member of the party since 1924, was commissioned to design

[43] For the details of Hitler's decision, see Brenner, *Kunstpolitik*, pp. 82–86.

[44] Cited in Lane, *Architecture and Politics*, p. 183, footnote 71.

[45] On Hitler's first meeting with Troost, see Ziegler, *Adolf Hitler*, pp. 188–189. See also Speer, *Erinnerungen*, pp. 52–55; *Inside*, pp. 39–43.

the House of German Art on Prinzregentenstrasse and the new party headquarters on the Königsplatz in Munich. The *Führer* revered him as "one of the greatest German architects" and "the instructor of our age,"[46] and bestowed on him the title of professor. "That man revolutionized the art of building," reminisced Hitler later.[47] After Troost's death in 1934, Hitler annually laid a wreath on the grave in Munich's North Cemetery. Rarely did Hitler respect any man; but this admiration of a "genius" seems to have been genuine, at least in his applause for Troost's ability to create impressive, monumental state architecture. There is much truth in the claim: "What Dietrich Eckart was to the *Führer* in the field of ideology, so also was Professor Troost in the field of architecture."[48] Besides his penchant for neo-classicism, Troost had other qualities which endeared him to Hitler. According to the *Führer*, Troost was a genius, yet was modest and had to be persuaded to enter his designs for the House of German Art contest.[49] Further more, he expressed in his plans the strength and reserve of the "Teutonic" soul and he did not compose intellectual treatises on how to revamp society. Hitler maintained that so out of joint were circumstances in Germany before 1933, Troost would have languished in obscurity under the "November system."[50]

Troost's distaste for *Bauhaus* architecture and his love for a simplified but traditional classicism[51] made him the ideal man to express Hitler's need for monumental "community" architecture. Before he received Hitler's commissions, his activities help indicate what many hoped for in German architecture of the Third

[46] Domarus, *Reden*, p. 707 (July 19, 1937; opening of the House of German Art), and p. 779 (January 22, 1938).

[47] S.C., p. 212 (January 13, 1942).

[48] *Adolf Hitler: Bilder aus dem Leben des Führers*, Hamburg, 1936 cited in Armand Dehlinger, *Architektur der Superlative: Eine kritische Betrachtung des NS-Bauprogramme von München und Nürnberg*, microfilmed manuscript, Institut für Zeitgeschichte, Munich, n.d., p. 21.

[49] Domarus, *Reden*, p. 707 (July 19, 1937).

[50] S.C., p. 212 (January 13, 1942).

[51] Troost sought to revive an early classical or "Doric" architecture. (Correspondence with Gerdy Troost, November 29, 1969.)

Reich. He designed villas for industrialists in the "Munich style": "simple German gabled house[s] higher than wide, with windows cozily placed in whitewashed walls, with charming shutters and broad groups of windows on the main floor."[52] In this phase of his career, Troost belonged to that school of architects, which included the more racist Schultze-Naumburg, who were trying to revive a traditional type of dwelling.[53] This appealed to Nazi ideologues, but not to Hitler. It was Troost's neo-classical work, especially the remodeling of the party's Brown House in Munich in 1931, which really impressed him.[54] The Hall of Banners and the Senate Chamber accorded with Hitler's sense of pomp. (See illustration no. 25.) In 1934, therefore, he commissioned Troost to design the new art gallery of Munich, which was to be the first monumental edifice of the new Reich. For this reason, Speer calls Troost "the real initiator of the Hitler style."[55]

Troost did not live long enough to create any monumental "community" buildings other than the House of German Art and the new party offices in Munich. His place as semi-official architect was taken by Speer, a younger man, but also a neo-classicist, and influenced by Hitler's first favorite. Speer is well known as the war criminal sentenced in 1946 to twenty years in Spandau prison for his use of slave labor when he was minister of armaments and war production. But it is his earlier career as designer of the Berlin Chancellery, of parts of the Nuremberg Party Rally Grounds, and consequently as leading architect of Nazi Germany that is most significant in this context.

[52] Hans Kiener, "Germanische Tektonik," p. 183.

[53] Troost "rejected everything alien to the [German] way of life," said Kiener, cited in Teut, *Architektur*, p. 185.

[54] See Adolf Dresler, *Das Braune Haus und das Verwaltungsgebäude der Reichsleitung der NSDAP*, Munich, Eher, 1939. (Dresler was a Nazi journalist from Munich.)

[55] Correspondence with Albert Speer, November 27, 1967. The plans for the museum were completed after Troost's death by his wife, Gerdy. It is described below in Chapter XI. Troost also designed the public rooms of the North German Lloyd's steamers. Kiener praises their "beautiful and effective propaganda for the German way of life." (Cited in Teut, *Architektur*, p. 184.) Hitler appreciated these rooms, too. (Correspondence with Gerdy Troost, November 29, 1969.)

The young Speer had three outstanding characteristics; a strong ambition, a deep nationalism, and a thorough (but not unusual) political naïveté. His ambition enabled him to reach two high positions in the Nazi state, that of Hitler's chief architect, and that of minister of armaments. His nationalism made him want to build magnificent buildings for a revitalized Germany. His naïveté allowed him to maintain, until at least 1966, that he had little to do with the Nazi ideology. It is true that he was not interested in the politics of Weimar Germany. He was one of those ambitious young nationalists who were attracted to the party as to a *Bewegung* (movement) that would spiritually revive the Fatherland. For Speer, party membership and acceptance of government commissions meant fulfilling patriotic duties, as well as personal ambitions. "I scarcely felt myself to be a member of a political party," he writes; instead, he was "a follower of Hitler,"[56] and — he might have said — a part of a *Bewegung*, the aims of which seemed to him not crassly political, but patriotic, even spiritual (in an antimaterialist sense). In the thirties, he never seemed to have understood the implications of this movement, which was, in reality, lead by power-hungry, if not nihilistic, politicians. This fault he later (in 1968) attributed to his "inadequate political schooling."[57]

Insofar as it expresses German strength, his architecture might be called "Nazi," but he was himself not "Nazi" in any narrow or doctrinaire sense. To be sure, his buildings were not the product of a generous cosmopolitan mood; they were not perhaps beautiful architecture. But lack of beauty should not be equated with the political consequences of the Nazi state. In this period, many other architects, such as Rudolf Wolters, Speer's official biographer, thought that Speer and his monumental works expressed all that was best in the nationalist movement; for them, his archi-

---

[56] Speer, *Erinnerungen*, p. 34; *Inside*, p. 17.

[57] Speer, *Inside*, p. 19; this remark is not in the original German *Erinnerungen*. However, he does note he felt himself to be "Hitler's architect. Political events did not concern me." (*Erinnerungen*, p. 126; *Inside*, p. 112.)

tecture was "rooted in the new life." [58] and in their books and articles, they tried to analyze the "German" or "National Socialist" qualities of these buildings.

Born in 1905, Speer was educated at several technical universities, and graduated in 1927 from the Berlin Technical University.[59] He was appointed first assistant to Professor Heinrich Tessenow (1876–1950) to tutor his students and assist him in his studio. At the same time, he began to practice as an architect himself, deeply influenced by Tessenow's stark but still traditionalist style. In 1931, he first heard Adolf Hitler speak to a group at the Berlin Technical University and became "fascinated" [60] by the *Führer*. Influenced by this speech, and by his own students, he joined the National Socialist party the same year.[61] In 1932, the party gave him his first commissions to remodel the party headquarters in the capital. Speer soon gave up his assistantship at the university, and, in 1933, he became commissioner for the technical and artistic organization of the rallies in the Reich Propaganda Bureau. In his capacity, he organized the 1933 May Festival on the Tempelhof Field, where he used the "cathedral of light" effect which later became famous at Nuremberg. In the fall of the same year, he organized the party's first great harvest festival rally on the Bückeberg near Hameln.[62] The most impor-

[58] Wolters, *Albert Speer*, p. 14.

[59] Although Speer, as a young nationalist, joined the party in 1933 (two years before many others felt it wise to join for career purposes), there is little evidence that he was ever seriously politically orientated, and Wolters exaggerates in saying that, even as a student, Speer was a Nazi ("gläubig"; a believer). (*Albert Speer*, p. 6.) Of course, during the war years, he was not unaware of what he felt was his potential political power. (*Inside*, p. 342; *Erinnerungen*, p. 353.)

[60] "Die Bürde werde ich nicht mehr los," *Spiegel*, XX: 46 (November 7, 1966), 48. On his life up to 1931, see his *Erinnerungen*, pp. 19–35; *Inside*, pp. 3–20.

[61] It was probably both ambition and nationalism that led him to join the S.A. in this year and to assume (wrongly, he maintains) that he had become a member of the S.S. in 1932. (*Erinnerungen*, p. 36; *Inside*, p. 22.)

[62] A series of similar commissions followed immediately: planning the Tannenberg Festival on the occasion of Hindenburg's funeral in 1934, redesigning the Kroll Opera House for Reichstag sittings, and transforming the Berlin Lustgarten on the occasion of the Olympic Games.

tant year for Speer was 1934 when he was only twenty-nine years of age; he had so impressed Adolf Hitler with his backdrops for mass meetings, that he was given the position of leader of the Beauty of Labor Office in the German Labor Front in which he tried to improve the working environment of proletarians. As a member of the staff for the organization of the party's rallies, he began work on the party grounds in Nuremberg. He also made additions to the old Reich Chancellery in Berlin,[63] redesigned the German embassy in London, and designed the German pavilion for the Paris World's Fair of 1937. Later, he was appointed general building inspector for the capital of the Reich, in which role he planned a fundamental remodeling of Berlin. Hitler was so pleased with his work that he granted him the Golden Medal of the party in January 1938 and commissioned him to design and build a new chancellery for Berlin.[64] (See illustrations no. 15–23, 29, and 42–43.)

Speer, despite this apparent participation in things Nazi, preferred to consider his work in a European setting. Around 1900, European architects were searching for a new medium to express their awareness of a changing society and their disgust with the overladen historicism of the late nineteenth century. *Jugendstil* and neo-classicism were part of this mood. By the nineteen-thirties neo-classicism, although not triumphant, was expressed through

[63] Speer, *Erinnerungen*, p. 47; *Inside*, p. 34.

[64] Speer's other works include the temporary decorations on Unter den Linden in Berlin for special occasions, and, on a smaller scale, a studio for the sculptor, Joseph Thorak, in Bavaria. (See photos in Wolters, *Albert Speer*, pp. 65 and 67.) On Speer's work in the London embassy, Wilhelm Lotz wrote: "For the first time, German skills and German sense of form are consciously displayed in the entire furnishing and arrangement of details." ("Die deutsche Botschaft in London," *Moderne Bauformen*, xxxvii (1938), 345–346.) (Lotz, a writer on architecture and applied arts, was an assistant to Speer in the latter's Berlin office.) Aside from becoming minister of war production after Fritz Todt's death in 1942, Speer was in charge of the reconstruction of bombed cities. In 1938 Goering had appointed him to the Prussian Council of State. He won the Golden Medal of the Hitler Youth in 1940, and was a member of the Senate of the Reich Culture Chamber, the Prussian Academy of Arts, and the Academy of Architecture. He became in 1942, general inspector for war and energy and leader of the party's Central Bureau of Technology.

several important buildings in France, Italy, and Russia. In Paris, Auguste Perret designed the Museum of Public Works (1937). In Rome, Marcello Piacentini planned one of the main buildings of the University of Rome with a pillared portico (1936). Moscow's Red Army Theater (1940, designed by K. S. Alabyan and V. N. Simbirtzev) is a good Russian example, as is the building for the Supreme Soviet in Kiev (1939, V. I. Zabolotni).[65] Moreover, the Russian pavilion (designed by B. M. Iofan) at the World's Fair of 1937 in Paris neatly complements Speer's neo-classical German pavilion. (See illustration No. 30.) With Russia, Italy, and Germany all building in this fashion one is tempted to say that this style is typical of totalitarian dictatorships. But the French examples as well as others from America (such as Washington, D.C.) support Speer's view of the nonideological character of the movement. In the thirties, in fact, neo-classicism was the official style of many countries. As for Speer, he rightly felt part of this modern neo-classical movement. His Berlin Chancellery and his Zeppelin Field in Nuremberg are good examples of the use of simplified colonnades, heavy cornices, and porticoes. Thus in their historical context, the "patriotic" or "Nazi" qualities of these buildings are less obvious. Even when he was working on them, Speer says that he stood aside from the political and ideological rivalries within the party and concerned himself with designing, planning, and organizing.[66] Public statements by him on ideological matters are indeed rare, and there is little reference in his few writings to the concept of "community," although he was more concerned with public housing than was Hitler.

However, nationalism and romantic interest in the past which

[65] For photographs of these buildings, see Bruno Zevi, *Towards an Organic Architecture*, London, Faber and Faber, 1950, p. 48ff.

[66] Speer, *Erinnerungen*, p. 126; *Inside*, p. 112. Geoffrey Barraclough doubts the truth of this statement ("Hitler's Masterbuilder," *New York Review of Books* (January 7, 1971), p. 11.) However, Barraclough tends to ignore the peculiarly German educational and psychological background of men like Speer, which could lead to a naive optimism about human nature and politics.

is evident in the ideology did dominate his outlook.[67] Wolters was quite correct in describing him as "a true follower" of Adolf Hitler.[68] Wolters praised Speer for keeping only a small, young staff, and for avoiding excessive bureaucracy (a factor which also helped to endear him to Hitler, who hated officialdom). There may be some idealizing in this picture of the young artist who did not like to make speeches, and who preferred to work alone in his studio at Obersalzberg; yet Wolters' view of Speer as a youthful nationalist is substantially correct and could be a description of many younger party members. Wolters stresses that Speer was part of that nationalistic generation frustrated by the absurdities of the Weimar era; the Nazi movement appealed to his "uncommonly faithful and fresh, youthful optimism."[69]

Speer himself has gone to great lengths to stress that he was not trying to create a "Nazi" style, but rather to revive and update an old style. "I loved Gilly," he says, "and revered Schinkel."[70] He saw a revival of neo-classicism as the answer for modern architects who no longer wished to build in the neo-baroque and neo-Gothic. Hitler, whose taste in 1932–1933 was turning to the neo-classicism of Troost, gave the young Speer a chance to build as he wished. Like his idols, Schinkel and Gilly, Speer dreamed of monuments that might last for centuries. Upon his release from prison in 1966, he maintained that his structures were not designed with a view to expressing the National Socialist ideology, despite what propagandists or his accusers claim.[71] If his buildings were used by the state as propaganda, he believed that it was not his responsibility. If Hitler used his buildings to

[67] Speer's love of wild Alpine landscapes and his remarkable "Theory of Ruins" are described in his *Erinnerungen*, pp. 26 and 29; *Inside*, 10 and 56.
[68] Wolters, *Albert Speer*, p. 63.
[69] *Ibid.*, p. 68. He admits to having "strong nationalistic feelings." (*Erinnerungen*, p. 26; *Inside*, p. 9.)
[70] Correspondence, November 24, 1967. In his memoirs, Speer describes his 1935 trip to Greece, during which he was deeply impressed by the simple Doric style of structures like the rebuilt Stadion in Athens. (*Erinnerungen*, p. 76; *Inside*, p. 63.
[71] Correspondence, November 24, 1967.

glorify the state and party, this was not his own intention. He felt
that the *Lichtdom* (cathedral of light) effect, for example, was
simply a method of illumination, and was to serve no symbolic or
psychological purpose. (See illustration no. 44.) Any building
which is made more beautiful or more impressive could be said
to serve the propaganda purposes of that building's owners. If
Nazi architects and propagandists fastened their attention upon
his "Aryan" neo-classicism and made them nationalist propaganda,
Speer said this was none of his business. He loved the monumental
neo-classical style for its own sake. In building the party's "community" buildings, his aim was simply to execute the commissions
well, and to construct large, impressive, yet usable buildings. Here
he believed that his responsibility ended.[72]

However, in his memoirs (published in 1969), Speer states
that he designed his buildings in less innocence. They were intended to "spell out in architecture the political, military, and economic power of Germany."[73] His admiration for Hitler and his
love of Germany blinded him to the possible political consequences of his work. Consumed by ambition and probably by a
desire for power, too,[74] he was "wild to accomplish things," and
admits that he would have done nearly anything to further his
career.[75] Still, he does not seem to have thought of his works or
their style as being quintessentially German.

Moreover, although he approved of monumental buildings,
even Speer may have doubted the wisdom of the neo-baroque
trend which Nazi monumentality took into the planning of the
forties. "Above all, in the later buildings," he says, "I did not like
the pomposity and the ornamentality." This gaudiness made him

    [72] "Die Bürde werde ich nicht mehr los," *Spiegel*, XX:46 (November 7,
1966), 52–53. "Above all," he writes, "I was an architect." (*Erinnerungen*, p. 35;
Inside, p. 21.)
    [73] *Erinnerungen*, p. 153; *Inside*, p. 138.
    [74] *Erinnerungen*, p. 23; *Inside*, p. 7. Speer recalls that in his youth he par-
ticularly enjoyed the power of the coxswain of a rowing team.
    [75] *Erinnerungen*, p. 44; *Inside*, p. 31.

"uncomfortable." [76] Yet he had no serious disagreements with Hitler on the neo-classical "community" architecture which was actually built. This complex outlook, despite the semidisillusionment later, enabled young Speer — and probably other architects as well — to produce structures which, in their grandiosity, still seem to express the fervent nationalism of that age.

Speer maintains he developed a much more practical concern for the masses than did his *Führer*; he disagreed with Hitler when the latter wanted a resumption of monumental building after the victory over France in 1940. During the war, he says, he turned away from monumental classicism, opposing the construction of expensive "community" edifices and looking ahead to postwar housing problems. [77] He foresaw the need for a million workers to rebuild the damaged cities as well as 400,000 to 600,000 apartments in huge complexes for young married people. In order to solve the housing crisis in three years, he estimated that 2.5 million conventional dwellings would also have to be built. [78] But this program was for the future. In a speech of April 18, 1942, Speer declared that material used in building was often lost to the armaments industry, and the 1.8 million laborers in the building industry were misapplied. [79] Eventually and of necessity, the monumental building program was scaled down; Hitler had increasingly less time to concern himself with it anyway. At the same time, Speer was put in charge of reconstruction of bombed cities, a position in which he had little opportunity to act but one which

[76] "Die Bürde werde ich nicht mehr los," *Spiegel*, XX:46 (November 7, 1966), 50. (Hereafter cited as *Spiegel*, Nr. 46, 1966.) Speer admits that his own planning for the new Berlin had become very florid and had little to do with his original "Doric" ideals. (*Erinnerungen*, p. 174; *Inside*, p. 184.)

[77] Interview with Speer, June 13, 1968, in Heidelberg-Schlierbach; see also his *Erinnerungen*, p. 327–328; *Inside*, p. 315.

[78] Cited in Eugene Davidson, *Trial of the Germans*, New York, Macmillan, 1967, p. 498. Significantly, even in considering more mundane human needs, Speer emphasized the great size of the enterprise. See also I.M.T. *Trial*, XVI (June 20, 1946), 480.

[79] *Ibid.*, p. 482. See also Speer, *Erinnerungen*, pp. 63–84; *Inside*, pp. 50–70.

allowed him to turn his mind away from the monumental to the practical demands of working-class homes.

Given Hitler's opinion of Speer's abilities and his love of architecture, not to mention Speer's own ambition, the real architect and the would-be one worked together well. Their closest contact came in the years 1937 to 1939, when the Nuremberg buildings were going up and plans for all Germany were being outlined. Hitler was usually fair and generally agreed with his architect. He seems to have used Speer as a sounding board for his ideas, a carefully chosen sounding board, for he knew that Speer was not *avant-garde*. Perhaps he sensed the young man's ambition as well. He would come to Speer's office on the Pariser Platz and would pencil in his own touches to Speer's sketches for new buildings. Speer maintains that he (Speer) tried to differentiate between his own projects and those of Hitler. For example, the *Führer's* proposals for an arch of triumph did not please him, and because he did not regard himself as a mindless executor of Hitler's ideas, he would not accept responsibility for them. When the plans were enlarged in his office, he put three small stars under them, to indicate that these were Hitler's ideas and that he "had nothing to do with it."[80] Even though Hitler often begged him to put his signature on his (Hitler's) sketches, Speer claims that he refused. His plans for the Chancellery or the Zeppelin Field were not influenced by Hitler's taste, nor did he try to copy or imitate the *Führer's* style. He maintains, too, that in the early years of their relationship, he managed to restrain Hitler's still rather baroque taste.[81] Given Hitler's attitude to artistic creativity, these statements appear to be true.

Despite his protégé's stubbornness, Hitler gave Speer an almost completely free hand in his work. In a nineteenth-century romantic way, Hitler considered him a genius,[82] and expected

[80] Interview, June 13, 1968.
[81] Gilbert, *Nuremberg Diary*, p. 142.
[82] Interview, June 13, 1968.

nothing explicitly political from him.[83] Yet Hitler made unusual social and personal demands on him. The *Führer* seems to have identified himself with this young architect and derived relaxation from discussing projects with him at any time of day. Not only did he often invite Speer for dinner, but would call him late at night. As Speer relates, "It often happened that an adjutant would call me up at ten or eleven o'clock . . . 'Come over here, he must see plans, he wants to be diverted.' Then he would study some of my plans until three in the morning."[84] Speer did not object to this treatment. He was flattered by such attention, and his ambition was inspired by the "chance to be able to build without limits," and "to play a role in the history of art."[85] Thus the two men preserved a symbiotic relationship for almost a decade.

The architecture which the Nazis praised as having been created by the Third Reich was not only monumental and neoclassical, but included various other styles of building, from rural settlements to factories. However, neither Speer nor Hitler directly influenced much of the non-monumental building in the thirties. This less impressive sphere was more permeated with purely ideological concerns (such as defending the health of the "Aryans" against racial pollution) than was the construction of monumental buildings. Moreover, much that was written on architecture was not in line with the opinions of the "official" intellectuals or architects, and the "nationalist" theory of architecture, with its political implications, existed before 1933. The *völkisch* outlook dominated Rosenberg's philosophy, and even Speer was influenced by passionate nationalism. Hitler and Goebbels were less sincerely nationalist, but their government benefitted from both *völkisch* and right-wing nationalist approval.

[83] Neither, if the architect's widow is correct, did Hitler intervene much in the work of the Troost studio after Troost's death. (Correspondence with Gerdy Troost, November 28, 1969.)

[84] *Spiegel*, Nr. 46, 1966, p. 48.

[85] *Ibid.*

CHAPTER FOUR

The Nationalist View
of Architecture

THE NATIONALIST view of architecture that prevailed, with
state approval, in the Third Reich, was complex, even contradictory at times, for party leaders and nationalist commentators did
not always have the same aims. Hitler and Goebbels were more
concerned with monumental public buildings than with *völkisch*
structures. For them, good "German" architecture was massive,
neo-classical and urban. The *völkisch* critics, such as Schultze-
Naumburg, had not usually considered large public buildings, but
rather smaller, indigenous structures in a rural or village setting.
There were, therefore, two schools of architectural thought within
the nationalist ideology: the right-wing nationalist group and the
völkisch group, two schools that were not always mutually exclusive, yet both fervently nationalist, and often using the same vocabulary (such as the word *Volk*). For example, writers such as
Troost and Rittich approved of both types of architecture, and
Hermann Goering, who commissioned the monumental Air
Ministry in Berlin, also revelled in the *völkisch* Karinhall.

Some writers on architecture in the Third Reich were Nazi
officials, bureaucrats, intellectuals, or political leaders within the
party structure. Others, not always hard-line Nazis, merely hoped

that the party would do something about the architectural crisis.[1] Nevertheless, most writers were nationalist, and believed that Germany's "political and spiritual revival" should be evident in its architecture. That "the reawakened will of the Volk" should find expression was deemed a law of nature, and it was believed that the Nazi party had led Germany back to its natural foundations. The writers of the period looked back to ancient Greece, and to the German past, seeking manifestations of the "will" of the Volk; but there was not always agreement that, at any one period in German history, this "will" flourished. Consequently, the writers urged "Aryan" architects to listen to the voice of their blood and to the voice of the Führer and his ideology. If they did so, the best qualities of the Volk would appear in the buildings they designed. Of course, the Volk must also be taught and examples must be set. Hence to express support for good "German" architecture, these writers produced a flood of books and articles explaining why some buildings were appropriate for Germany.

In the six years of Nazi peacetime rule, it proved impossible to develop any theories on good German architecture into a thoroughgoing program. Indeed, no architectural program was ever written up.[2] Hitler did not care enough about such a scheme; besides, he was too pragmatic to pin himself down to any rigid doctrine before he had the means to execute one. Yet writings on the subject envisaged a program which would permanently alter the face of Germany. The relatively free and even chaotic growth of German cities and their architecture in the preceding century was to end, and was to be replaced with a centralized control over every aspect of building and of the use of the landscape. Although this aim might seem admirable, it was often inspired by the al-

---

[1] One nationalist writer prefaced his study of the preservation of artistic monuments with a statement of Hitler that he and his party would protect "the great traditions of our Volk." (Paul Clemen, Deutsche Kunst und die Denkmalpflege, Berlin, Deutscher Kunstverlag, 1933, Vorwort, p. viii.)

[2] On the relatively mild Gleichschaltung of architecture, see Lane, Architecture and Politics, pp. 169–184; and Brenner, Kunstpolitik, pp. 118–130.

leged foreign suppression of the German spirit in the past and in
the present. Moreover, control over building was defended by one
member of the League for the German Homeland (*Deutscher
Heimatbund*) as being part of Prussian tradition. In the eighteenth century, he wrote, the power of the state was ruthlessly employed to control both public and private building. Not only high
administrative officials, but the Prussian king himself, took an
interest in the development of cities. In those days, local architects worked together closely in characteristically Prussian fashion, their aim being — and here the writer cited Moeller van den
Bruck's *Der preussische Stil* — to unite the "small with the great,
the individual with the whole."[3] Thus some degree of guidance
and control seemed to be a basic attribute of German life, he
said. What could be more natural than for architecture, the "syn-
thesizing art," to express this quality of the *Volk*? Consequently,
every city should have certain characteristics, such as a main axis
and an Adolf Hitler *Platz*, in common with other cities and should
be linked with other centers by the *Autobahnen*. The topography
of Germany would be unified, and speedy communications would
create a spiritual unity among the population. The word *Aufbau*,
which means both building and synthesis, is found frequently in
writings of the period, expressing the idea that not only was Germany to be built up and made strong, but every aspect of German
life, of individuals and of communities, was to be linked together
in a new communal synthesis.[4]

Other reasons contributed to the great interest in architecture
in this period. Understandably, many desired the repair of damage
done to German cities by one hundred years of factory and tene-

[3] Werner Lindner, "Grundlagen und Ziele des Bandes," *Die Landschaftlichen
Grundlagen des deutschen Bauschaffens: Der Osten*, ed. by Julius Schulte-Frohlinde, Munich, Callwey, n.d., pp. 12–14.

[4] "Building" and "rebuilding" Germany was a popular phrase in much of
the propaganda of the period. After the party came power, Goebbels wrote: "Now
we have the whole Reich in our hands. We can therefore begin rebuilding
[*Neubau*]." (*Vom Kaiserhof*, p. 278.)

ment growth. The *völkisch* school was part of this urban reform movement and tended to give the campaign a racist slant. When fine old buildings were demolished to make room for department stores or when industrial smokestacks were built higher than church spires, these nationalists often detected what they thought was the work of the anti-German foreigner or, "worse," the work of the Jew. Moreover, the traditionalists who hated the style of the *Bauhaus* or of Le Corbusier rallied to the party and its anti-Marxist appeal, hoping that the Third Reich would stop the spread of "Bolshevik architecture." The temporary success in Russia of *avant-garde* architects like Ernst May particularly disturbed traditionalists and seemed to substantiate their worst fears. Furthermore, Hitler's own interest in building meant that at least some steps would be taken to purge Germany of these influences.

Finally, architecture was propaganda. Many of the writers expressed a vivid awareness of the psychological power of individual buildings and of the manner in which the common people could be impressed by a government that builds. "The influence of the individual of structured space, especially the interior space in which he works, is very strong," said a writer in the official *Die Kunst im Dritten Reich*.[5] Commenting on the tasks of the government agency, The Beauty of Work, one architect wrote: "We now know how important every object in our environment is, because through its language it determines our feeling for life."[6] Some writers were more explicit, stating that the ideology itself must speak from the new architecture. National Socialism, wrote an art historian, "unconditionally demands the totality of all crea-

[5] Ernst Sagebiel, "Festliche Räume der Luftfahrt," *Die Kunst im Dritten Reich*, II:1 (January 1938), 169.

[6] Karl Kretschmer, "Uber die Aufgaben des Amtes für 'Schönheit der Arbeit,'" *Die Form*, Berlin, July, 1934, cited in Teut, *Architektur*, p. 282. So important was architecture to the Nazi leadership that a crisis in the labor market emerged in the summer of 1935. Excessive building made it difficult for employers not in the building industries to find workers. Moreover, the rearmament program was retarded temporarily due to building expenditures in 1937. (T. W. Mason, "Labor in the Third Reich," *Past and Present* (April 1966), p. 126.)

tivity. . . . Therefore its buildings must bear witness to its will."
Architecture, he continued, is "the ideology become stone"; it is
"a political confession."[7]

Deliberate rationalization for the massive building program
undoubtedly was one motive for this literature,[8] but it was also
out of nationalist zeal that writers explained the importance of
architecture. It is the "queen of the fine arts," said Wolters and
a "self-justifying necessity" for "powerful epochs"; "races and their
leaders feel an inner duty and compulsion to document themselves
and their age in stone monuments."[9] "If a race is strong, healthy,
beautiful, and gifted, then its architectural garment will show it,"
said Schultze-Naumburg, who was convinced that these adjectives
applied to the German race.[10] "Stones never lie," wrote another
architect.[11] Most writers agreed with the architect Winfried
Wendland, who noted that "all great conservative epochs have a
special relationship to architecture," the art which "stands nearest
to the state."[12] Most felt that the state, with its nationalistic ideology, had a duty to revivify the *Volk* and draw out its talents.[13]

[7] Rolf Badenhausen, "Betrachtungen zum Bauwillen des Dritten Reiches,"
Zeitschrift für Deutschkunde, cited in Wulf, *Bildende Künste*, p. 250. See also
Fritz Todt's introduction in Fritz, *Strassen und Bauten Adolf Hitlers*, Berlin, Ver-
lag des Deutschen Arbeitsfront, 1939, p. 7.)

[8] It is quite possible that when party men like Fritz Todt or Robert Ley
called their undertakings "community" enterprises, they were rationalizing their
own "empire-building"; using this label may have been a way to justify the ex-
penses involved. However, most of the commentators do not seem to have had
this "axe to grind."

[9] Wolters, *Albert Speer*, p. 7.

[10] Schultze-Naumburg, *Städtebau* in *Kulturarbeiten*, Vol. IV, Munich, Callwey, 1909, p. 39. See Teut, *Architektur*, p. 63, note, for the details of his long
career from his series *Kulturarbeiten* (1903–1917) to his resignation in 1939 from
the post of Director of the Weimar Academy. Another, sympathetic account of his
work is found in Ziegler, *Adolf Hitler*, pp. 205–211.

[11] Otto Kloeppel, "Der Baukünstler: Ein Träger nationalsozialistischer Weltanschauung," *Die Bauzeitung*, Stuttgart, Heft 9 (September 1934), cited in Teut,
Architektur, p. 134.

[12] Winfried Wendland, *Kunst und Nation: Ziele und Wege der Kunst im
neuen Deutschland*, Berlin, Reimar Hobbing, 1934, p. 5. Wendland was a professor in the Berlin Academy of Art and advisor to the Prussian Ministry of Religion.

[13] Rudolf Wolters, an architect and author of a biography of Speer and of
other works, was one of these patriots who claimed to have a social conscience.

"Building," explained Baldur von Schirach, Reich youth leader, "is something like a religion, which means that it has less to do with stone and mortar than with experience and faith."[14] The majority of these commentators agreed with Hitler's view of Nazi architecture as "the Word in stone."[15]

The new architecture, therefore, would be both documentary and didactic. It would record the German renaissance and would teach Germans and foreigners the truths of the ideology. In the past, a faith that had moved mountains had also moved men to build monumentally. For Wilhelm Pinder, a Munich university art historian, the new German architecture would record Germany's "ascent from despair and need."[16] At the same time, for Gerdy Troost, wife of the architect Troost, the new architecture should be the "educator of a new *Volk*," teaching that life was tough and involved many difficult decisions.[17] Whereas this might be called the domestic task of architecture, there was also a role for German buildings in world affairs. Expressing and embodying the values of the German people, the new architecture would represent the "will" (*Wollen*) of the *Volk* to other peoples and to future history.[18] This was the oft-stressed function of *Representation*, so important to Hitler.

Architecture was also to be a weapon to secure respect for

[14] Cited in Heinrich Hartmann, *Werkhefte für den Heimbau der Hitler-Jugend*, ed. by Reichsjugendführung der NSDAP, Leipzig, Skacel, 1937, I, 17. Hartmann was an *Oberbannführer* and leader of the Fine Arts Office in the Central *Kultur* Section of the Propaganda Ministry.

[15] Few architects objected when the government "coordinated" the League of German Architects and other related professional organizations in 1933. (See Teut, *Architektur*, pp. 69–70 and 92–93.)

[16] Wilhelm Pinder, "Architektur als Moral," *Gesammelte Aufsätze aus den Jahren 1907–38*, Leipzig, Seemann, 1938, p. 204. Pinder, 1878–1947, was an art historian.

[17] Gerdy Troost, ed., *Das Bauen im neuen Reich*, Bayreuth, Gauverlag Bayrische Ostmark, 1938, I, 10.

[18] Wilhelm Lotz, "So baut Europa," *Europa: Handbuch der politischen, wirtschaftlichen, und kulturellen Entwicklung des neuen Europa*, ed. by Deutsches Institut für aussenpolitische Forschung, Leipzig, Helingsche Verlagsanstalt, 1943, 1943, p. 177. This book was given an introduction by Joachim Ribbentrop, the Nazi Foreign Minister.

the German people in perilous times and dangerous localities. On the role of architecture in the reconquered east, the architect Julius Schulte-Frohlinde wrote: "we are fighting for Germany, for the maintenance and recovery of the soul of our people, which is mirrored most visibly in our craft and architectural *Kultur*."[19] The German mission in the East could be fulfilled in part through architecture. To execute this mission in, for example, the *Wartheland* (western Poland), all architectural defects and deformities had to be removed, especially modern flat roofs.[20] "Everything ugly, unclean, aimless, . . . that is . . . Polish buildings, should be removed," said another writer, to create a purely "German" environment.[21] Part of this program included building and repairing the homes and barns of German peasants, and the construction of "castles of the dead" (*Totenburgen*) as monuments to those who died in the crusade against the Slavs.[22] Architecture, then, had a definite role to play in politics. For one writer, the new Germany needed "a unity of politics and architecture," such as he believed had existed in antiquity and in the Renaissance. "Contemporary German architecture," he wrote, "is not concerned with technical questions or aesthetic values but rather with a political form of life which speaks out of a building."[23]

If architecture was a political weapon, it followed that architects could be compared to soldiers in a crusade, and crowds to

[19] Schulte-Frohlinde, ed., *Die landschaftlichen Grundlagen des deutschen Bauschaffens: Der Osten*, p. 7. (Schulte-Frohlinde was head of the architecture section of the Labor Front.)

[20] Hermann Wagner, "Wohnungspolitische Aufgaben in dem Reichgau Wartheland," *Bauen, Siedeln, Wohnen*, Berlin, 1940, cited in Teut, *Architektur*, p. 345. Wagner was a government official in Posen.

[21] "Richtlinien für die Pflege und Verbesserung des Ortsbildes im mdeutschen Osten," *Der soziale Wohnungsbau in Deutschland*, Berlin, Heft 2 (1941), cited in Teut, *Architektur*, p. 346.

[22] See also Bruno Schier, "Der deutsche Einfluss auf der Hausbau Osteuropas," *Nationalsozialistische Monatshefte*, VIII (1937), 398–409. Dr. Schier was a professor of German anthropology.

[23] Jürgen Petersen, "Albert Speer — Über einen deutschen Baumeister," *Das Reich*, January 11, 1942, cited in Wulf, *Die bildenden Künste*, pp. 256–257. Petersen was editor of *Das Reich*.

armies of the faithful. In the new *Volk* community, all must serve the great idea. The architect "must believe [. . . muss gläubig sein]," said Wolters; he must be prepared to give his utmost for the *Volk* and their ideology.[24] Perhaps the best statement of this viewpoint is found in an article by Hubert Schrade, "Der Sinn der künstlerische Aufgabe und politischer Architektur."[25] The party rallies in Nuremberg, in particular that of 1933, resembled a monument to the fallen, said Schrade; the climax came when the *Führer* and the chief of staff walked through the assembled ranks of men on the Luitpold Field and laid a huge wreath on the actual monument. Great crowds of people had gathered, not in unruly mobs, but rather in response to the call of a "form-giving will" (*ein formender Wille*), surrendering to a strong original form of communal existence, following a traditional soldierly precedent. It was wonderful to see the masses saved from disorder and formlessness, and individuals saved from atomization. Now all Germans were united in a communal experience, as if in an army expressing their genuine "will to form" (*Formungswille*), a development which was impossible in the "individualist age," a completely "unarchitectural" period. Thus the rally became "human architecture," the "expression of our inner lives." Looking to the future, this writer wanted to see permanent structures built for this communal experience; he felt, that it was the patriotic duty of German architects to volunteer to produce these *Volk* halls.[26]

Serving the community was often presented as the highest moral goal for the individual architect, as well as for the citizen.

[24] Rudolf Wolters, *Vom Beruf des Baumeisters*, Berlin, Volk und Reich, 1944, p. 69. Hitler had called poets, singers, and architects "fighters" in a speech (September 7, 1937). (Baynes, *Speeches*, p. 594.)

[25] Hubert Schrade, "Der Sinn der künstlerischen Aufgabe und politischer Architektur," *Nationalsozialistische Monatshefte*, V:5 (June, 1934) 508–514. Schrade was professor of art history at the University of Heidelberg. The idea of the new Germany was "soldierly, serious, simple, large," said another writer, and its architecture should reflect this. ("Vom Bauen des dritten Reiches," *Baugilde: Zeitschrift der Fachgruppe Architekten in der Reichskammer der bildenden Künste*, XVIII:15 (May 25, 1936) 426.)

[26] Schrade, "Der Sinn," pp. 510–511.

This otherwise politically neutral idea takes on explicit Nazi overtones in Pinder's essay, *Architektur als Moral*, in which he
wrote that "great architecture . . . is always the face of a su-
perindividual whole." In all great periods, he continues, when
an ideology triumphs, architectural accomplishments are commissioned by the whole community. In such epochs, the architect
should not seek an egotistical self-expression, but rather an expression of the common feeling. Then, his buildings will serve the community and therefore will be morally good. "We look back to the
time when architecture was still the language and the countenance
of the *Volk*, and building a sacred procedure undertaken by the
whole community."[27] The role of the community was also important for a writer in the official *Baugilde*. In great epochs, he said
the "outlook of the community takes architectural form," and
monumental buildings serve the communal life of the *Volk*. It
is the people themselves who both grant commissions and create
plans, with the result that buildings become the "symbol of the
unity of the Reich," or "the stone heralds of this great idea."[28]

The *Führer* believed that the finest buildings were "community" architecture, structures built by the collective will of
the people and (more important to him) representing the power
and authority of the *Volk* state. Sympathetic commentators agreed:
compared to the significance of the "Aryan" race and its state, the
individual German was unimportant. The most important aim of
the Nazi building program was generally believed to be the ele-
vation of the community and the common good above the individual through the magnificence of "community" buildings, particularly those in which thousands could congregate. "The individual human being should not take himself as the measure of
these buildings," wrote one art historian, "but should rather see in
them the all-embracing will of the people."[29]

[27] Pinder, "Architektur als Moral," pp. 206–207.
[28] "Vom Bauen des Dritten Reiches," p. 425.
[29] Wolfgang Müller, "Deutsche Baukunst," *Das Reich*, Nr. 16 (April 20),
1941, p. 15, cited in Georg Hellack, "Architektur und bildende Kunst als Mittel
nationalsozialistischer Propaganda," *Publizistik*, 1960, p. 86.

However, some Nazi-approved writers on architecture were concerned to defend the individual — not his political rights, but his identity as a German faced with the more harmful aspects of modern urban mass society. A desirable sense of oneness in the German national community in no way suggested collectivism, which was "Bolshevik."[30] When one writer maintained, in a discussion of village life, that the German individual "stands at the center of all planning,"[31] he represented the *völkisch* rejection of modern urban life and its occasionally dehumanizing effects. Yet individual self-expression by the architect and expensive indulgence in "individualizing" a private home were still frowned upon. And most commentators agreed with Wilhelm Lotz, an assistant to Speer, when he declared that a building should not be an end in itself, but must be built as a manifestation of the creative life of the *Volk*.[32]

The new German ideology was "close to nature, [and] life-affirming";[33] the new architecture should therefore be a living part of the German community, in harmony with the German landscape, and rising organically out of the German soil. Natural stone was chosen for the new buildings, because it was native to Germany — "the German soil offers [it] in rich variety" — and because it could bind buildings "organically with . . . the native landscape."[34] Thus nationalist and *völkisch* writers looked beyond individual buildings and cities to study the countryside and rural life; this led them to a consideration of the problem of "living space."

Space or *Raum* has two different meanings in this literature. In the first place, *Raum* refers to German living space in the old

[30] Karl Willy Straub, *Architektur im Dritten Reich*, Stuttgart, Akademischer Verlag Dr. Fritz Wedekind, 1932, pp. 36–37. (Straub was connected with the anti-*avant-garde* group of architects, the "Block".)

[31] Erich Kulke, in Werner Lindner, et al., *Das Dorf: Seine Pflege und Gestaltung*, Munich, Callwey, n.d., p. 218.

[32] Lotz, "So baut Europa," p. 177.

[33] Kretschmer, "Uber die Aufgaben," cited in Teut, *Architektur*, p. 282.

[34] Hans Stephan, *Baukunst im dritten Reich*, Berlin, Junker und Dünnhaupt, 1939, p. 10.

Reich and in the new Europe, and to the importance of organizing and controlling this area. The newly recovered *Lebensraum*
in the east would have to be supplied with German cities and
German architecture so that the space itself would be "Teuton-
ized." The German "will to build" would embrace the entire German living space.[35] The other use of the term *Raum* includes the
view that ideal Nazi buildings themselves should communicate
a sense of spaciousness; the new streets and squares in each rebuilt
city should be large and wide, with distant vistas of huge monuments.[36] Youth centers, too, should have wide halls and spacious
rooms.

The best German buildings of the past were spacious, like
the medieval hall churches. Whereas classical art and architecture
had been "spaceless," German architecture had always been "spacious, bound by space, conditioned by space." (There is an implied rejection of the styles of antiquity here which is unusual in
this literature.) All Germanic building, from the migration period
onward, expressed the "yearning search for the eternal," a quality
found in both the Romanesque cathedrals, with their continually
flowing lines, and in the "boundless height" of the "forest of columns" of the Gothic churches.[37] A typical German building suggested infinite distance. "Oriental" and "Bolshevik" architecture
was only two-dimensional, whereas "Nordic" buildings were three-

[35] Rudolf Wolters, *Neue deutsche Baukunst*, Prague, Volk und Reich, 1943,
p. 9. "A new ordering of the German living space" was a goal also held by Gottfried Feder, Commissioner for Settlement. (Feder, foreword to *Die neue Stadt*,
Berlin, Springer, 1939. Feder was a construction engineer, an economics "expert,"
and one of the founders of the party. Later he became leader of a new government
office, the Reich Work Community for Research into Space.) See also the section
on "The Ordering of Space" in publication of the Reichsheimstättenamt (Reich
Homestead Office) of the Labor Front, *Städtebild und Landschaft*, Berlin, Verlag
der Deutschen Arbeitsfront, 1939, p. 2. General Nazi works on the problem of
space include Hans Grimm's *Volk ohne Raum*, 1926, and Ludwig Ferdinand
Clauss' *Die nordische Seele: Eine Einführung in die Rassenseelenkunde*, 1936.

[36] For Hitler's views of the importance of spaciousness in buildings, see *S.C.*,
p. 425 (May 1, 1942); *Tischgespräche*, p. 304. On the "will to space," see Hartmann, *Werkhefte*, pp. 32–33.

[37] Wendland, *Kunst und Nation*, p. 26.

dimensional.[38] Space was important, therefore, not only in foreign and military policy (as "living space"), but also as a concept in the design of buildings and cities (as the quality of spaciousness).

Along with symmetry, which Rosenberg stressed, a general rectilinear appearance was common in the Nazi-approved buildings of this period.[39] This was part of the drive for clarity (believed to be a German quality) in architecture. Hitler's words — "to be German is to be clear"[40] — were often quoted, and the highest praise a writer could bestow on a new structure was to call it "clear." (The lines of Bauhaus-type architecture were also rectilinear but without the symmetry and traditional connotations of approved architecture in the Third Reich.)

Most writers who were able to appear in print agreed on the importance of "community buildings" and the rejection of modern architecture. They disliked most developments in German architecture and city growth since 1850; they were upset at the expansion of an apparently dehumanized technology; they were also depressed by the political and social upheaval in the Germany of the twenties and by the predictions of doom fashionable among followers of Oswald Spengler (author of The Decline of the West, 1918) and other cultural pessimists. In this mood, they searched in the German past for signs of an architecture that was genuinely German.

[38] Ludwig von Senger, in Blick in die Zeit, Berlin, April 26, 1935, cited in Wulf, Die bildenden Künste, p. 302. Von Senger was a professor of art and a painter.

[39] A rectilinear plan makes for "simple and clear" building, wrote Hartmann. (Werkhefte, p. 36.) "Prehistoric racial laws," he added "begin . . . to exert an influence again. We remember that the oldest Germanic house known to us had a rectilinear plan." (Werkhefte, p. 122.)

[40] This quotation prefaced the title page of Hartmann's Werkhefte. It was originally part of Hitler's speech on July 18, 1937 at the opening of the House of German Art in Munich. (Domarus, Reden, p. 706 [July 19, 1937]; Baynes, Speeches, p. 587.)

CHAPTER FIVE

Contemporary Attitudes to German Architecture 1000-1850: "Suppression"

WHEN FERVENT nationalists looked to the historical achievements of German architecture, they found little that was encouraging and often they were in disagreement. The diversity of opinion on past styles partially explains why no unified style was developed by the Nazi government. Invariably, however, architecture was regarded as a mirror in which was reflected the health of the German community in any given period. Moreover, views on the history of German architecture were united by one idea, that the creative instincts of the German people had always been smothered or misdirected by foreign styles. This conflict meant that the German *Volk* were still searching to express themselves in a style purely their own.

The classical culture of the ancient world was held by Hitler and Rosenberg to have been of "Nordic" origin. It was typical of the Nazi attitude that the cover of the official publication *Kunst im Dritten Reich* showed the helmeted head of a classical goddess with Grecian features.[1] This was considered fitting and a natural

---

[1] The same symbol appeared on the cover of the catalog for the first German Architecture and Crafts Exhibition of 1938. (*Erste deutsche Architektur — und*

consequence of racial affinity. Germans in the thirties, it was maintained, were conscious again of their blood relationship with the ancient Greeks.[2] The voice of the blood determined the sense of beauty, said the *völkisch* architect German Bestelmeyer, and since the Germans were racially related to the ancient Greeks, they could understand the classical concept of beauty.[3] Like the modern Germans, the ancient Greeks also defended true *Kultur* from the onslaught of "Asia." "Again and again Hellas and the Near East clash," wrote Rosenberg in his diary, "decadent Cretan culture, matriarchal, etc. on the one hand, and on the other, robust strength of form, patriarchal."[4] Another architect echoed this thought, seeing ancient Greek culture and its values as the "strongest opposition" to the "colored races of Asia and Africa."[5] Research apparently proved this; Professor A. Baeumler, director of the Institute for Political Education, made a trip to Greece, and returned, having found "confirmation of our views," wrote Rosenberg.[6] This attitude also occurs in an article by an art historian on the uncontrollable element in the "Nordic" character. The classical style, he wrote, acts as a necessary counterweight against that tendency of the "Aryan" mind to be abstract, to become alien to reality, and to destroy form (as, for example, in *art nouveau*). Tending to formlessness, this dark side of German character could reject the concept of community. But the other

Kunsthandwerkaustellung: Im Haus der deutschen Kunst zu München, 22. Januar bis 27. März 1938, Munich, Knorr und Hirth, 1938; this publisher was controlled by the party's *Zentralverlag*.

[2] Troost, *Bauen*, I, p. 5.

[3] German Bestelmeyer, "Baukunst und Gegenwart," *Zentralblatt der Bauverwaltung*, Berlin, Heft 17 (1941), cited in Teut, *Architektur*, p. 133. *Bestelmeyer* was a member of the Munich School to which Troost also belonged.

[4] Rosenberg, *Tagebuch*, p. 33 (May 17, 1934).

[5] Kloeppel, "Der Baukünstler," p. 134.

[6] Rosenberg, *Tagebuch*, p. 33 (May 5, 1934). The alleged relationship between ancient Greece and modern Germany was underlined by Wolters, whose illustrations include seven examples of classical cornices, from the Theseion (a Doric temple) in Athens to Albert Speer's Chancellery in Berlin. (Wolters, *Vom Beruf des Baumeisters*, pp. 110–113; examples of colonnades, from the Parthenon to Speer's Zeppelin Field in Nuremberg are given, pp. 114–119.)

side sought self-expression through discipline and rules, adherence to norms, simple functionalism and objective clarity. This two-sidedness, however, was as much Greek as German, because both were "Aryan."[7] Greek civilization being a "source of life" for German civilization, said Lotz, it was only to be expected that a "renaissance of the Greek way" should include building as the Greeks did.[8]

Less was written on Roman architecture, but a good deal was produced on the building of those Germanic tribes that helped to bring about the decline of the Roman Empire. Romanesque architecture was sometimes seen as a mixture of Germanic and Roman elements, but more often as a genuinely German style, misused. The achievements of the Greeks, it was usually held, were taken over by the Romans, who built bigger although not better, after which the Teutonic tribes brought their energy and imagination to the Roman achievements, creating a new "Nordic" synthesis. Thus the Romanesque cathedrals of the time of Emperor Henry I (919–936) were "an expression of the purest Nordic character."[9] Early Romanesque was "an absolutely Germanic style," representative of the strong emerging Teutonic state, a new state inspired by a new ideology.[10] Schultze-Naumburg noted that, although the Germans learned from the Romans how to build

[7] Georg Weise, article in *Zeitschrift für Deutschkunde*, 1935, cited in Wulf, *Die bildenden Künste*, p. 261.

[8] Lotz, "So baut Europa," p. 173. "What we see in them . . ." said Kurt Karl Eberlein, "is ourselves." (*Was ist deutsch in der deutschen Kunst?* Leipzig, Seemann, 1934, p. 64.) This art historian was co-chairman of the fine arts section of the *Volk* culture office in the Education Ministry. Less was written about Roman culture and architecture, probably because the Romans (despite the size of the buildings) represented an alleged racial decline from the height of Greek purity. Praise was given, however, for the Roman architect Vitruvius (c. 27 B.C.), who worked inspired by a "strongly held philosophy of life," under "a towering *Führer* personality, Augustus." (E. Stürzenacker, "Die deutsche Baukunst und die Antike," *Baugilde*, XX:19 (July 5, 1938), 624.)

[9] Otto Riedrich, "Die Germanische Seele im Zeitalter der Gotik," *Odal: Monatschrift für Blut und Boden*, 1936, cited in Wulf, *Die bildenden Künste*, p. 185. (Riedrich was an art critic.)

[10] Wendland, *Kunst und Nation*, p. 24.

with stone, German works were not "imperfect imitations of Roman models." The Germans would build only as Germans and never as Romans. To be sure, they learned from Rome the art of cutting stone and of vaulting, and took over Roman floor plans, but their structures looked very different from those of Rome. They showed the special qualities of the Germans; "that steel-hard strength and ruthlessness, which, beside the cool logic of the Roman original form (*Grundform*), bears witness to an inflexible self-will and a strange fantasy, which is not to be found in Roman buildings." Indeed, the new style should be called "German," said Schultze-Naumburg, "not Romanesque."[11] (See illustration no. 7.)

The "controlled strength" and "restraint" of Romanesque buildings was praised also by a writer who introduced another idea more common in discussions of the Gothic: in "the early buildings of northern Italy, . . . the buildings of Saxony, Westphalia, . . . the Rhineland and . . . the land of the Franks and Swabia, one recognizes the same heavy weight on the soul. The Romanesque edifice weighed on the earth like the hand of papal Rome, on the spirit of the people."[12] Thus some writers, although seeing admirable German qualities expressed in Romanesque, nevertheless found this and the later Gothic period a time of "subjugation of the soul."[13] However, this did not prevent the round arch and the heavy appearance of the Romanesque from being used in the Third Reich, as in the Ordensburgen and in the Congress Hall in Nuremberg. Romanesque had too many qualities

[11] Paul Schultze-Naumburg, *Die Kunst der Deutschen: Ihr Wesen und ihre Werke*, Stuttgart, Deutsche Verlagsanstalt, 1934, pp. 14–15. "Although its name might mislead us to believe that it is of foreign derivation, Romanesque architecture is, in all its forms, Germanic." (From a program printed for the 1938 "Day of German Art," in Munich. Cited in Karl Arndt, "Zur Eröffnung der Grossen Deutschen Kunstausstellung durch Hitler: München, 10. Juli 1938, Haus der Deutschen Kunst," *Filmdokumente zur Zeitgeschichte*, Göttingen, 1968, p. 167.)

[12] Otto Riedrich, "Die Germanische Seele," p. 169.

[13] *Ibid.*, p. 169.

which were felt to be essentially "Nordic" for the style to be rejected. For instance, an art historian wrote that the Romanesque
buildings suggested "intimacy, they offer protection, they breathe
calm and firmness, relaxation, and peace in their strong thick
walls." These virtues were just what Germany needed in any time
of trial.[14]

If there was some ambivalence in views of the Romanesque,
attitudes to the Gothic were even more divided. For one writer,
who was proud of the German cathedrals, there were two great
ages of architecture, the classical and the Gothic, and the Gothic
was firmly rooted in the classical tradition.[15] Yet another writer,
connecting Germanic wooden domestic architecture of eastern
Europe to classical Greek architecture, contrasted Germanic and
Greek building with the western "French" Gothic. For him, the
Gothic was developed in Latin France, and had no teutonic ancestry. Gothic architects strove to exhibit visually the laws of gravity
and to broadcast the triumph of individual accomplishment,
whereas genuinely "Nordic" architects balanced interior and exterior construction to delight the eye and to stimulate the mind
with an abundance of variety and scale. Columns and pillars revealed this contrast best: in the "Nordic" culture, the column
was naturally developed from wood and later transmuted into
stone; in the French culture, the pillar was simply what was left
after walls were almost eliminated. Hence, Gothic and "Nordic"
styles were representative of "two different worlds."[16] In the same
vein, Theodor Fischer, a respected older architect, declared in
1933 that the Gothic style was "magnificent, but French."[17] To
be sure, many architectural historians would agree that the Gothic
style was first noticeable at Saint Denis, near Paris (finished in

[14] Johannes Eilemann, *Deutsche Seele, deutscher Mensch, deutsche Kultur,
und Nationalsozialismus*, Leipzig, Quelle und Meyer, 1933, p. 14.

[15] Stürzenacker, "Die deutsche Baukunst," p. 623.

[16] Heinrich Franke, *Ostgermanische Holzbaukultur und ihre Bedeutung für
das deutsche Siedlungswerk*, Breslau, Korn, 1936, p. 147.

[17] Theodor Fischer, "Vermächtnis an die Jugend," *Die Bauzeitung*, Stuttgart Heft 32 (1933), cited in Teut, *Architektur*, p. 154.

1140), and that some of the best examples of the style are found in France (such as Sainte Chapelle, 1243–1248, in Paris, or the cathedral at Chartres, 1194–1506). However, it is typical of this nationalist attitude to stress the "unGermanness" of the style and to erect something purely "German" against the foreign style. At the very least, the German Gothic cathedrals had to be viewed as more German than French.

Hence, the German cathedrals were, in the words of one writer, "livelier, more passionate and masculine" than the feminine Romanesque. Their striving vertical lines revealed the German struggle for expression. The Gothic German experienced "a humility, a self-discipline before the ultimate, before the *Führer*, before God." Gothic churches, particularly the hall churches,[18] revealed more joy in responsibility and the presence of a class of leaders unfortunately prevented from wielding complete authority.[19] Whereas Hitler preferred bright airy *Volk* halls, this writer found that the half-darkness of the cathedrals, as "in the tops of intertwined beechtrees" was German.[20]

Rosenberg attempted an authoritative estimate of the Gothic as "the first embodiment of the dynamic Western soul in stone . . ."[21] But it was more Germanic than European; pointed arches, flying buttresses, ribbed vaulting were all ways in which the Germanic spirit sought to express its will. The "Nordic soul" struggled away from all things material (except, of course, the sacred soil), seeking to escape the pressure of horizontal weight and to overcome all the heaviness of the world: it wanted "no functionalism . . . but rather to express a very definite agitation of soul." The Gothic style, then, was totally German, despite the

[18] A *Hallenkirche* has side aisles with very high ceilings. The cathedral of Strasbourg, a hall church, was praised by Wendland (*Kunst und Nation*, p. 33), as well as by Hitler, who planned to make a national monument of it.

[19] Eilemann, *Deutsche Seele*, pp. 14–15. To Jürgen Peterson, on the other hand, the Gothic was "feminine" and the Romanesque was "masculine." Albert Speer — über einen deutschen Baumeister," *Das Reich* (January 11, 1942), cited in Wulf, *Die bildenden Künste*, p. 257.

[20] Eilemann, *Deutsche Seele*, p. 15.

[21] Rosenberg, *Mythus*, pp. 352.

fact, as Rosenberg admitted, that it originated in northern France. In the early Middle Ages, he explained, northern France was "completely Germanic." Then with the hall-church phenomenon and the arch allegedly becoming more pointed sooner in Germany than in France, only in the Reich did the Gothic fully mature.[22] If a great ideology should inspire German hearts again, Rosenberg believed the "Gothic soul" would also reawaken.[23]

Nazi monumental architecture was characterized by horizontal rather than vertical lines, as well as by an earthbound appearance: indeed, it was praised for its sobriety and weight. Those most closely connected with the building program in the thirties — Speer, Troost, Hitler — obviously did not listen to Rosenberg on this matter.

The tragedy of the German Middle Ages, for Rosenberg and others, including Hitler, was the inhibiting presence of the Roman Catholic Church, the "embittered enemy of the German feeling for nature."[24] "This heroic race," said Schultze-Naumburg, "could not follow with an upright heart the doctrine of renunciation and humility which Christianity demanded of it."[25] Suppressed by rigid doctrine and foreign control, the German spirit could never achieve creative freedom in this period.

Yet most Nazi writers were enthusiastic about the age and its architecture. The racist Hans Günther, for example, did not doubt that the Gothic style was purely German in origin. He cited the Milan cathedral, which, while Gothic, was a "half-understood" Gothic, begun by a German architect, Heinrich von Gmund, but altered later in a non-Germanic direction toward the horizontal and the overdecorated.[26] (Incidentally, this is good example of how notable buildings outside the Reich could be claimed for the Volk.) For another writer, the decorative profusion of the Gothic

---

[22] Ibid., pp. 357–358.
[23] Ibid., pp. 356–357. Rosenberg wrote this in 1930.
[24] Ibid., p. 359.
[25] Schultze-Naumburg, Kunst der Deutschen, p. 20.
[26] Günther, Rasse und Stil, Munich, Lehmann, 1926, p. 97.

church is a "joyful expression of the repossessed freedom of the Germanic soul"; medieval artisans were "sacred soldiers [creating] the revalidation of German right and German freedom."[27] In reality, then, these cathedrals had allegedly nothing to do with church dogma. One writer saw originality and racial progress in German Gothic cathedrals. Up to the Gothic period, he said, the seats of the clergy were raised in the chancel; now this changed, for in most German Gothic churches the Romanesque habit of elevating the chancel was abandoned. "Only . . . a *Führer* alienated from the *Volk* needed (and needs) an elevated throne. . . . The good German person certainly wanted his *Führer* to supersede him in insight, education, knowledge and, above all, in character. . . . But he also demanded that his *Führer* eternally stand on the same soil as himself, the soil which nourishes our blood and deeds, our existence and our future."[28]

Many German writers found it difficult to reconcile their hostility to "foreign" Catholicism — or to Christianity itself — with their need to claim for Germany the great medieval cathedrals. Hitler himself had been vague on this issue, but most right-wing nationalists would probably have taken comfort in Hermann Goering's generalization that "everyone finds it obvious that the great art of the Middle Ages was bound up with the Aryan race."[29] A more objective and defensible view maintained that in the Middle Ages there was a desirable unity of man and his technology, a more human scale to architecture, and a greater degree of social cohesion than in twentieth-century Germany.[30] (See illustrations nos. 6 and 8.)

The Renaissance revived classical building patterns and motifs; but, perhaps because this style left fewer monuments in Germany (outside of, for example, Augsburg), the writers on

[27] Riedrich, "Die germanische Seele," p. 186. Note the way Riedrich compares the artist to the soldier.

[28] Eilemann, *Deutsche Seele*, p. 15.

[29] Hermann Goering, *Reden und Aufsätze*, Munich, 1942, p. 182.

[30] Wolters, *Vom Beruf des Baumeisters*, p. 13.

architecture were not interested in it. Schultze-Naumburg was critical of what he found: pompous façades for the purpose of display and buildings "sitting like foreign bodies in the whole German scene."[31] For Fischer, the Renaissance was a "foreign [welsche] invasion."[32] Günther thought Gothic was far superior, because it was an art native to the Germans, expressing the whole community, whereas in the Renaissance building styles represented only the interests of the upper class and appealed more to reason and the educated appreciation of art among an elite.[33]

Opinions were more varied on the baroque period, for which Germany (especially Bavaria) could boast many examples. Hitler always liked this style, but its general reception among commentators was not favorable. It was usually regarded as another foreign style and, worse, a Catholic one. The irony here is that the theatricality of the baroque was similar to that of Nazi representative and "community" architecture; both styles are, in part, stage settings for great shows.

Pinder, one of the few who had some favorable generalizations to make about the baroque, called it a heroic style.[34] Another art historian was more cautious, maintaining that the baroque and rococo were foreign influences at first, but were soon Germanized. For example, whereas the architect François Cuvillies was a foreigner, his creations were German.[35]

Insofar as it was "an art of space,"[36] the baroque was Germanic. For Günther, too, the baroque was a manifestation of the "Dinaric" race, but, happily, the best examples of the German baroque had been transformed by the "Nordic" spirit; he cited the

[31] Schultze-Naumburg, *Kunst der Deutschen*, p. 44.

[32] Fischer, "Vermächtnis. . . ," p. 154.

[33] Günther, *Rasse und Stil*, p. 159.

[34] Pinder, "Architektur als Moral," p. 210.

[35] Cuvillies (1695–1768) was born in Flanders and trained in Paris; his work includes the interior of the *Amalienburg*, a rococo hunting lodge on the grounds of *Nymphenburg* palace near Munich, 1734–1739. (Werner Hager, *Die Bauten des deutschen Barocks: 1690–1700*, Jena, Eugen Diederichs, 1942, p. 8. The Diederichs publishing house had long printed *völkisch* works.)

[36] Hager, *Bauten*, p. 54.

Church of Our Lady (1726–1738) in Dresden, which revealed "self-discipline of the feelings, and Nordic austerity and strength," an "inner veracity," and a "Nordic" "trend to objectivity."[37] (See illustration no. 9.)

Rosenberg, in contrast, found little to praise in the baroque. A "Jesuit style," it amounted to "an almost purely sensual mixture of a powerful will to decorate and a complete artistic degeneration."[38] For Rosenberg, of course, anything associated with Catholicism was suspect. Schultze-Naumburg, too, suggested that baroque churches did not satisfy the religious needs of Germans.[39] But it was Fischer again who applied the standard criticism of almost all previous styles to the baroque: "The homeland of our great German baroque," he said, "was south of the Alps."[40] For most writers, therefore, the baroque, like Romanesque, Gothic, Renaissance, might have much to admire, but it was not German.

Eighteenth-century neo-classicism, and particularly the Greek revival, were much better received in the literature of this period.[41] Writers lauded von Knobelsdorff, Langhans, von Klenze and especially Gilly and Schinkel, all German architects of the eighteenth and early nineteenth centuries.[42] Hitler selected Speer and Troost, twentieth-century classicists, and consequently a form of classicism (strictly speaking, a simplified "Doric" style) to express the representative needs of the Third Reich in monumental "community" buildings. It is not accidental that the House of German Art built in Munich in 1935 resembles the Old Museum

[37] Günther, *Rasse und Stil*, p. 94. The Dresden *Frauenkirche* was also praised by Wendland, *Kunst und Nation*, p. 33, in a similar context.

[38] Rosenberg, *Mythus*, p. 375.

[39] Schultze-Naumburg, *Kunst der Deutschen*, p. 72.

[40] Fischer, "Vermächtnis," p. 154.

[41] A rare dissenting opinion was that of Fischer: "We are justifiably proud of our classical age, but it was not German or native to us." ("Vermächtnis," p. 154.)

[42] Georg Wenzeslaus von Knobelsdorff (1699–1753) designed the Berlin Opera House and Sanssouci for Frederick the Great. Carl Gotthard Langhans (1732–1808) built the Brandenburg Gate. Leo von Klenze (1784–1864) was active in Ludwig I's Munich.

by Schinkel in Berlin (1828).[43] (See illustration no. 10.) The
modern German neo-classicists wanted to recall this period, perhaps the only period when German (and particularly Prussian)
architects achieved as much fame as other Europeans in this field.
Praise for Greek styles also suited the racial aspects of the ideology — the Greeks as "Aryans," and the nationalist aspects —
Prussia as the leader of Germany. The style itself was respectable
and could be well adapted to impressive representative buildings.
Writers often cited from Schinkel's written works as if from an
architectural Bible.[44] Even non-Nazi and non-German critics
would agree with Wolters' statement that the age of Schinkel
was "the last golden age of architectural creativity";[45] yet, critics
in the Third Reich put an ideological value on the style of the
period.

Prussia could boast the best examples of this architecture.
Here the simplest buildings had a "noble monumentality," which
was thought worth copying.[46] Moreover, some of the leading architects of the period were felt to have the right attitudes. In short,
they would have made good Nazi architects. They were both
heroic fighters and obedient servants, and their architecture constituted "the expression of the state and its heroic idea."[47] Most
writers approved and cited Moeller van den Bruck's book, *Der
preussische Stil* which expressed similar feelings about Prussian
architecture, wherein, said one commentator, "the inner relationship of the north German individual with classical Greece again
found a clear expression."[48] Yet, far from being dryly antiquarian,
soldier-architects like Schinkel were said (correctly) to be aware

[43] Or that Schinkel's plan for Schloss Köstriz (1802), is echoed in the Air
Ministry designed by Sagebiel in Berlin. (See Alste Oncken, *Friedrich Gilly
1772–1800*, Berlin, Deutscher Verein für Kunstwissenschaft, 1935, p. 93.) Karl
Friedrich Schinkel built also the "New Watch" and the royal theater in Berlin.

[44] For example, Rittich, *Architektur und Bauplastik*, pp. 156 and 168.

[45] Wolters, *Neue deutsche Baukunst*, p. 7.

[46] Lindner, "Grundlagen und Ziele," p. 12.

[47] Wendland, *Kunst und Nation*, p. 6.

[48] *Ibid.*, p. 25.

of technological advances in building. Schinkel was enthusiastic about cast iron and knew of the possibilities of glass and steel in building.[49] As will be seen, architects in the Third Reich, when imitating past forms, were always proud to note that they used the most up-to-date technical means — but not for the sake of technological modernity alone (the sin of the *Bauhaus*).

In his book, *Gilly: Wiedergeburt der Architektur*,[50] Alfred Rietdorf described a man whom Hitler and the Reich Chamber of Culture would have approved thoroughly. The architect Friedrich Gilly (1772–1800) lived in a time when the peoples of Europe sought change and turned back to their racial origins for inspiration. Thus, said Rietdorf, the Germans rediscovered their "awareness of the whole," their "feeling for totality." Gilly was led by this movement to study prehistoric graves, which influenced his sense of monumentality and stimulated his "feeling for the Fatherland." At the same time, he developed his "feeling for history and attraction for distances." His talent, however, was rooted in his surroundings; his gifts were not analytical, but "an organic endowment."[51] Compared to later architects of the nineteen-twenties, he was a builder for the *Volk*, not an intellectual drawing complex impractical schemes. Gilly wanted to create a "new Greece," "free of Roman falsifications," and a classicism uncorrupted by baroque additions. Although at first he favored Rome and the round arch as models, he soon adopted Athens and the Acropolis as the ideal, and proceeded to make plans for monumental, "earthbound" buildings, such as a templelike monument to Frederick the Great (1797). For the Third Reich, this was his most significant plan, "a protest" said Rietdorf, ". . . against the Church. Its brightness was to drive out the darkness of the cathedrals." It was the "symbol of a new order."[52] Obviously, Rietdorf interpolated the main

[49] *Ibid.*, pp. 6–8.
[50] Alfred Rietdorf, *Gilly: Wiedergeburt der Architektur*, Berlin, Hans von Hugo, 1943.
[51] *Gilly*, p. 6, and pp. 13–17.
[52] *Ibid.*, pp. 19–20 and 45.

tenets of the contemporary nationalist theory of architecture into Gilly's work. Rietdorf deduced that neo-classicism was more natural for the Germans from Gilly's note that, although the French triumphed with the Panthéon in Paris, they ultimately failed to build well in this style. French architects, such as Claude-Nicolas Ledoux (1736–1806), evidently missed "the Prussian education, which Gilly had enjoyed," a training that developed the whole personality, "in the service of [the] Fatherland." But Rietdorf became even more precise. Gilly was impressed by a Parisian republican festival on the Champs de Mars and Rietdorf saw this ceremony as a precedent for the Nazi May 1, 1933 celebrations and the party rally grounds in Nuremberg.[53] Rietdorf seemed to believe that Gilly would have approved of what the Nazi government was doing for Germany. At least now — in the Third Reich — Germans could understand what Gilly was trying to do. Out of their new communal experience Germans were building sacred places, parade grounds, congress halls, communal houses, barracks, stadiums, and sport halls, filling them with the people of a new epoch, meeting together to celebrate. "To the age of Gilly, this experience is not foreign." Gilly did not build for mundane purposes, and Nazi planners, too, sought to overcome the trivial with a style which was monumental: "We want to bear witness and to build permanently," an aim "common to that age and to ours."[54] In this way, one writer sought a respectable precedent for the monumental "community" architecture of the Third Reich.

Whereas the Romanesque, Gothic, Renaissance, and baroque periods were viewed critically by these writers, the neo-classical age usually received general approval. It seemed to be the only time when the "German spirit" escaped suppression by alien fashions and was able to express itself in a form appropriate to its nature. Unfortunately, this freedom did not last and, in the later nineteenth century, German building fell into decadence.

[53] *Ibid.*, pp. 80, 108, and 84.
[54] *Ibid.*, pp. 128–130.

CHAPTER SIX

Contemporary Attitudes to German Architecture since 1850: "Decadence"

HITLER'S VIEW of nineteenth-century German architecture was not original nor peculiarly "Nazi." Even before he went to Vienna as a youth, objective critics had begun to lament this period of imitation. In Germany, moreover, nationalists who wrote on the nineteenth century linked the decline of architecture to political, social, and racial problems and hence to ideological issues. The age was repeatedly termed "the period of decay." This may seem paradoxical at first, given the political unification during 1866–1871. Yet the view is symptomatic of the widespread disillusionment with Bismarck's Reich and its weaknesses, particularly the lack of social and political unity apparent after 1890. Many *völkisch* writers, in particular, were shocked by the rapid industrialization of German society in the last quarter of the century and its destruction of old ties binding Germans together as members of a family, a village community, or a class; hence the longing for new "community" architecture.[1]

[1] It was the constant reiteration of the "community" goals of the new regime which led Wolters to support it. ("Versuch einer Rechtfertigung: Brief von Rudolf Wolters an Alfons Leitl," *Baukunst und Werkform*, 1952, cited in Teut, *Architek-*

In 1900 Germany represented "an architectural junk heap," said the architect Wolters.[2] Paul Schmitthenner, an architect who favored traditional styles, believed that the Thirty Years War had not destroyed as much of cultural value as had the senseless building of the nineteenth century.[3] What had caused this phenomenon? The most popular answer was that the liberal and materialistic ideology of the middle class dominated German building, resulting in disastrous consequences for German cities and the German landscape.[4] Seeking only profit, the middle class built ugly factories, not only destroying the appearance of beautiful old towns, but wrecking the surrounding countryside. Unhealthy tenements were built to house the workers, while clumsy villas, with imitation foreign styles, were constructed to house the *nouveaux riches*. As the industrial metropolis grew, and the old crafts succumbed to mass production, all sense of a German community vanished. The typical German bourgeois was vividly described by Gerdy Troost as "indifferent to race, un-*völkisch*, unsocial, devoid of any deep connection with the community, wedded to money and machines, misled by Jews, and driven closer and closer to destruction."[5]

The editor of *Der Baumeister* (a journal) was specific. The Memorial to Kaiser Wilhelm I (1896) at the Porta Westfalica was a "monstrosity"; the German pavilion at the Paris World Exhibition of 1900 was "one of the ugliest ever built"; the expansion of the Reich Post Office in Berlin (built in Italian baroque 1871–1873, enlarged 1893–1898) was ugly; the city halls of Dresden and Kassel, the Hamburg Railway Station, the Spa Pavilion at Wies-

tur, pp. 368–372. Wolters had gone to Russia in 1932, attracted by what seemed to be the ideal social goals of their government.

[2] Wolters, *Neue deutsche Baukunst*, p. 8.

[3] Paul Schmitthenner, *Die Baukunst im neuen Reich*, Munich, Callwey, 1934, p. 6.

[4] This view is similar to that of the "National Bolsheviks," who sought a socialist solution to Germany's problems, yet within the framework of national loyalty.

[5] Troost, *Bauen*, I, 9.

baden, the Bismarck monument in Hamburg, the Municipal Museum in Altona, the new Civic Theater in Cologne — all represented "an indescribably chaotic epoch in German architecture."[6] (See also illustrations nos. 5 and 11.)

Many writers believed that liberalism, rationalism, and materialism had produced this chaos. Beginning with the French Revolution, a materialist conception of history spread throughout Europe, as reflected in laissez-faire, the doctrine of the industrial middle class.[7] In architecture, it meant that anyone could build as he wished; there was no ruling hand to create order.[8] Living like Renaissance princes in colonies of villas, the newly rich industrialists concentrated on building more sumptuous "palaces of capital" and more factories.[9] Their luxurious mansions cost great sums, but they regarded every other type of building solely according to what they believed to be its function, to make money. Calculating reason, therefore, dominated architecture, and the importance of beauty, and Germanness was forgotten. "*Bauspekulation*, a foreign ugly monstrosity, [crept] over our land," said Schultze-Naumburg in 1909.[10] Later, in the thirties, Werner Lindner, another *völkisch* writer, found the same phenomenon, the "soil profiteer," who made money trafficking in "plots of sacred German earth." This type of German, possessing no real "will to build," admired what was done abroad and ignored German needs or achievements.[11] In the nineteenth century particularly, he in-

[6] Rudolf Pfister, introduction to *Bauten Schultze-Naumburgs*, Weimar, Alexander Duncker, n.d., pp. v–vi. (As editor of *Der Baumeister* after 1928, Pfister (a traditionalist) abandoned the publication's former *avant-garde* stand.) The buildings of the imperial post office were denounced as an "outrage" by Werner Lindner as well. (*Die Stadt*, p. 594, and illustrations, pp. 593–595.)

[7] Schultze-Naumburg, *Die Kunst der Deutschen*, p. 81.

[8] This phenomenon was a "child of the French Revolution," continued Gottfried Feder, a consequence of "architectural liberalism." (*Die neue Stadt*, p. 10.)

[9] Wolters, *Albert Speer*, p. 6.

[10] Paul Schultze-Naumburg, *Städtebau* in Vol. IV of *Kulturarbeiten*, Vol. IV, Munich, Callwey, 1909, p. 31.

[11] Lindner, *Die Stadt*, p. 22. On the same theme see Stephan, *Die Baukunst im Dritten Reich*, p. 6; and Troost, *Bauen*, I, 9.

dulged in "an orgiastic worship of styles."[12] The result was that "a foreign criterion" was again applied to German building, which suppressed the creative strength of the race.[13]

In the late nineteenth century, German cities increased greatly in size and population. The "asphalt waste of the metropolis" was detrimental to the "German instinctive feeling for culture,"[14] for it was a human ant heap wherein German existence became almost oriental in its aimlessness and passivity.[15] Schultze-Naumburg repeated the popular nostalgic and nationalist view that the older German cities were themselves genuine works of art, made so by the talented craftsmen who lived and worked in them. But, with its mass production, the new industrial city had destroyed craftsmanship. Thus, a great crime had been committed against Germany: "Our cities carry the contemporary mark of Cain in stone and brick."[16]

Most of these writers stressed that the sense of a community was lost and that only "the whim of the individual"[17] determined the appearance of cities: each rich man could build what, where, and as he pleased. The most imposing buildings in any German city usually represented individual ambition, not the values of the community.[18] "The more the *Reich*, the *Volk*, and the family dissolved," wrote the architect Hans Stephan, "the more so did the architectural body of the city."[19] This disunity of the architectural scene was believed to be symbolic of the spiritual and political

[12] Pfister, *Die Bauten Schultze-Naumburgs*, p. vi.

[13] Rosenberg, *Mythus*, p. 379. Most of the nineteenth-century styles were "un-German," said Schmitthenner. ("Tradition und neues Bauen," cited in Teut, *Architektur*, p. 123.)

[14] Troost, *Bauen*, I, 9.

[15] Schultze-Naumburg, *Städtebau*, p. 480.

[16] Schultze-Naumburg, *Städtebau*, p. 479.

[17] Troost, *Bauen*, I, 9.

[18] "The architecture of the liberal epoch," wrote one writer, did not represent "the soul of a *Volk* or a community," but expressed only "the private soul." (Hartmann, *Werkhefte*, p. 106.) Good "German" architecture, on the other hand, should express the soul of the *Gemeinschaft*.

[19] Stephan, *Baukunst im Dritten Reich*, p. 6.

condition of Germany. Had there been a *Volkstaat* in existence, as after 1933, this would not have occurred; but Germany was not yet a real community and had no leadership, only "an administration for the execution of laws."[20] The collapse of medieval organic communal ties and the decline of crafts was due, said Schulte-Frohlinde, to the liberal introduction of occupational freedom, the abolition of corporations and guilds, and the triumph of the machine.[21] Moreover, the training of architects with textbooks alien to *völkisch* life, removed the earth from under the young builders' feet, with the result that buildings were no longer "bound by blood to homeland and *Volk*,"[22] and no longer symbolized the existence of a community. Hence no truly monumental buildings were constructed, only palatial banks and railway stations, having little relationship to the life of the people. Whereas in the old days, cities grew up around cathedrals or castles which "ordered" the landscape around themselves, few modern German cities had a central focus to give a sense of unity to their inhabitants.[23]

Also lacking was strong leadership, wrote the Nazi economist Gottfried Feder.[24] Germany needed "the supreme patron, the strong state, whose resolute will stands behind the work of the builder," said Wolters.[25] The Nazi revolution would provide this, as well as the ideals with which to motivate building. Those like Schultze-Naumburg, who had called for new ideals and for leadership as early as 1909,[26] hoped that the political changes of 1933 would bring these into existence.

These views reflected the general discontent with nineteenth-century architectural development of various German (and European) circles. The *art nouveau* movement, in Germany and Aus-

---

[20] Wolters, *Neue deutsche Baukunst*, p. 8.
[21] Schulte-Frohlinde, *Die landschaftlichen Grundlagen*, p. 7.
[22] *Ibid.*, p. 8.
[23] Wolters, *Neue deutsche Baukunst*, p. 14.
[24] Feder, *Die neue Stadt*, p. 13.
[25] Wolters, *Albert Speer*, p. 5. See also his *Vom Beruf des Baumeisters*, pp. 29–32.
[26] See his introduction to Straub's *Architektur im dritten Reich*, pp. 3–4.

tria known as *Jugendstil,* sought a more fluid, less heavy style of
interior decoration. At the same time, Walter Gropius, later
founder of the *Bauhaus,* produced his model factory with walls of
glass at the *Deutscher Werkbund* Exhibition in Cologne in 1914.
The *Werkbund* itself was founded in 1907 by progressive manu-
facturers and architects for the exchange of ideas. Here lay some
roots of modern European architecture. Yet by 1914 there were
two other important reform movements in Germany, *völkisch*
thought and a revival of classicism. An attempt at a starker classicism was evident in, for example, the work of Heinrich Tessenow
(1876–1950), an architect who influenced Speer. But stronger
than this movement was the *völkisch* trend, not only in architecture, but also in literature. A typical example of the search for
genuinely German architecture at this time is Albrecht Haupt's
book on Germanic building.[27] The work, although preceding
Nazism, must have influenced many men who later looked to the
Nazi movement for the realization of their nationalist ideals.
Haupt's study, which concentrated on early medieval architecture — buildings like Theodoric's tomb in Ravenna and the Caro-
lingian chapel at Aachen [28] — tried to show how all the best accomplishments of European architecture were a manifestation of
the "Nordic" spirit. Schultze-Naumburg was also active on the
fringes of this movement, although he confined his studies to Germany itself.[29] Fischer, originally an imitator of historical styles,
also turned in this direction, seeking a style which was closer to
German tradition; his rediscovery of the expressive qualities of
stone influenced many of his pupils, such as Paul Bonatz, and his

[27] Albrecht Haupt, *Die älteste Kunst.* Young Speer had read this book.
(*Erinnerungen,* p. 28; *Inside,* p. 11.)

[28] A few of his discoveries would not have pleased some nationalists: he
noted that the early Germans built with flat, wooden roofs (p. 122) and later
adopted the round arch (p. 138.)

[29] On the *völkisch* movement in general, see Mosse, *Crisis of German Ideology.* For an autobiographical look at the movement in the twenties, see Ziegler,
Adolf Hitler, especially pp. 25–68.

search for a more genuinely *völkisch* style explains his nationalist utterances in the early part of the Third Reich.[30]

The irony of the later Nazi building program is that the state tended to ignore the *völkisch* exponents and concentrated its efforts on building in a neo-classical vein. Yet ideologically, the *völkisch* writers were more deeply concerned with race than any others, while the neo-classical movement was international in scope. The neo-classicism of Speer and Troost was neither purely *völkisch* in inspiration nor purely blood-oriented, and it was not rooted in only German traditions. It became the task of architects to make neo-classicism fit in. This was even more difficult because there was a European classical revival in the twentieth century, a movement which could claim Speer, and Mies van der Rohe of the *Bauhaus*, as exemplars. Few of these architects, to be sure, advocated a complete return to the ancient Greek or the late eighteenth-century styles. But as in the works of Auguste Perret in France, ornate capitals were avoided, mouldings around windows and doors were simplified, cornices were reduced in size, and superfluous decoration was avoided.[31] Perret, Speer, and even Mies van der Rohe would agree on this style.[32]

It is also ironical that both the Nazis and the Bolsheviks favored neo-classicism in the thirties. The best examples are the pavilions of Germany and of Russia at the 1937 Paris Exhibition; Speer's tower was neatly complemented by the massive Soviet pavilion directly across the street on the right bank of the Seine.[33]

[30] Paul Bonatz, *Leben und Bauen*, Stuttgart, Engelhorn, 1950, pp. 44–45.

[31] Perret was the only French architect to resist the trend to functionalism in his country, wrote Lotz ("So baut Europa," pp. 179–180.) Lotz approved heartily of the architect's Museum of Modern Art and Museum of Public Works in Paris, both in a simplified neo-classicism.

[32] Nor were all supporters of the German neo-classical revival Nazis or even right-wing nationalists. For example, Hans Vogel's *Deutsche Baukunst des Klassizismus* (Berlin, Mann, 1937) is neither Nazi nor *völkisch* in inspiration, although its subject matter concerned the most "approved" age of German architecture. Vogel had also been a lecturer and museum curator.

[33] Paul Dupays, *Voyages autour du monde; Pavillons étrangers et pavillons coloniaux à l'exposition de 1937*, Paris, Henri Didier, 1938.

(See illustrations nos. 29 and 30.) Yet it was explained that the Russian style was "barbaric formalism," draped with a "small classical mantel," whereas the Nazi style was pure "Nordic."[34]

Neo-classical buildings, however, were only part of the Nazi building program. Moreover, a few Nazi sympathizers did not even approve of this trend. Pinder disliked Troost's "Doric" House of German Art, and favored a return to more purely German, that is, *völkisch*, medieval and rural styles. Wolfgang Willrich, a *völkisch* painter and writer, opposed classicism, too, preferring medieval styles. "Those temple mouldings and pillars," Winfried Wendland wrote, "belong under the bright blue sky of Greece . . . Our architecture had a different appearance; it was characterized by half-timbered houses with pointed gables, cathedrals with pointed archs and heaven-striving piers, statuary securely ensconced in niches and canopies."[35] Schultze-Naumburg himself, having sought to revive a pure German style since the turn of the century, could not approve of Nazi neo-classicism and was disappointed with the building program. The new Greek revival was merely a "theory of art, drawn up by intellectuals," not an idea which derived from the life of the *Volk*.[36] Ironically this was the same objection which Hitler and others had to the *Bauhaus*! Obviously it was all a matter of what one considered "German."

As for *art nouveau*, although a few writers praised it,[37] Rosenberg called it an "infamous . . . crime in the arts and crafts."[38] *Jugendstil*, most thought, was not a "healthy" trend. The search for precursors led to those architects who worked in simplified traditional styles and who seemed to be trying to be "German" in inspiration. There was praise for Wilhelm Kreis (1873–1955) and his monuments to Bismarck, and for Peter Behrens (1868–1940) and his German Embassy in St. Petersburg, "a building in which

[34] Lotz, "So baut Europa," p. 174.
[35] Wendland, *Kunst und Nation*, p. 19.
[36] Schultze-Naumburg, *Kunst der Deutschen*, p. 87.
[37] Pfister, *Bauten Schultze-Naumburgs*, p. vi.
[38] Rosenberg, *Mythus*, p. 378.

the future Greater German Reich is presaged."[39] Heinrich Tessenow (1876–1950), Fritz Schumacher (1869–1947), and Hermann Muthesius (1861–1927), were said to have "recognized the collective task"[40] of German architects, a task which included not simply esthetics or engineering, but also social and political problems. Schmitthenner praised this prewar trend towards a "more healthy form of building," and the new awareness of tradition and landscape.[41]

Although historians might deny the existence of "Nazi" or "German" buildings before 1933 — or at any time — what some German critics thought was good in twentieth-century architecture shows what they wanted developed after 1933. Some "approved" architects were neither party members nor even *völkisch* in sympathy. Some received few or no commissions after 1933. But their selection for praise reveals what some critics thought "German" architecture should be like.

Particularly in 1933–1934, there was no hard line on this issue, because of the conflict between the antimodern Rosenberg clique and the Goebbels group with their acceptance of modern architecture, and because of Hitler's indifference and pragmatism. Symptomatic of this relative freedom was the appearance of a book, *Kunst und Nation* by Wendland in 1934, in which some buildings in the "objective" style were praised, a form which other

[39] Wolter, *Albert Speer*, p. 5. Speer himself declares that, with this embassy, Behrens was one of the originators of the "Nazi style." (Correspondence, November 24, 1967.)

[40] Wolters, *Neue deutsche Baukunst*, p. 8. The career of Schumacher, who often designed in brick, is described in "Fritz Schumacher, Hamburg: Der Architekt, Städtebauer, und Kulturpolitiker, zu seinem 70. Geburtstag am 4. November 1939," *Moderne Bauformen*, XXXVIII (1939), 545–551. Muthesius was one of the founders of the German *Werkbund*, 1907.

Moderne Bauformen was one of the most widely read architectural journals in the Reich, and accordingly influential. It had supported the *avant-garde*, but during the Third Reich became — typically — more and more oriented to the traditional and to crafts. Yet even in 1940 (Vol. 39), it was able to discuss objectively the qualities of strip windows (p. 501) and tube chairs (p. 595).

[41] Paul Schmitthenner, "Tradition und neues Bauen," cited in Teut, *Architektur*, p. 122.

critics emphatically condemned. Schmitthenner of Stuttgart and
other architects (including Speer), who were using both traditional and *völkisch* styles, and materials such as brick were also
represented. Yet the real peculiarity of the book was an illustration
of a flat-roofed post office building in Munich with a decidedly
radical *avant-garde* appearance.[42] Wendland was not clear as to
what unified all these buildings, but he did stress simplicity and
the rejection of historical imitation. Moreover he also discussed
church architecture, including one church of his own design.[43]
Here was another paradox, given Hitler and Rosenberg's hostiliy
to Christianity. That this book could be published in 1934 was
symptomatic of the confusion and caution in leading circles. It
was still too soon, and Nazi power was still not secure enough, to totally alienate either *avant-garde* architects or Christians.

As it turned out, an architectural counterrevolution never
occurred. In 1934, a progressive architect could still defend the
flat roof,[44] and as late as 1936 there appeared a noncommittal
article, "An Architect Visits Berlin," which included photos of
Hugo Häring's *avant-garde* work in Siemensstadt and of Mies van
der Rohe's stark apartments on Afrikanische Strasse, both in Berlin.[45] These were presented side by side with works of more obviously "Nazi" architects, Werner March and Ernst Sagebiel. The
individual architects who supported the Nazi building program
were not always second-rate or sycophants. The Artists' Council of
the Reich Chamber of Fine Arts boasted the membership of such

[42] Wendland, *Kunst und Nation*, p. 70. He praised expressionism in the same
book.

[43] *Ibid.*, pp. 65–68. Wendland was also advisor on art to the Reich Cultural
Committee of the German Faith Movement (a pro-Nazi Protestant group), and
one of the founders of the Evangelical Reich Office for Church Art, under the
protection of Reich Bishop Müller, Hitler's appointee.

[44] Hugo Häring, "Bemerkungen zum Flachbau mit Beispielen grundsätz-
licher Art," *Moderne Bauformen*, XXXIII (1934), 619–632. Häring (1882–1958)
worked with Gropius on the Berlin-Siemensstadt development.

[45] "Ein Architekt besucht Berlin," *Moderne Bauformen*, XXXV (1936), 417–
424. Emil Fahrenkamp's Shell Haus (1928–1931), with its undulating facade, was
also illustrated.

respected — and not necessarily "Nazi" — names as Fritz Höger (1877–1949) and Tessenow, architects who hoped that the new regime would shore up traditional developments and combat the undesirable aspects of modern urban life. Nevertheless, the critics were mistaken in considering these men and their works as forerunners of any "Nazi" style. Their support of the ideology was not political. What united them in support of the government's program was their hope for cultural reform.

Of course, the government often encouraged these men to remain active. Another paradox of the architectural policy during the Third Reich is that Peter Behrens remained head of the Department of Architecture at the Prussian Academy of Fine Arts in Berlin. Behrens was one of the leaders of architectural reform at the turn of the century and was a major designer of factories and office buildings in brick, steel, and glass. His A. E. G. Turbine Factory in Berlin (1908–1909), although usually considered abroad as a pioneering work, presumably was, to the Nazi critics, a "palace of capital." Yet he was permitted to design an office building, again for A. E. G., during the Third Reich.[46] Official architectural policy was still flexible enough to allow him to continue to work. Moreover, he was praised by Speer, and was internationally famous. Under these circumstances, it was unwise for the government to restrict his activities, even if it so desired.

In fact, during the Third Reich, mere opposition to *Bauhaus* architecture was enough to gain official approval for almost any architect, as with German Bestelmeyer (1874–1942). A member of the Munich School to which Troost also belonged, he had been trained under Fischer. He was praised by Schultze-Naumburg in a lecture in 1931,[47] because he aligned himself with supporters of traditional styles. In 1934, he became head of the Munich Academy of Art, to which he enlisted Alexander von Senger, the

---

[46] Troost, *Bauen*, I, 78. Yet this structure had the familiar "Nazi" horizontal lines, symmetrical wings, and heavy classical cornice.

[47] Cited in Brenner, *Kunstpolitik*, p. 19.

passionate opponent of "Bolshevik" architecture; later he designed
a *Luftwaffe* office building on the Prinzregentenstrasse in Munich.
This traditional building and his other works were singled out for
praise in the later thirties.[48] An article he wrote in 1934 sums up
his ideas and probably drew the approval of Nazis. Admiring von
Senger's criticism of Le Corbusier, he found that, in the twenties,
architecture was petrifying into mere "architectural technology,"
creating "soulless" buildings. The flat roof, he said, was simply not
practical for Germany's climate.[49] His 1928 alliance with Schultze-
Naumburg, Schmitthenner and others into The Block, a group of
architects determined to combat the experiments of the *Bauhaus*,[50]
made him acceptable.[51]

In a position similar to Bestelmeyer's was another Nazi-
approved architect, Paul Bonatz (1877–1951), a member of the
Stuttgart School and professor at the technical university in that
city. He tended to favor a radically simplified neo-Romanesque
style, as in his Basel Museum or his Stuttgart Railway Station, although he maintained that he never adhered to one style.[52] He,
too, had been trained under Fischer,[53] but, unlike him, was never
a party member, although he accepted the position of architectural expert and advisor to Fritz Todt, general inspector for German road building, and built two major bridges for the Autobahnen.[54] He accepted these commissions, as well as the one to
design the huge new railway station planned for Munich, for the
engineering challenge they offered.[55] The government tried to
make good use of his talents and name, but found him unreliable.
He disliked Troost's renovation of the Royal Square in Munich,

[48] See, for example, *Moderne Bauformen*, XXXVIII (1939), 558, wherein his office building on Leipzig's Augustusplatz is described.

[49] German Bestelmeyer, "Baukunst und Gegenwart," pp. 127–131.

[50] For the Block's "Manifesto," June, 1928, see Teut, *Architektur*, p. 29.

[51] Feistel-Rohmeder, *Im Terror des Kunstbolschewismus*, p. 36.

[52] Bonatz, *Leben und Bauen*, p. 185.

[53] See the chapter "Im Bannkreis Theodor Fischers," *Leben und Bauen*, pp. 43–50.

[54] See the chapter "Die Autobahn," *Leben und Bauen*, pp. 158–170.

[55] Bonatz, *Leben und Bauen*, p. 179.

and said so: twice he was investigated by the police, who accused him of aiding Jews and being openly critical of Hitler.[56] It seems that as with Fischer and Bestelmeyer, Bonatz, although no historical imitator, was approved because he was not in the *avant-garde* and because his works were in styles vaguely "German." Thus Friedrich Tamms expressed the party's official approval in *Kunst im Dritten Reich*,[57] and Schultze-Naumburg expressed the *völkisch* school's approval, calling the Stuttgart Railway Station (a stark Romanesque building of stone, built 1913–1927) "a modern technical buiding in the best sense of the word."[58] Despite continuing "approval" and commissions, Bonatz felt obliged to leave Germany for Turkey, because of disagreements with Hitler over his plans for the Munich Railway Station.[59]

A third architect acceptable to the Nazis was Schmitthenner, also from the Stuttgart School. He was praised in 1931 by Schultze-Naumburg,[60] and his books were approvingly cited. "The monuments of German Art," he wrote, "are definitely rooted in German *Volkstum*, the character of which is affected by that piece of earth to which its fate is bound." In 1934 he saw Hitler as the "unknown stonemason," who correctly appraised Germany's dangers, rallied the *Volk* together, and began building defences.[61] His belief that the traditional methods and styles in architecture revealed best the German character [62] led to his appointment as expert group

[56] *Ibid.*, pp. 151–154, and 168–169. See also Speer, *Erinnerungen*, p. 94; *Inside*, p. 80.

[57] "Paul Bonatz," *Kunst im Dritten Reich*, VI:12 (December, 1942), 218–237. See also Friedrich Tamms' book, *Paul Bonatz: Arbeiten aus den Jahren 1907 bis 1937*, Stuttgart, Hoffman, 1937, wherein Bonatz' works are described as being "serious, manly [and] German" (p. 7).

[58] Schultze-Naumburg, *Kunst der Deutschen*, p. 112. See also "Technisches und monumentales Bauen: Arbeiten von Paul Bonatz aus den Jahren 1907–39," *Moderne Bauformen*, XXXVII (1938), 1–16.

[59] Bonatz, *Leben und Bauen*, pp. 179–180; see also Dehlinger, *Architektur der Superlative*, p. 15.

[60] Lecture cited in Brenner, *Kunstpolitik*, p. 19.

[61] Paul Schmitthenner, *Die Baukunst im neuen Reich*, pp. 17–18.

[62] Cited in "Arbeiten von Paul Schmitthenner," *Moderne Bauformen*, XXXIX (1939), 408.

leader for fine arts in the Kampfbund. However, despite official
approval, his enthusiasm did not bring many large commissions.

A final example is Tessenow, cited by one critic as a fore-
runner in the "Nazi style."[63] His Festival House in Hellerau, near
Dresden, was built in 1910–1912 along "Doric" classical lines.[64]
Tessenow wanted, along with Nazis and *völkisch* writers, to restore
the craft tradition and the small town environment over that of
the metropolis; he believed that style evolved from the *Volk*. He
was, however, an opponent of the Nazi party. He was still praised
for recognizing the need for a new, but not too *avant-garde* architecture.[65] In the thirties his activities were not important, but his
name was influential.

One irony of this search for ideological ancestry includes
Schultze-Naumburg, who had been fighting since the turn of the
century for a reform of German architecture and cities. In the
twenties he became the first chairman of The Block, and in 1930
was appointed director of the Weimar Academy of Architecture,
Fine Arts, and Crafts. He was also art advisor to the Nazi Minister of the Interior in Thuringia, Wilhelm Frick, for a short time
in the same year. In 1933 he supported the Third Reich in the
hope that the *völkisch* aspect of its ideology would lead to re-
forms.[66] Despite his "almost naïve faith in Hitler,"[67] he was not
patronized by the new state, nor does his work appear often in the
officially published books on "the buildings of the movement."

[63] Rittich, *Architektur und Bauplastik*, p. 127. According to Speer, Tessenow
stood close to him in his thinking: "However, after 1933 he severed ties with me,
since he could not approve of the new tack my interests were taking." (Correspondence, November 27, 1967.) Tessenow was approvingly quoted by the Nazi
sympathizer, Böckler, in his *Landschaftsgemäss Bauen?* p. 43 (on the lack of harmony in German creative life). Although Nazi students flocked to his seminars
in Berlin, he remained critical of the party. (Speer, *Erinnerungen*, p. 31; *Inside*,
p. 14.)

[64] Hans Weigert, *Geschichte der deutschen Kunst*, Vol. II: *Von der spät-
gothischen Plastik bis zur Gegenwart*, Frankfurt, Umschau, 1963, pp. 266–267.

[65] Wolters, *Neue deutsche Baukunst*, p. 8.

[66] See his praise for Hitler in the preface to the second edition of his *Kunst
der Deutschen: Ihr Wesen und ihre Werke*, Stuttgart, Deutsche Verlagsanstalt,
1934, pp. 5–6.

[67] Dehlinger, *Architektur der Superlative*, p. 58.

Schultze-Naumburg's own style was a domestic *Biedermeier*, neither *völkisch* in the sense of peasant architecture, nor monumental or neo-classical, but rather a simple, dignified, and comfortable style which did not accord completely with either Hitler's thought or the two main strands of nationalist thinking on architecture.[68] Schultze-Naumburg, says Speer, was "a bourgeois architect" and hence his architecture did not please Hitler.[69] The *Führer*, often derogatory of the architect in conversation, was particularly displeased with his renovation of the Nuremberg Opera House.[70] According to Schultze-Naumburg's colleague, Ziegler, Hitler valued him only as a teacher and writer on art, not as an architect.[71]

These so-called forerunners were important: they rejected the new lines of the *Bauhaus*; they stressed traditional (although simplified) and usually "German" (*völkisch*) styles; they liked to build with local materials and favored crafts. Only in these respects could they be called "Nazi." Citing them as pioneers of Nazi design gave the new regime and its supporters a sense of dignity and respectability, for they were well known and competent. Yet their influence on architecture in the Third Reich was less than might be expected.

Obviously, some critics opposed modern functional architecture of the *Bauhaus* and of other pioneers. It would be superfluous here to detail their attack before and after 1933.[72] One of the most

[68] When he retired in 1939, *Art in the Third Reich* devoted only two pages to a summation of his career. (Robert Scholz, "Paul Schultze-Naumburg," *Kunst im Dritten Reich*, July 1939, III:7, 214–215.) There was also the book by Rudolf Pfister, *Die Bauten Schultze-Naumburgs*, and an approving reference to him in Paul Schmitthenner, *Die Baukunst im neuen Reich*, p. 13. In 1943, he was still considered an expert on traditional *Kultur*, and was quoted by Böckler (*Landschaftsgemäss bauen?*, pp. 24 and 48.

[69] Interview with Speer, June 13, 1968; and correspondence, November 24, 1967. See also Speer, *Erinnerungen*, p. 77; *Inside*, p. 64.

[70] Dehlinger, *Architektur der Superlative*, pp. 24–25.

[71] Ziegler, *Adolf Hitler*, p. 205.

[72] This has been done competently by Lane, *Architecture and Politics*, pp. 11–68 and especially pp. 69–86 ("Controversy over the Bauhaus"), pp. 125–145 ("Debate over the New Architecture"), and pp. 147–167 ("The New Architecture and National Socialism").

interesting of these attacks was Karl Willy Straub's book *Architektur im Dritten Reich*, written in 1932, which is quite constructive as Straub describes what good German architecture in the future would be. There would be no flat roofs or bare surfaces, but rather sloping roofs and moderate decoration; modern technology would be used as a means, not as an end; good architecture of the past would be valued.[73]

However, few writers combined their criticisms with constructive or comprehensive suggestions as did Straub. For the *Bauhaus*, denunciation ruled. The modern style of the twenties was criticized for reflecting the same malaise as did that of the nineteenth century. The spirit was the same; only the form had changed.[74] The "engineer art" of the present was as unacceptable as the pseudo-baroque of the previous century.[75] The period of the twenties was seen as the lowest point of German architectural — and political — history. All sense of community was gone. According to Nazi art expert Werner Rittich, architects built only for individuals or small groups of self-seekers, often Jews, or they built only to suit themselves.[76] Their plans were often the product of overintellectual musings, unrelated to the real needs of Germans. But what was worse, many architects had fallen victim to the Marxist ideology, with its materialism and its hatred of tradition. The new buildings of concrete, glass, or steel did not fit the old cityscapes, while the progressive destruction of the German landscape proceeded apace. Perhaps the most devoted campaigner against modern architecture was Alexander von Senger.[77] Preservation of a racially pure style was endangered, he said, by Bolshevism in architecture (epitomized by Le Corbusier

[73] Straub, *Architektur im Dritten Reich*.

[74] Schmitthenner, "Tradition und neues Bauen," p. 123.

[75] Rosenberg, "Revolution in den bildenden Künste," *Völkischer Beobachter*, July 7, 1933, 2nd supplement.

[76] Rittich, *Architektur und Bauplastik*, p. 5.

[77] See particularly his *Krisis der Architektur*, Zürich, Rascher, 1928; and "Baubolschewismus und seine Verkoppelungen mit Wirtschaft und Politik," *Nationalsozialistische Monatshefte*, V (1934), 497ff.

(1887–); the machine was destroying the crafts, and now — thanks to Le Corbusier's concept of the house as a machine for living — it would destroy human life itself. Antimaterialist, von Senger found the middle class as wicked as the Marxists, for both were obsessed with only economic concerns. Together, they represented "mammonism [and] Bolshevism."[78] The implied solution was a national dictatorship over art and architecture. The *Deutsche Kunstkorrespondenz*, a column by Feistel-Rohmeder, was also in the vanguard in the fight against "Bolshevik" architecture, as typified by the *Bauhaus*. The latter school, with its "nihilist style," produced "garbage-can architecture."[79] Like von Senger, this writer implied that "Jewish finance" was behind the desecration of the German landscape. Germany's solution to the problem was Hitler.[80] There were other writers who played the same theme. Some were propagandists for the party; others were well educated nationalists. Yet most agreed that modern architecture was not only un-German, but was part of either a Jewish or Marxist plot to destroy Germany. In short, modern architecture was "Jewish-Bolshevik."[81]

Something which particularly annoyed the critics about the Communist ideology was its deterministic denial of free will. Often these writers wanted to stress that the German *Volk* could build if it so wished, and could thus express its "will" to greatness,

[78] Von Senger, "Baubolschewismus," p. 504.

[79] Feistel-Rohmeder, *Im Terror*, pp. 62 and 177.

[80] *Ibid.*, pp. 145 and 177. "If only the leading personalities in the German government would not try to keep him [Hitler] from office — the only man who could end the Bolshevik danger" (p. 177).

[81] Wilhelm Kreis' phrase was typical. (A memorandum of March 16, 1944, cited in Wulf, *Die bildenden Künste*, p. 143.) Despite the condemnation of *avant-garde* architects who were also Jewish, the anti-Semitism of the ideology actually played a lesser role in the *Gleichschaltung* of architecture than might at first be expected, although synagogues were destroyed, as in the pogrom of 1938. Julius Streicher justified his order to tear down the Nuremberg synagogue in the spring of 1938 because it was "an oriental monstrosity of a building" and "for reasons of city architecture" rather than because of any vicious influence it may have had. I.M.T., *Trial*, XII, 324–325.) The Law for the Restoration of the Professional Bureaucracy of April 7, 1933 drove many "non-Aryan" architects from their jobs.

regardless of what economic conditions might prevail at any time: hence the stress on "will" and the "will to build" in this literature.

These crusaders could not claim much success before 1933. They rejoiced, however, at the work of Wilhelm Frick. They were able to drive the *Bauhaus* from Dessau to Berlin and then to see its demise in 1933. Although they greeted the advent of Hitler as the beginning of their architectural revolution, they were to be disappointed, for, as has been seen, Hitler had little interest in their denunciations, but fostered monumental neo-classicism, and even gave qualified support to functionalism.

Before 1933 there are few clues what the new "Nazi" or "genuinely German" style would be. Only Straub, cited above, offered some concrete suggestions. It was not even clear that the new architecture would not be slightly "modern" in the *Bauhaus* sense. Around 1934, however, an eclectic trend could be detected. There should be no need, said a typical critic, for disputes over flat roofs or pointed roofs. Much that was traditional was good, he claimed, and should be preserved and used; much that was new was also good. The important thing was the spirit in which the building was erected.[82] The new materials, steel and concrete, offered new challenges and new opportunities; they were the building materials of the twentieth century, just as stone after 800 and brick after 1100 were the then current German materials.[83] There may be a deliberate echo in these statements of Hitler's conciliatory remarks made in the same period on the same subject. For whatever reasons this eclectic pragmatism was to be the tone of much of the literature.

By 1933 the one universal cry of the patriotic critics was to defend Germany from foreign influences corrupting its urban and rural landscape: "In Germany, we want to build German."[84] But

[82] Wendland, *Kunst und Nation*, pp. 49–50. Rittich expressed the same eclectic idea (*Architektur und Bauplastik*, p. 155).

[83] *Kunst und Nation*, p. 11.

[84] *Ibid.*, p. 49. Similarly, Straub wrote that the new style would be a "national style." (*Architektur im dritten Reich*, p. 11.)

what was the "German style"? Ziegler wrote in 1937 that "it is wonderful to see how more and more a National Socialist style is developing."[85] Nearly thirty years later, Ziegler wrote that the Nazi monumentalism was the ideal "German style" a "thoroughly self-willed and strong style, with the stress on the horizontal. . . . It derives, to be sure, from the Renaissance style, but also has Romanesque elements, . . . It has massive weight and is a militant style, the self-assertion of the *Volk.*" Its qualities were those of "Nordic sobriety," "austere beauty," and "clear harmonies." He believed that it was not merely neo-classicism, but a "thoroughly original architectural style."[86] Wolters also believed the monumental architecture of the Third Reich was the best German style; it was original and had no predecessors. Its singularity, he said, was found in the spirit it expressed.[87] "The fundamental tone of the new style," wrote another critic "is determined by the heroic tone of the National Socialist ideology. Simplicity and uprightness of attitude demand also a simple and upright architectural expression."[88]

Yet no overall unity of style developed. For example, only the state's representative buildings were neo-classical; its new rural settlements were *völkisch*; its military schools were Romanesque. But this situation was not without significance. Inadvertently, the different styles represented different aspects of the ideology. This lack of stylistic unity in the building program was also symptomatic of Hitler's indifference to any architecture other than the monumental and of the eclectic, pragmatic theory of architecture which was developing. He did not forbid other styles as long as these could be rationalized as "German."[89]

[85] Ziegler, *Wende und Weg*, p. 12.

[86] Ziegler, *Adolf Hitler*, pp. 191–192, and 196. Ziegler has not found it necessary to alter many of the opinions he held in the twenties and the thirties. Modern architecture is "Oriental" (p. 103); German cities are being "degermanized" (p. 189).

[87] Wolters, *Neue deutsche Baukunst*, p. 12.

[88] Stephan, *Baukunst im dritten Reich*, p. 10.

[89] Thus, ironically, Nazi pronouncements on the role of architecture remain true, although in an unintended way. Architecture was "the visible *Kultur* of an

However, given the lamentations over the buildings of the past century, it is not surprising to find a great longing for a new architectural unity to express the new national unity. In the words of one commentator, the struggling tendencies of Nazism would come to an artistic expression as did the Gothic. Not that Nazism would use Gothic for self-expression, he said, but it was inevitable that when a *Volk* was transformed by a totalitarian movement and a unity of faith, then art and architecture must experience the same revolution.[90] An article, "Der Deutsche Stil des 20. Jahrhunderts," expressed the hope that future generations would have as clear a concept of a Nazi style as they did of Renaissance or Gothic.[91] Schulte-Frohlinde of the Labor Front wrote that the new buildings "must all express the same spirit and must therefore all resemble each other to a certain degree."[92]

Yet for some writers — perhaps in a mood of rationalization — a visual sameness for all new buildings was not really important. At the first German Architecture and Crafts Exhibition in 1938, some visitors complained that there was no unity of style; some models were in the classical, some in the Romanesque, some in the *völkisch* style. This was irrelevant, wrote Rittich, for whom such questions were a manifestation of historicism and related only to the superficial aspects of architecture.[93] "We could choose a unified style for all buildings," said Rittich, "but, if we did, buildings would lose their character and would not be the embodiment of

age," said Otto Kloeppel ("Der Baukünstler," p. 134), and Schulte-Frohlinde said it was "the outward expression of the mood of our time" (*Die landschaftlichen Grundlagen*, p. 8.).

[90] See, for example, Hannes Kremer, "Kulturkritik und Weltanschauung," *Die völkische Kunst*, Heft 1 (1935), cited in Wulf, *Die bildenden Künste*, p. 127. (Kremer was a bureaucrat in the propaganda division of the party.)

[91] Rudolf Ramlow, "Der deutsche Stil des 20. Jahrhunderts," *Bausteine zum deutschen Nationaltheater* (Organ der NS-Kultur-gemeinde), III:4 (1935), 98. Ramlow was a lawyer and writer.

[92] Julius Schulte-Frohlinde, *Bauten der Bewegung*, 2nd ed., Berlin, Wilhelm Ernst, 1939, p. v. This was the first volume in a series published by the building administration of the Prussian Ministry of Finance.

[93] Rittich, *Architektur und Bauplastik*, p. 151.

the spiritual and material drives of our contemporary life and thought." All good German buildings will express the same mood, whatever their style.[94] Rittich was not disturbed that representative buildings used the colonnade, the Ordensburg used the tower, and the Hitler Youth hostels used traditional local styles in harmony with the landscape. Whether Rittich was rationalizing the diversity of opinions on architecture which were allowed to flourish, these opinions and styles represented a reality — the different, sometimes contradictory, facets of the multifaceted ideology. For example, Wendland wrote that there was no calm or balance in genuine German architecture; symmetry was not the highest goal for the German architect, but rather continual agitation, because the German soul must "search and seek eternally and even farther afield."[95] This attitude parallels the dynamism of the Nazi movement, and reflects the belief that, like the tribal migrations of the Dark Ages, it was a primordial urge that could not be restrained. But this view of ideal German architecture was very different from Rosenberg's or Rittich's view, which expressed the contemporary need for order. The latter wrote that "harmony in mass, clarity in structure, and balance in relationships between weight and support" were "Nordic."[96] In the end, the problem of style remained unresolved. The National Socialist ideology contained conflicting trends, and so did the body of thought on architecture which thrived along with it.

While stylistic questions absorbed writers, the architect and his role also concerned them. Most believed that the inner attitude of the architect was more important than style.[97] An article, "Der Baukünstler, ein Träger nationalsozialistischer Weltanschauung," admonished architects to express the best instincts of the Volk. They had "the sacred duty" to follow the directions of the Culture Chamber and to create "new values." They should not

[94] Ibid., p. 165.
[95] Wendland, Kunst und Nation, p. 27.
[96] Rittich, Architektur und Bauplastik, p. 154.
[97] Ibid., p. 156.

set themselves apart.[98] "Our duty," said another writer, "is to take part, to serve with our talents the whole community. We are not here only for the upper ten thousand, but for the whole *Volk*."[99] The artist or architect was expected to give up his "so-called freedom to a higher will," that of the state. He must allow himself to be "incorporated into the whole." The Nazi state demanded that he find a way "out of his individualization to a union with the community."[100] The "spiritual attitude" of the artist should be akin to that of the soldier, said another writer; he should not only extract from himself the best qualities of the race, but he should feel like a soldier, "who lives in obedience, surrounded by great chaos"; in this way he learns to respect and honor "the organic."[101] The call for "spiritual mobilization"[102] was answered, for example, by Wendland, who announced in 1934 that "with their art, architects are ready for service."[103]

One sign of this service was a large collection of books and articles on good "German" architecture, past and present. Some of these writings appeared in the party press, but many were independent, although state-approved, productions. The ideas expressed in this literature were not new after 1933; most of them had circulated in the twenties. The writers almost always said

[98] Otto Kloeppel, "Der Baukünstler," pp. 134–135.

[99] J. Elfinger, "Kampf für eine gesunde Baukultur," *Baugilde: Zeitschrift der Fachgruppe Architekten in der Reichskammer der bildenden Künste*, XL:34 (December 5, 1936), 1034. The same idea was expressed by Hubert Schrade, "Der Sinn der küunstlerische Aufgabe und politischer Architektur," *Nationalsozialistische Monatshefte* (1934), pp. 510 and 512.

[100] Wendland, *Kunst und Nation*, pp. 13 and 52. The architect, said Karl Vogel, must "serve the whole." ("Nationalsozialistische Architektur," *Nationalsozialistische Monatshefte*, IV (1933), p. 326; Vogel was a Bohemian sculptor.) See also the section on the "creative personality" in Hartmann, *Werkhefte*, pp. 125–126.

[101] Richard Pfeiffer noted that this was the goal of Prussian military training. ("Die seelische Haltung des Künstlers im Dritten Reich," *Die völkische Kunst*, I (1935) 29.)

[102] From the "Proclamation" of the *Kampfbund*, printed in its *Mitteilungen*, III:7/12 (1931), 69.

[103] Wendland, *Kunst und Nation*, p. 12.

that good architecture should serve the community, thus allowing the community to express its will and its faith. Unity, both in the plan of a particular building and within the community, was often stressed, although respect for — and rationalization of — diversity was sometimes found. Clarity, simplicity, and sobriety, alleged virtues of the German individual and the German community, were to be expressed in German architecture. Racial health was also to be served by the style and mood of buildings, which could stimulate the best qualities of the *Volk*. Needless to say, foreign styles were intolerable. Space was another important factor; both the whole "living space" of Germany, and the microcosm of the city, its avenues, vistas, and squares. Architecture conceived with these "German" ideas in mind was considered good "German" architecture.

CHAPTER SEVEN

Architecture Representative of the New Germany

WHEN DISCUSSING ideal "German" architecture, although architects and critics agreed on many points, they did not necessarily
follow a narrow party line, dictated by Hitler; rather, the party's
political aims paralleled *völkisch* and right-wing nationalist
thought. Some commentators, such as Adolf Dresler, were more
politically oriented, concerned more with the power of the party
than with the well-being of the *Vaterland* or the *Volk*. Others, such
as Ziegler, were more esthetically oriented. Yet all wanted to express through architecture what they thought was, or should be,
suitably "German" values, and most were approved by the party.
Besides Speer, Gerdy Troost, author of *Das Bauen im neuen
Reich*, was probably closest to Hitler personally.[1] An interior decorator and the widow of Paul Ludwig Troost, she designed the
rooms of the Munich *Führer* Building. Her book, in two handsome
volumes, was printed by the party publisher in Bayreuth, and
was representative of what the party considered acceptable architecture and acceptable commentary on buildings. Significantly, it

---

[1] "Hitler frequently listened to her," notes Speer, and her negative view on
modern architecture was the same as the *Führer's*. (*Erinnerungen*, p. 63; *Inside*,
p. 50); so, too, was her pragmatism and flexibility. Her views reflected the thinking
of many traditional oriented Munich architects and do not seem to have been
cynically geared to those of Hitler.

was an amalgam of *völkisch* ideas and Nazi political jargon.[2] Other writers, such as Wolters or Rittich, were not as close to the center of things as was Frau Troost and their works were not always published by the party press or related publishing houses; however, their comments were similar to hers. Works on architecture published after 1933 were sometimes the product of the Party's *Zentralverlag* (central press) in Munich; but others were put out by independent publishers (such as Callwey, of Munich), some of whom, however, had been publishing hypernationalist works for many years. Books on ideal German architecture were not the products of totalitarian thought control, but reflected a wide body of thinking which coincided with a political ideology, a theory of architecture which existed even before the founding of the party it supported, and which grew out of an extremely nationalistic, often race-oriented rejection of the modern world. Obviously, books and articles in praise of Gropius or Le Corbusier could not be published in the Third Reich, but those books on architecture which were published by no means followed a government-directed line.[3]

[2] After her husband died, Frau Troost was given the title "Professor" by Hitler, who, according to Zoller, "respected her, because of the artistic confidence with which she continued the work of her husband." He also commissioned her with the decoration of his apartments in Berlin, Munich, and Berchtesgaden. (Zoller, *Hitler Privat*, p. 109.)

[3] Typical of the wide range of publishable ideas was Wilhelm Müseler's *Peoples and Epochs in European Art* (1942), in which the author (an art historian) stressed that Germans must not reject the artistic accomplishments of foreign nations simply because they were not German achievements, (p. 32), and emphasized the similarities between the landmarks of European art and architecture. Of course, Müseler made no reference to Slavic art and noted that all western-European peoples have a strong admixture of "Nordic-Germanic" blood (p. 6). Although the book was not narrowly National Socialist, it was a suitable brick in the edifice of European "unity," which the government was trying to construct in 1942. (Wilhelm Müseler, *Europäische Kunst — Völker und Zeiten*, Berlin, Safari, 1942.) An even more noncommital — but, of course, anti-*Bauhaus* view — was that of Karl Scheffler, in "German Architects," *Deutsche Baumeister*, Leipzig, List, 1939; a new architecture, he hoped, would express the national spirit, but would be possible only when the "vital strength" [*Lebensgefühl*] of all Europe revived [p. 291].

Strictly speaking, there were as many as four styles of architecture acceptable to these theorists, and to Hitler and the party.[4]
Literature from both the party presses and from more independent sources, shows that a form of classicism dominated the larger
buildings planned and erected. There was also a concerted effort
to preserve and revive the indigenous styles of the various areas
of Germany. This was the *völkisch* trend. The authorities and commentators also accepted the *Biedermeier* domestic style, as exemplified by Schultze-Naumburg's homes. The *völkisch* movement
drew its models not only from various geographical areas within
the Reich but also from historical periods, leading to overlapping
of these two trends. Some critics would have considered "Doric"
classicism to be *völkisch,* because they deemed it "Aryan;" the
same held true for the Romanesque style, which was to be revived.
Consequently, to devout racists, both these trends could be considered acceptable as *völkisch* architecture. And, to these people,
all the approved buildings, because "genuinely German," were
"community architecture." This obviously allowed for much latitude in what was to be built. It also led to paradoxes, for even
structures with Egyptian or oriental connotations were somehow
"German," or inspired by the *völkisch* spirit.

The *völkisch* writers were always at a disadvantage in their
fostering of the truly indigenous styles because Hitler himself,
political leader of Germany and presumedly the official spokesman
for its ideology, did not adhere wholeheartedly to the "Aryan"
myth — although he was undoubtedly anti-Semitic. He allowed
völkisch propaganda to circulate and *völkisch* buildings to go up,
but he cared very little for the idealized Teutons and their barrows
or the romanticized peasants in their half-timbered cottages, both
of which the *völkisch* writers extolled.

Most writers wanted splendid buildings of which Germans

[4] This does not mean that some "modern" or "functional" structures were
not built with the party's blessing. However, these did not concern Hitler, as they
were in industry and in technical buildings of the Luftwaffe. Hitler had himself
allowed room for "functionalism" in his outlook.

could be proud. For Adolf Hitler, representative state and public buildings in an impressive neo-classical style were the form of architecture which Germany needed most. He wanted to display the revived and invincible power of his Germany to the world, specifically to diplomats, ambassadors, and visiting dignitaries.[5] This is not a peculiarly Nazi view, of course; all countries use imposing buildings as propaganda. But given the condition of Germany after 1918, the drive to build representative edifices was understandably strong, not only in Nazi political circles. Hitler also wanted to remind Germans of the presence and authority of the party and the government in every town of the Reich. Even small buildings could have a monumental and representative character, the significant factor being the idea they symbolized.[6] Again, architecture was propaganda, not aimed abroad in this case, but directed at the German people themselves. Finally, the larger representative buildings, such as those in Berlin, Munich, and Nuremberg, were designed as monuments which could stimulate pride in the national community. Rittich expressed a typical view of this role for representative architecture when he said that representative buildings were those which "grow out of the life, the behavior, and the thought our our time . . . which not only only are commissioned by the community itself, but which are regarded by the community as the embodiment of the significance, the character, and the inner attitude of our *Volk*."[7] Implicit here is the idea that the German people should learn a lesson from

---

[5] For this reason, Hitler wanted representative buildings to be large — so that, as he said, other nations would know that "we take second rank to no other people." (Cited in Speer, *Erinnerungen*, p. 82; *Inside*, p. 69.) Not only was architecture to impress the foreigner, but books about the new buildings were directed at the foreign market. One of these was printed with an English and an Italian commentary. (Georg Fritz, *Strassen und Bauten Adolf Hitlers*, Berlin, Verlag der Deutschen Arbeitsfront, 1939).

[6] Rittich, *Architektur und Bauplastik*, p. 134. Teut writes that "architecture in the Third Reich, as no other art, contributed to the representing and the stabilizing of the Nazi form of authority." (*Architektur*, p. 7.) Even a Hitler Youth home could be representative. See, for example, the plans for the *Heim* to be built at Herringen, in Hartmann, *Werkhefte*, p. 83.

[7] Rittich, *Architektur und Bauplastik*, p. 28.

this architecture. Because most "Nazi" architecture was didactic, nearly every government or party-financed building could be called "representative," but the best examples were the new Chancellery in Berlin, the Munich party headquarters, and some lesser party and government buildings.

Perhaps the most important building, representative or otherwise, constructed in the Third Reich was Speer's new Chancellery on Voss-Strasse in Berlin, built in 1938–1939. (See illustrations nos. 15–23.) The old Chancellery was actually a complex of several buildings, on the corner of Voss-Strasse at Wilhelmstrasse, near Wilhelmsplatz. These older buildings included the nineteenth-century Borsig Palace (directly on the corner) and dated even as far back as 1739 when Count von der Schulenburg first built a home on the site. In 1871, Bismarck purchased the complex and had it remodeled for the needs of the new German Reich. In 1929–1930 the architect Jobst Siedler made an addition on Wilhelmstrasse in a stark modern style; this stood between the Borsig Palace and the older Schulenburg palace. (See illustration no. 13.) Wolters lamented that the builders of this addition did not "risk a self-confident, original façade," but he found this typical of the age, since the structure "vacillates between right and left . . . a compromise, and thus a true symbol of its time." The "boring"[8] façade of this addition was later altered by Speer, who built a balcony onto a window of the first floor at Hitler's office, from which the Nazi chancellor could review marches. (See illustration no. 14.) In 1939 Hitler himself wrote an interesting description of why he decided to build a completely new structure. When he took office, the Chancellery had been ruined, he said, "by tasteless renovations," "disfigured with overloaded refinements," its pompous plaster ornaments failing to hide the

---

[8] Wolters, *Albert Speer*, p. 37. This structure was retained in Speer's new Chancellery. Wilhelm Lotz noted that it was "the only attempt made in the age of the 'system' to erect a representative state building." ("Die Errichtung der neuen Reichskanzlei," *Die neue Reichskanzlei*, ed. by Albert Speer, Munich, Eher, 1940, p. 40. See the photograph of the addition on p. 26.)

absence of genuine building materials and of proper proportions.[9] The Chancellery garden to the rear had been allowed to go to seed, and, since the revolution of 1918, the buildings themselves had begun to decay. "Since my predecessors could count on a period in office of only three, four, or five months, they saw no cause to clean out the dirt left by those who had occupied the house before them." Thus by 1934 the ceilings and floors were rotten, and the whole structure "filled with a scarcely bearable evil smell." (This was symbolic of the state in which the "November criminals" had left Germany.) Hitler decided on a complete renovation. With the help of Leonhard Gall, an interior decorator from Troost's studio, he first planned a large reception room to hold over two hundred people and new offices for the chancellor and the president. The old rooms, he said, were to cease to look like the office of "a representative of a cigarette and tobacco company."[10] For the exterior, Speer was commissioned to add the aforementioned balcony, in Hitler's words, the structure's first "architecturally respectable element."[11]

Yet these changes were only a beginning. Two factors influenced Hitler to build a totally new chancellery. His plans for Berlin involved making Voss-Strasse a major thoroughfare, where a monumental building would not be out of place. Moreover, he said: "I had decided in December and January, 1937–38, to solve the Austrian problem, and to erect the Greater German Reich,"[12] a decision which called for a suitable representative palace. So on January 11, 1938, he commissioned Speer with the task of designing and building it within a year, by January 10, 1939.[13]

[9] Domarus, *Reden*, p. 1033 (from an article in *Kunst im Dritten Reich*, July, 1939).

[10] *Reden*, p. 1034. Hitler wanted to be able to stand on a balcony, rather than to stand in a window, because on a balcony, he could be seen from three sides by the crowd.

[11] Speer, *Erinnerungen*, p. 47; *Inside*, p. 34.

[12] Domarus, *Reden*, p. 1034.

[13] Renovating older buildings was acceptable for the Labor Front, but not for Hitler; he said that he was too proud to live in the palaces of former ages.

The work could not begin until the houses on Voss-Strasse had been torn down, and it was not until the end of March 1938 that actual construction began. Although this left only nine months in which to complete the job, the Chancellery was actually built in that short time, thanks, according to Hitler, to the "architectural genius" of Speer, and to the "particular capacity for work of the Berlin laborers," who on this job "outdid themselves." [14] Eight thousand construction workers heard the same compliment in Hitler's speech on January 9, 1939, at the opening of the chancellery. [15] This was "community" architecture and Hitler sought to underline the fact. The short period in which the Chancellery was constructed was praised by others, too, and taken as evidence of the renewed vitality of Germany. There were other difficulties in its construction. The location itself was not ideal, the site was elongated, yet narrowly confined between Voss-Strasse and a park; there were no other monumental structures in the neighborhood to relate to the new building. These difficulties might have hindered the successful completion of the building.

Nevertheless, writers agreed with Hitler that the result was admirable. Speer himself does not consider it one of his better works, for he lacked time enough to devote to its planning. [16]

The street front of the new three storey Chancellery stretched down Voss-Strasse from Wilhelmstrasse to Hermann Goering Strasse (formerly Budapesterstrasse) and Voss-Strasse itself was widened to give a better view of the building. The structure had to correspond to "the representative stature and spatial size of the concept of the new Reich," [17] and there is no doubt that it did. The neo-classical façade had three sections, a central portion set back sixteen meters from the street, and two flanking symmetrical

(Cited in Speer, *Erinnerungen*, p. 538; see also pp. 116–130 for Speer's description of the building of the chancellery; *Inside*, pp. 532, and 102–116.)

[14] Domarus, *Reden*, p. 1035.
[15] *Reden*, p. 1030–32.
[16] Interview with Speer, June 13, 1968, in Heidelberg-Schlierbach.
[17] Wolters, *Albert Speer*, p. 32.

wings. Not only was the middle part recessed, but it was several meters higher than the wings. Nevertheless, due to an optical illusion, it seemed to be only as high as the wings.[18] The central section was of cream limestone, but in the wings, only the base, cornice, and window frames were of this material, the remaining surfaces being of yellow stucco. Otherwise, the Chancellery's colors were beige and brown, "the natural colour of the genuine materials."[19] The windows of the wings were linked by horizontal string courses, giving the building an appearance of "severe, disciplined organization and order."[20] Two pillared portals, in the wings, each surmounted by eagles bearing wreathed swastikas,[21] gave access from Voss-Strasse. This façade was illuminated by night with spotlights based on buildings on the opposite side of the street. On Wilhelmstrasse, a large double portal was built into the older structure, giving access to the Court of Honor.[22]

The appearance of the Chancellery was typical of most representative "Nazi" buildings. Its lines were mainly horizontal; a heavy cornice defined the roof and the solidly framed windows marched in military order. Its classical lines were singled out for comment by many writers. The façade, wrote Lotz, could be compared with the best façades of the Italian Renaissance, but kept its "genuinely German character" and its "concise austerity."[23] Giessler found this austerity "Prussian," and compared the façade

[18] Lotz, "Die Errichtung," p. 42.

[19] "Die Errichtung," p. 44.

[20] Speer, "Die neue Reichskanzlei in Berlin," *Moderne Bauformen*, XXXVIII (November 1939), 527.

[21] These omnipresent symbols implied that the activity of other political parties — indeed all political life in the democratic sense — had ceased in Germany: the new government was to be the eternal government of Germany, for it truly embodied the *Volk*. All new government buildings would naturally bear the Nazi symbol. The presence of the initials, A. H., on crests over interior doors, almost suggested the founding of a Hitler dynasty.

[22] Service buildings and quarters for the guards, three-storey structures in a traditional *Biedermeier* or domestic classical style, stretched along the Hermann Goering Strasse. They were also designed by Speer.

[23] Lotz, "Die Errichtung," p. 42.

to the works of Gilly and Schinkel.[24] Thus the building's appearance was deemed appropriate to its representative function.

The garden façade of the Chancellery was softer in appearance and boasted more decoration. The central part of this side of the building was dominated by six pairs of fluted columns of Lahn marble ten meters high, topped by partly gilded bronze capitals; behind these was Hitler's office. To the left of this vaguely Egyptian portico, an arcade marked the dining room. Besides a fountain, in the garden were two powerful bronze horses (by the sculptor Joseph Thorak) and another bronze sculptural group, a man wrestling with a bull (by Louis Tuaillon), all symbolizing strength.[25]

However imposing the exterior of the Chancellery might be, it was the theatrical interior which was designed to stun the visitor. The eastern part comprised offices and work rooms, and surrounded the Court of Honor; the western section also contained administrative offices, and a smaller courtyard. But between these two wings were the ceremonial, representative chambers of the palace, through most of which the visitor had to pass in order to meet the *Führer* in his office or his reception room. Walking through these rooms, wrote Wolters, was like seeing "a magnificent play."[26]

After the bronze doors on the Wilhelmstrasse had opened to admit his car, the visitor would be driven into the Court of Honor. This "calm and almost solemn"[27] courtyard, like a large grey-walled room open to the sky, served not only to impress visitors, but also as a parade square for military reviews or demonstrations. (Its pavement was divided into square motifs for this purpose.)

[24] Giessler, "Symbol des Grossdeutschen Reiches," *Die neue Reichskanzlei*, p. 14.

[25] See the photographs of the garden in Speer, *Neue Reichskanzlei*, pp. 38–43. From the garden there was an entrance to the famous bunker. For a description, see Zoller, *Hitler Privat*, pp. 148–150, or Trevor-Roper, *Last Days of Hitler*, p. 108.

[26] Wolters, *Albert Speer*, p. 44. This walk was 250 meters long.

[27] Rittich, *Architektur und Bauplastik*, p. 56.

The visitor faced the entrance portal, in a correspondingly serious mood, flanked on each side by a pair of smooth columns, which echoed the attached columns placed against the walls of the court at intervals. Two large statues by Breker, *The Party* and *The Army*, guarded the portal.[28] As he walked up the ten steps to the porch, the guest passed under another eagle with outstretched wings and wreathed swastika over the portal. Nearly half of the floor area of the porch was occupied by the bases of the four columns, each eight times as high as a man.

From this porch, through a high, narrow door, the visitor entered a marble-walled antechamber; here he was likely to find a peculiarly Hitlerian sight — vases brimming with flowers, a scene repeated often in the Chancellery and the Munich party buildings.[29] The antechamber led on to the first truly representative area, the rectangular Mosaic Room.[30] Its walls were of red-grey marble from Austria, and the floor, of deep red Saalburger marble; pillars, also of red marble, flanked the mahogany doors at either end, and eagles in relief stood over the portals. The room was lit by a large window in the ceiling, and at night by lights concealed above the cornice. Much of the Mosaic Room, particularly the recesses for the doors, was Roman in inspiration.[31] Square patterns of mosaic characterized the floor, and vertical rectangles of mosaic covered the walls. Executed by Hermann Kaspar, a professor at the Munich Art Academy, these mosaics represented eagles, oak leaves, torches, and other familiar symbols of the Nazi movement. The Mosaic Room was to awe the visitor; its monumental propor-

---

[28] See the photographs in Speer, *Die neue Reichskanzlei*, pp. 23–24. On the importance of sculpture and reliefs in architecture, see Rittich, *Architektur und Bauplastik*, esp. pp. 170–182. The sculptor Breker, in his memoirs, writes that these two figures were intended to symbolize "the intellectual" and "the guardian of the state." (*Paris, Hitler et moi*, p. 36.) In Rittich's work, one finds the more ideological labels (*Architektur und Bauplastik*, p. 62.)

[29] See the photo of this room in Wolters, *Albert Speer*, p. 39.

[30] See the color photographs in Speer, *Die neue Reichskanzlei*, p. 52.

[31] Rudolf Wolters, "Werk und Schöpfer," *Die neue Reichskanzlei*, p. 52.

tions, towering above one, were supposed to achieve an existence of their own, apart from any human reference.[32]

Out of the rather dim light of the Mosaic Room, the visitor passed into the brighter Round Room, also lit from the ceiling through a glass cupola. As in the Mosaic Room, the wall was divided into severely rectangular patterns by inlaid marble.[33] The floor was divided into geometrical rays, including swastika patterns. Over the doors, marble reliefs by Breker were installed.

From the Round Room, the visitor passed into the most impressive of the representative chambers: the Marble Gallery, or Long Hall, "longer than the famous Hall of Mirrors in the Palace of Versailles."[34] To the visitor's left, nineteen high windows in deep marble niches looked out onto Voss-Strasse — for the Marble Gallery formed the recessed part of the street façade. It was actually a corridor, punctuated with five massive doors on the wall to the visitor's right, the center one of which led into Hitler's office. The walls were hung with tapestries and imitation candelabra. Clusters of furniture grouped around carpets offered the visitor rest. At the far end of the gallery a door led into the Reception Room. Here Hitler's New Year's reception took place, as well as other formal occasions. Two huge four-tiered crystal chandeliers from Vienna hung from the ceiling, and these walls were also decorated with tapestries. Four French windows opened onto a terrace. (Despite its lavish accoutrements, Hitler considered this room too small.)

The visitor might have one further monumental impression, if he were invited into Hitler's office, which adjoined the Marble Gallery and had a view of the garden.[35] Here the walls were of

[32] Wilhelm Lotz, "Die Innenräume der neuen Reichskanzlei," *Die neue Reichskanzlei*, p. 64.

[33] There are photos of this room, and of two Breker statues (*Man of Thought* and *Man of Action*) in Speer, *Neue Reichskanzlei*, pp. 55–61. It was 14.25 meters in diameter.

[34] Rittich, *Architektur und Bauplastik*, p. 63. See the color photograph in Speer, *Neue Reichskanzlei*, p. 66. This was 12 meters wide and 146 long.

[35] See the photograph in Rittich, *Architektur und Bauplastik*, p. 87. Hitler's private living quarters were also attached here.

dark-red Linbacher marble, the wall panels of polished wood, and the floor of Ruhpoldinger marble. The ceiling was coffered in palisander wood. Five high window-doors gave access to the garden. Tapestries covered the walls and over a large fireplace hung Lenbach's famous portrait of Bismarck. The huge dimensions of the room dwarfed the heavy desk in the corner and the absence of any hanging light fixtures accentuated the impression of empty space. This was apparently intentional, for furniture had been chosen by Speer which would remain subordinate to the sense of spaciousness.[36] "Great thoughts arise here," wrote Lotz. "Decisive conversations with small groups of experts take place here, and one enters this room with a sense of respect, because the great creative mind of the man who works here lends to the room's form an air of solemnity."[37]

The other larger rooms of the Chancellery were less imposing. The comfortable dining room, with its fifteen French doors, looked out through the arcade to the garden. The Cabinet Room was similar in its outfitting to the *Führer's* office, with dark-wooden panelling and deep-red leather chairs.[38]

No other German building of the thirties had as much written about it as the new Chancellery. It became a symbol of the revival of Germany, of the triumph of Nazism, and of the future glories of the German *Volk*. In the series of magnificent representative rooms, one architect detected "the marching step of the movement."[39] The Chancellery was a "community" building, produced by the will of the *Volk*, a "communal labor of a thousand hands." It showed that the German people could not be prevented from

[36] Lotz, "Die Innenräume," p. 79.

[37] "Die Innenräume," p. 79. This office recalls Mussolini's giant workroom in the Palazzo Venezia in Rome — which might have inspired it and Hitler's office in the Brown House.

[38] This room, with its swastika decorations on chairs and table covering is illustrated in Speer, *Die neue Reichskanzlei*, p. 84; the dining room is shown on pp. 99 and 102. Hitler's Hall of Models was a large room in the upper storey. There was also a library.

[39] Wolters, *Albert Speer*, p. 50.

expressing their "unified will."[40] Wolters added that the building
revealed "the well-balanced will of a self-aware and strong age."[41]
Above all, writers stressed that the Chancellery reflected the age
of the *Volk* community. No one individual stood out as the creator,
but the work of many individual craftsmen was melted together.[42]
Even the role of Speer, Hitler's young "genius," was minimized
by Breker, the sculptor, who wrote that architect and assistants
worked together harmoniously in "common labor," always coop-
erating, never disputing.[43] Moreover, this palace was not built
to glorify the *Führer*; Lotz explained that it was the German *Volk*,
in the person of Hitler, who received guests here.[44] Thus, as the
people thought of Hitler welcoming foreign dignitaries in the
sumptuous surroundings of this palace, ostensibly their own creation, they should be proud of their Fatherland.

To illustrate the building's organic connection with all Germany, it was pointed out that stone from all the German *Gaue*
were used; marble from the Lahn valley, from the Bavarian woods,
from Thuringia, from the Kelheim region, from the Jura, and
above all from the recovered East Mark (Austria).[45]

Writers stressed the symmetry and "clarity" of the building's
lines, linking this to the sense of strength it should exude, the
feeling of security and order it should produce, and to the disciplined labor of its creators and the new discipline of the revived
Germany. In one short paragraph, Lotz referred to "the symmetrical division of the whole structure," "the symmetrical division
aligned on a north-south axis," and the "perpendicular, rectilinear
placement of the rooms"; the "symmetrical division of the interior
determines the outer form," he wrote; forms were seen in "rhyth-

[40] Herbert Hoffmann, "Die neue Reichskanzlei," *Moderne Bauformen*,
XXXVIII (1939), 527 and 524. (Hoffmann was editor of this journal.)
[41] Wolters, *Albert Speer*, p. 33.
[42] *Albert Speer*, p. 49.
[43] Arno Breker, "Zum Bau der neuen Reichskanzlei," *Die neue Reichskanzlei*,
p. 59. There were no "discussions or experiments."
[44] Lotz, "Die Errichtung," *Die neue Reichskanzlei*, p. 26.
[45] Die Innenräume," p. 90.

mical ranks."[46] Obviously, there was nothing here of the provocative asymmetry of the *Bauhaus'* creations.

On the contrary, the Chancellery, with its avoidance of experiment and with its luxurious, comfortable furniture, gave off an air of respectability. It was not an intrusion into Berlin's architectural traditions, for it carried the same lines which the soldier king, Frederick the Great (1740–1786), had stamped on the city.[47] Its exterior was characterized by the austerity and "clarity" peculiar to the old Prussian capital.[48] Breker described how, in the designing and construction of the building, Speer, "in Prussian fashion, indicated the march route" and all workers were "united in step."[49] There were no discussions or disputes in this essentially military undertaking. Giessler, in the same volume, found that the "wonderful discipline" exhibited by the German people in the difficult year of 1938 was "eternally symbolized"[50] in the Chancellery, and Wolters found the architectural elements of the Chancellery "simple, clear, and soldierly."[51] Thus, present national unity and past German traditions were unified in a new architectural symbol. Speer and his assistants had "continued a great tradition and further developed it."[52]

The Nazis declared that their movement embodied an idealist reaction to materialism, and the architect Giessler saw the Chancellery as a symbol of a refutation of liberalism. Materialism, he said, played no role in the building's creation, but rather it was the realization of an idea, German greatness. "The scale of old princely palaces is surpassed," he wrote "not in decoration or in the expanse of the rooms but rather through the comprehensive

[46] "Die Errichtung," p. 39.

[47] *Ibid.*, p. 26.

[48] Rittich, *Architektur und Bauplastik*, p. 64.

[49] Breker, "Zum Bau der neuen Reichskanzlei," p. 59.

[50] Giessler, "Symbol des grossdeutschen Reiches," *Die neue Reichskanzlei*, p. 10. Troost saw "concentrated serenity and disciplined power" in the Chancellery. (*Bauen* I, p. 52.)

[51] Wolters, *Albert Speer*, p. 33.

[52] Hoffmann, "Die neue Reichskanzlei," p. 524.

spiritual nature" of the building.[53] He also noted that the construction of the Chancellery marked the return of authority and
law to Germany, as opposed to the liberal chaos of the preceding
decades. Comparing Hitler to the Italian architect Brunellesco
(1377–1446), Giessler claimed that both had saved "discarded
values" from capricious abuse in a lawless age.[54] Thus indirectly,
at least, the Chancellery reminded these Germans of Hitler's allegedly great service to the moral health of the Fatherland.

In his new home and office building, Hitler finally was able
to rival the Habsburg glories of Vienna, such as the Hofburg
palace. He called it "the first building constructed under the
Great German Reich," an edifice which would last centuries.[55] It
had also an immediate value for Hitler's ego. Privately, he said
that "when one enters the Reich Chancellery, one should have
the feeling that one is visiting the master of the world."[56] In the
last days of the war, he would not leave the vicinity of this building, a tangible sign of his own glory.

As to the genuine materials and natural colors, the allusions
to the age of Pericles, the Renaissance, and the Greek Revival,
and as to the frank use of symbols, the Chancellery was the perfect
embodiment of "representation" thinking on architecture. Some
of these comments are probably a rationalization of the building
program, and certainly there must be an element of political justi-
fication in writings on the monumental buildings. For example,
Lotz noted that the quarry workers, who had earlier drifted
into less traditional jobs, were back at work in their ancient pro-
fessions in the Lahn valley, thanks to the building of the Chan-

[53] Giessler, "Symbol des grossdeutschen Reiches," p. 12.

[54] He cited Hitler's 1937 Culture Speech: "Our opponents will come to realize
it, but above all our followers must know it: our buildings are built with the aim
of strengthening . . . authority." (Giessler, "Symbol des grossdeutschen Reiches,"
p. 14.)

[55] Baynes, *Speeches*, p. 601 (January 9, 1939, at the opening of the Chancellery). Hitler meant that only after *Anschluss* of Austria in 1938 did the "Great
Reich" exist.

[56] S.C., p. 103 (October 21–22, 1941.)

cellery and other structures.[57] Thus, the building program provided work for the unemployed. Another critic wrote, perhaps
wishfully, that Hitler built the Chancellery as a "comprehensive,
peaceful work of reconstruction."[58] No man planning war would
spend so much money and effort on beautiful buildings. Ostensibly Hitler's main concern was for the well being, in peace, of his
German people. That he cared nothing for his subjects became
apparent only during and after the war. Such cynicism may also
have motivated some of the writings. Yet, most nationalist writers
rejoiced over the new Chancellery.

The Chancellery was destroyed during and after the Second
World War. Already in 1940 it felt the effects of total war, as the
enormous bronze doors on Wilhelmstrasse were removed, melted
down for the arms industry, and replaced by large brown wooden
ones. By 1943 the palace had been bombed. Goebbels reported in
his private diary on November 24 of that year that the private
apartments of the *Führer* had been hit, and a big fire started in
the Hall of Models. On November 26 he wrote that the Chancellery "looks terrible. All the rooms that were formerly so beautiful,
and so dear to us are now destroyed, either burned out or full of
water." On November 27 he visited Hitler's rooms, which were
"completely destroyed." "It makes me sad," he wrote, "to find
these rooms, in which we enjoyed so many hours of spiritual up-
lift, in such a condition."[59] In April 1945 Russian shells began to
make direct hits on the building. Colonel General Gotthard Hein-
rici described the complex as it looked in the month: there were
"huge craters, lumps of concrete, smashed statuery, and uprooted

[57] Lotz, "Innenräume," p. 98.

[58] Hoffmann, "Die neue Reichskanzlei," p. 251. In 1943, Gerdy Troost noted
that the *Führer*'s "will to peace" was proved by his *Kultur* program, the monumental buildings, the reform of whole cities and the planned housing projects;
completion of these enterprises required a long period of peace. (Troost, *Bauen*,
II, 5.)

[59] Joseph Goebbels, *The Goebbels Diaries 1942–43*, translated by Louis P.
Lochner, New York, Garden City, 1948, pp. 519–532.

trees"; the building's windows were "great black holes."[60] In
May 1945 however, at the end of the war, the Chancellery walls
were still standing in what was to become the Russian sector of
Berlin. Attaching as much political importance to the building as
did Hitler and his supporters, the Russian razed the ruins and
used the stones to build their war memorial in Berlin-Treptow.
Today the site of the Chancellery is a grassy mound at the nearly
deserted corner of Wilhelmstrasse (now Otto-Grotewohlstrasse)
and Voss-Strasse.

Before he built the Berlin Chancellery, Hitler created in
Munich a new center for the party itself. Two large structures,
the Administration Building, and the *Führer* Building, on Arcisstrasse, were to be part of a renovation of the Königsplatz, which
included the construction of two Temples of Honor as well.[61]
Because of its special role as the city where the party had been
founded, Munich had a particular significance for the Nazis. It
was called the "capital of the movement," and was to be fundamentally remodeled. The Administration and *Führer* buildings
were the first steps in the plan to give Munich the suitable monumental and representative buildings it lacked.

Before the party got these spacious offices, it had moved
from location to location in Munich, settling finally in 1924 in
unprepossessing quarters on Schellingstrasse. Hitler decided in
1930 that a more imposing center for the party was necessary,
and so the former Barlow Palace[62] on Briennerstrasse was purchased, renovated, and opened in January 1931 as the Brown
House. (See illustrations nos. 24–25.) It was Troost's redesigning
of the interior, partly on Hitler's own plans, which impressed the
Führer and which set a standard for future Nazi interior decora-

[60] Cited in Cornelius Ryan, *The Last Battle*, New York, Simon and Schuster,
1966, p. 259.
[61] See below, chapter nine.
[62] See Adolf Dresler, *Das braune Haus*, p. 13. Built in 1828, this three storey
patrician mansion was in the "traditional simply Biedermeier style." (*Ibid.*, p.
14.) (See illustration no. 24.)

1
The *Bauhaus*, Dessau. In its appearance alone, Gropius' school symbolized the *avant-garde*. (Hans M. Wingler, *The Bauhaus. Weimar, Dessau, Berlin, Chicago*)

2
The town of Melsungen in Hessen. The ordered and picturesque Germany which the *völkisch* experts wished to preserve. (Toni Schneiders)

3

The Museum of Fine Arts, Vienna. Hitler was more impressed with the neo-baroque building than with its contents. (National Archives)

4

The New Hofburg, Vienna. The Habsburg palace in the neo-baroque which Hitler first loved. (National Archives)

5
The Berlin Protestant Cathedral. Too small, said Hitler, but the neo-baroque style was
suitably impressive. (National Archives)

6
Strasbourg Cathedral. Despite his ambivalence towards the Gothic style, Hitler planned to convert the church into a monument to the German unknown soldier. (Staatsbibliothek, Berlin)

7

Worms Cathedral. "Not Roman-esque, but German" (Schultze-Naumburg). (Library of Congress)

8

Freiburg Cathedral. German, or French? (Library of Congress)

9
The Church of Our Lady, Dresden. "Germanized" Baroque. (Library of Congress)

10
The "Old" Museum, Berlin. The popular and officially approved neo-classicism of Schinkel. (Staatsbibliothek, Berlin)

11
The City Hall, Munich. Neo-Gothic "decadence" of the nineteenth century. (Staatsbibliothek, Berlin)

12
Modern apartments in Berlin-Britz. Flat-roofed, undecorated "architectural Bolshevism." (National Archives)

13
Addition to the Berlin Chancellery (1929–30). Symbolic of the Weimar Republic, said Rudolf Wolters, it "vacillate[d] between right and left" and was neither "self-confident" nor "original." (National Archives)

14
The "*Führer*-Balcony" added to the 1929–30 expansion of the Chancellery, Berlin. (Library of Congress)

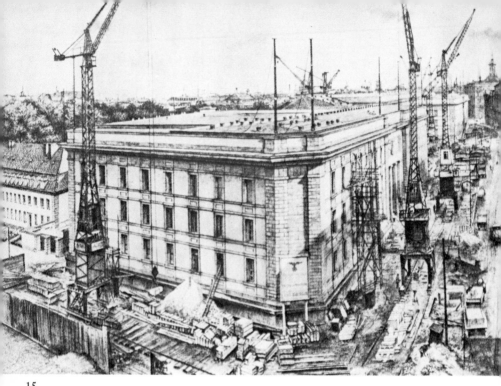

15
The Chancellery, Berlin.   Under construction: pride-giving work for unemployed laborers and craftsmen. (Library of Congress)

16
The Chancellery, Berlin. Vossstrasse portal. (National Archives)

17
The Chancellery, Berlin. Vossstrasse facade: an architecture of "discipline" and "order" (Speer). (National Archives)

18
The Chancellery, Berlin. The Court of Honor should help to give visitors the impression that they were in the presence of "the Master of the World" (Hitler). (Wolters, *Neue Deutsche Baukunst*)

19
The Chancellery, Berlin. The Mosaic Hall. (National Archives)

20
The Chancellery, Berlin. The Round Room. (National Archives)

21
The Chancellery, Berlin. The Long Hall: "longer than the famous Hall of Mirrors at Versailles" (Rittich). (National Archives)

22
The Chancellery, Berlin. Hitler's Office. "Great thoughts arise here" (Lotz). (Library of Congress)

23
The Chancellery, Berlin. The Reception Room was not large enough for Hitler. (National Archives)

24
The Brown House, Munich. (Library of Congress)

25

The Brown House, Munich. The Senate Chamber: a "solemn and dignified" meeting place for the non-existent party senate. (Library of Congress)

26

The *Führer* Building, Munich. The Arcisstrasse facade: "symbol of the fundamental strength which is renewing the German *Volk*" (Troost). (Library of Congress)

27
The *Führer* Building, Munich. One of the main staircases. (Library of Congress)

28
The *Führer* Building, Munich. The "Living Room": dignified respectability for formal Nazi occasions. (Library of Congress)

29

The German Pavilion, Paris Exhibition, 1937. Showing the German community's peaceful "will to culture." (Library of Congress)

30

Russian and German Pavilions, Paris 1937. The "cubic mass" of the German pavilion checks the "onslaught" of the Soviet building. (National Archives)

36
Olympic Square. (Library of Congress)

37
The Olympic Stadium, Berlin. Promenade. (National Archives)

35
The Olympic Gate. Parts of the grounds were to revive the mood of the original (Aryan Greek) Olympics. (National Archives)

33
Karinhall. Part of the interior. (Library of Congress)

34
The Olympic Stadium, Berlin. Ideal architecture for the experience of "community." (Under construction) (National Archives)

31
Hitler's Chalet above Berchtesgaden, under construction. (Library of Congress)

32
Karinhall. A combination of *Repräsentation* and *völkisch* traditionalism. (Library of Congress)

38
Sculpture on the Olympic Grounds, Berlin. (Library of Congress)

39
The May Field, Olympic Grounds, Berlin, with the Langemarck Tower. (National Archives)

40
Rear of the Langemarck Tower on the May Field, Olympic Grounds, Berlin. (Library of Congress)

41
The Party Rally Grounds, Nuremberg. A center for the "communal experience of the unity between *Führer* and *Volk*" (Troost). (National Archives)

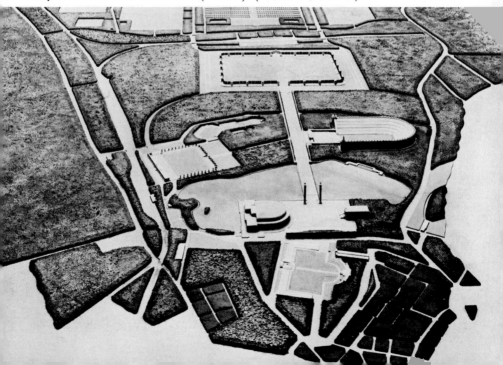

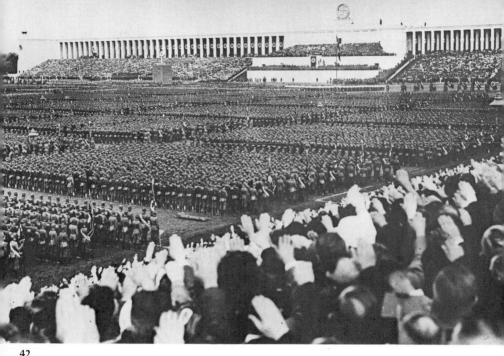

42
The Zeppelin Field, Nuremberg. The experience of "community" takes place. (National Archives)

43
The Zeppelin Field, Nuremberg. The rear of the main tribune has a suitably militant, fortress-like appearance. (Library of Congress)

44
The Cathedral of Light, Nuremberg. "A fantastic thing, like being in a Gothic cathedral" (Speer). (National Archives)

45
The Luitpold Arena, Nuremberg. The participants themselves become "human architecture" (Schrade). (Library of Congress)

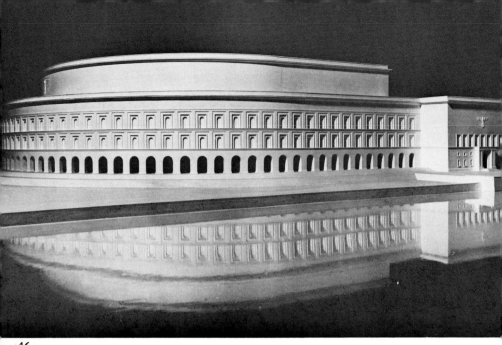

46
The Congress Hall, Nuremberg. A German Colosseum. (National Archives)

47
The Congress Hall, Nuremberg. Under construction (interior). (National Archives)

48
The German Stadium, Nuremberg. To be the largest of its kind ever built. (National Archives)

49
The March Field, Nuremberg. The largest of the *Aufmarschplätze* (designed for military reviews), its large building stones reflect the concern for genuine German materials. (Wolters, *Neue Deutsche Baukunst*)

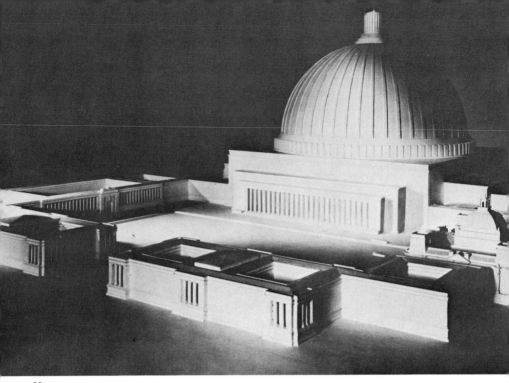

50
The *Volkhalle*, Berlin. The largest of the "People's Halls" planned for every German city. (Library of Congress)

51
The *Volkhalle*, Berlin. A German Pantheon, presumably for worship of Hitler alone. (Library of Congress)

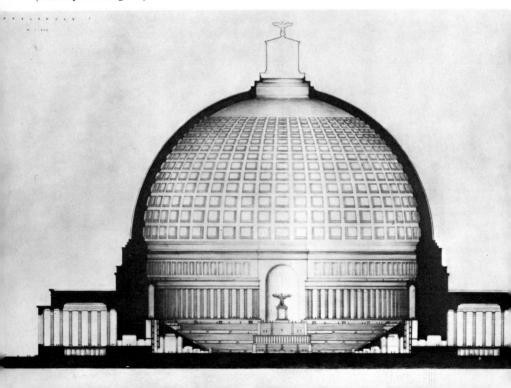

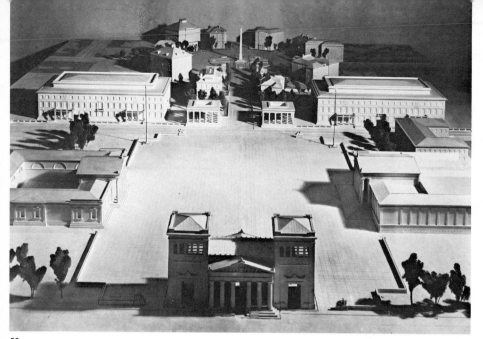

52
The Royal Square, Munich. "A community space of the *Volk*" (Troost). The Temples of Honor and Party Headquarters are to be seen in the background. (Library of Congress)

53
"Improvement" of the *Lustgarten*, Berlin. With the grass and shrubs removed, the "community" experience could occur. (Schinkel's Museum is in the background.) (Library of Congress)

54
The Dietrich Eckart Stage, Berlin. A *Thing*-place: a center for "community experience and experienced community" (Braumüller). (National Archives)

55
Air Ministry, Berlin. "Large . . . mighty, [. . . and . . .] soldierly" (Rittich). (National Archives)

56
Air Ministry, Berlin. Hall of Honor. (Library of Congress)

57
Army Barracks, in the Allgäu. Sober, economical, traditional, and somehow democratic
—therefore, typically German. (Troost, *Bauen im neuen Reich*)

58
The German Experimental Station for Air Travel. German functionalism, not "architectural Bolshevism." (Troost, *Bauen im neuen Reich.*)

59
The Tannenberg Memorial. A quintessentially Teutonic "community" building. (National Archives)

60
The Dnieper Monument. A sketch of one of the "Castles of the Dead," which would symbolize the triumphant liberation of Europe by the Germans. (Library of Congress)

Ordensburg Vogelsang; the tower. "An expression of our living

Ordensburg Sonthofen. "Like the castles of knights of an earlier

63
Ordensburg Crössinsee. The *Aufmarschplatz*, from the Hall of Honor. (Library of Congress)

64
The *Soldatenhalle*, Berlin. A planned Hall of Fame for military heroes. (National Archives)

65
The Royal Square, with Temples of Honor, Munich. Doric classicism, to reflect "a soldierly, disciplined feeling for life" (Troost). (National Archives)

66
A gas station on the *Autobahn.* Here was the place for the modern, streamlined look. (Library of Congress)

67
A gas station on the *Autobahn.* The more typical traditional design. (Library of Congress)

68
Waschmühltal Bridge, near Limburg. In harmony with the nearby Romanesque cathedral. (Wolters, *Neue Deutsche Baukunst*)

75
Apartment building, Nuremberg. Compare to illustration no. 12. (Troost, *Das Bauen im neuen Reich.*)

76
Opel factory, Brandenburg. Here avant-garde functionalism was considered typically German. (Troost, *Das Beuen im neuen Reich.*)

73
The National Socialist University, on the Chiemsee. (National Archives)

74
A Labor Front settlement, near Aachen. (Library of Congress)

71
The Baldur van Schirach Youth Hostel, near Urfeld. A south German *völkisch* structure (versus the Melle hostel), yet also designed with the same intentions. (Troost, *Bauen im neuen Reich.*)

72
The *Auslandshaus* of the Hitler Youth, Berlin. For young foreign tourists. (Library of Congress)

69
Krefeld Bridge. Reflecting its urban and industrial environment. (Troost, *Bauen im neuen Reich*)

70
The Hermann Goering Youth *Heim*, near Melle. Teaching traditional German values through traditional German architecture. (Wolters, *Neue Deutsche Baukunst*)

77
City of the Hermann Goering Works. An ideal "ordered" community. (Wolters, *Neue Deutsche Baukunst*)

78
The House of German Art, Munich. The facade of a "temple of art." (Library of Congress)

79
The House of German Art, Munich. Ceiling of the portico. (Library of Congress)

tion at the representative level.[63] On the ground floor was a large Hall of Banners (or of Honor), where old flags and standards of the movement, such as the Blood Banner of November 9, 1923, were hung in dignity. The paneled ceiling exuded the "German" virtues of "clarity and serenity."[64] A broad staircase led to an antechamber which included a bust of the late Dietrich Eckart, one of the party's founders, and two bronze tablets with the names of those killed in the 1923 putsch attempt. These tablets, along with two Munich S. A. standards, flanked the door to the Senate Chamber. The walls of this room were of palisander and walnut, expressing "solemnity and dignity."[65] The paneled ceiling was patterned with swastikas, and a long table with two rows of red-leather chairs with swastikas on their backs filled much of the room. One wall also inlaid with an eagle and swastika pattern. The design of the room, which probably inspired the Cabinet Room in the Berlin Chancellery, was Troost's, but Heinrich Hoffmann claims that Hitler himself first sketched a plan of the hall on the back of a menu in a Munich cafe.[66] Ironically, no senate ever met here — indeed, no party senate was ever constituted, and the hall became the office of Rudolf Hess (Hitler's deputy). The Senate Chamber was executed with dull sobriety. Here was the conference room, not for wild-eyed revolutionaries, or luxury-loving gangsters, but for an elite of statesmen from whom power and responsibility were unjustly withheld.[67] The opposition press,

[63] According to Schirach, the Brown House was supposed to set a standard for all future party buildings. (Baldur von Schirach, *Ich glaubte an Hitler*, Hamburg, Mosaik, 1968, p. 88.)

[64] Hans Kiener, "Germanische Tektonik," p. 186.

[65] *Ibid.* See also the photograph in *Erste Deutsche Architektur und Kunsthandwerkaustellung im Haus der deutschen Kunst zu München, 2. Januar bis 27. März 1938*, Munich, Knorr und Hirth, 1938, illustration no. 2.

[66] Hoffmann, *Hitler was my Friend*, p. 183. Dresler makes the same remark. (*Das braune Haus*, p. 10.)

[67] The Brown House had the desired effect on Richard Breiting, editor of the Leipziger *Neueste Nachrichten* who felt here Hitler lived "like a king," and he must become the future ruler of Germany. (Edouard Calic, *Ohne Maske: Hitler-Breiting Geheimgespräche*, Frankfurt, Societäts-Verlag, 1968, p. 19.)

said Dresler, wrote many lies about the furnishings of the chamber, but in reality, the furniture, especially the armchairs, were of "the simplest and yet most tasteful kind."[68] In the same manner, Dresler defended Hitler's study, a corner room, carpeted, with a round conference table in the center and Hitler's massive desk in a corner, combining "modern functionalism with artistic taste."[69] A portrait of Frederick the Great hung over the desk, and a painting of a battle in Flanders adorned the opposite wall so as to recall the Prussian tradition and the heroes of the Great War.[70] Brown was used throughout, because brown was "a German color."[71] Moreover, Hitler believed red, gold, and beige tones gave the most festive impression in representative rooms.[72] Thus the room was "functional" (as Dresler said) as it represented party ideals.

With its Hall of Banners, its Senate Chamber, and Hitler's office, and with its classical lines, the Brown House set a standard for later party buildings.[73] Yet, it lacked important attributes. It was not monumental enough, not large enough, and its location was not central enough. Feder laid down some qualities which the ideal House of the NSDAP should have in every German town. It must be easily accessible from all parts of the city, he said; located in the inner core of the town, but not in the business district. (Business activities were too materialistic.) In the future rebuilt city, it must be "one of the most important institutions." To render its significance visible, it should be surrounded "with a modest wreath of green and open space," preferably on a square.

[68] Dresler, *Das braune Haus*, p. 19.

[69] *Ibid.*, p. 20.

[70] Heiden claims Hitler designed his study after Mussolini's — a desk at the far end of a gigantic hall — and maintains that the effect failed; Hitler "often impressed visitors as a shy embarrassed creature, cowering unhappily behind his gigantic desk." (*Der Fuehrer*, p. 356.)

[71] Eberlein, *Was ist deutsch in der deutschen Kunst?* p. 27.

[72] Hitler told Ziegler this when they were discussing the renovation of the Weimar National Theater. (Ziegler, *Adolf Hitler*, pp. 89–90.)

[73] "We were, all of us, especially Hitler, extremely proud of the Brown House," wrote Hans Frank. (*Im Angesicht des Galgens: Deutung Hitlers und seiner Zeit auf Grund eigener Erlebnisse*, Munich-Gräfelfing, Beck, 1953, p. 92.)

At all events it should "rise with dignity above the rest of the neighbourhood." [74]

In Munich, where Arcisstrasse meets Briennerstrasse, almost on the Königsplatz, two suitable buildings for party headquarters, the Administration and *Führer* buildings, were built in 1935. (See illustration nos. 26–28.) Troost, on Hitler's command, may even have had the plans ready as early as March 1932.[75] On the exterior, they were identical, each three storeys high, with two "Doric" porticoes, echoing the forms of the two Temples of Honor, on either side of Briennerstrasse (which, in turn, separated the two buildings). These structures were also to reflect the Grecian lines of the early nineteenth-century Propylaen Gate (1846–1862) or the Glyptothek Museum (1816–1830) on the Königsplatz. Three *Führer* balconies on each building enabled Hitler to view parades or to make speeches while in the "capital of the movement." The usual eagle and wreathed swastika stood over each portico. Most of the windows were round arched, set deep in square frames. A heavy cornice at roof level and parallel string courses emphasized the horizontal lines of the three rows of windows.[76]

Of the two, the *Führer* Building is the more emblematic of Hitler's architectural aims, with its representative rooms for formal receptions. Like its twin, it was of pale-yellow Danubian limestone, with much dark-red Saalburg marble and yellow Jura marble on the inside. Leonhard Gall and Gerdy Troost, both of Munich, were charged with the interior decoration, and created a lobby with a red marble floor and marble columns. Two interior staircases which rest on "mighty columns" lead up to the upper storeys. The walls of the upper lobby were hung with tapestries, the lobby itself being furnished with tables and armchairs, "comfortably designed." Dresler stressed the warmth and comfort of

[74] Feder, *Die neue Stadt*, pp. 110–111.
[75] Goebbels, *Vom Kaiserhof zur Reichskanzlei*, p. 70.
[76] See the photographs in Troost, *Bauen*, I, pp. 13–18. The upper lobby is illustrated in a color photograph in Dresler, *Das braune Haus*, p. 33; the staircase, on p. 34.

these rooms, as well as their taste and beauty. The walls of the main reception room were covered with "beautiful paintings"; the adjoining room with a large fireplace had a "dark brown, warm stone," and "radiated comfort and serenity," an effect heightened by the red Saalburg marble of the hearth and the dark walnut panels of the wall. This so-called "living room" with its walls of reddish brown and paneled ceiling decorated in gold, giving the room "something uncommonly dignified," also boasted paintings by "famous old masters."[77] The dining room was correspondingly appointed, with the emblems of the movement, in particular the S.A. and the S.S., the Labor Front, and the Hitler Youth. The Great Hall, shaped like a half moon, was also paneled in wood, this time palisander, with door frames of red marble, "symmetrically arranged." Again there were tapestries on the wall and a large fireplace over which was a relief of *Day and Night*. The color impression was reddish brown, and the mental impression, comfort, warmth, and above all, respectability.[78] Here were no *"Bauhaus*-Marxist" tube-chairs or glass walls.

Hitler's carpeted office, with its view of the Königsplatz was also decorated in brownish red, had wood-paneled walls and a large marble fireplace. Its atmosphere, said Dresler, was "of the greatest serenity and dignity." It corresponded completely to the demands the *Führer* set for a room in which "great decisions" were made.[79] Paintings by popular nineteenth-century artists (Menzel, Feuerbach, Böcklin, and Lenbach) covered the walls.[80]

Although this headquarters was less imposing than the Ber-

[77] Dresler, *Das braune Haus*, p. 33.

[78] See the photograph on p. 37 of *Das braune Haus*. The Administration Building next door was also decorated in red-brown. (*Das braune Haus*, p. 39.)

[79] Dresler, *Das braune Haus*, p. 36.

[80] This was the room in which Hitler met Mussolini, Chamberlain, and Daladier in September 1938. (See *Ciano's Diary 1937–38*, London, Methuen, 1952, pp. 166–168.) Incidentally, these buildings were fully equipped with the latest lighting devices, were air conditioned, and contained large air-raid shelters. The apparent distrust of technology, which often appears in the Nazi or *völkisch* writings, is not reflected in any of the structures of the monumental, or representative "community" buildings.

lin Chancellery, an official book about it appeared from the party press. In this volume, Dresler described the two structures as "an expression of the National Socialist will to build."[81] Gerdy Troost reminded her readers that these were "the first monumental community buildings" constructed under Hitler, hinting that more were to come. "The clear symmetry, . . . the austere ordering of every detail, the noble stone of the mighty walls, columns and pillars . . . is a symbol of the fundamental strength which is renewing the German *Volk*." The buildings had the "natural clarity, the calm serenity of the strong, austere determination produced by a heroic mood."[82] Giessler agreed; the *Führer* Building, he wrote, was "a symbol of rediscovered faith in the future of Germany." It symbolized the ideological struggle, the uncompromising battle for power in the country, and showed with "Doric" austerity and severity the face of the militant party.[83] These representative buildings, therefore, were symbols of both the party itself and what the party was fighting for: the highest development of power and freedom of the German character with its innate virtues.[84] Yet Dresler was careful to remember that Germans could not live on ideals alone; he concluded his chapter on the *Führer* Building with a note that 250 workers and 100 craftsmen "found work and bread on this construction site."[85]

Monumental and symbolic though they were, these two buildings were not impressive enough. A new chancellery was planned for Munich, designed by Leonhard Gall.[86] This would far surpass the *Führer* Building in size and impressiveness. Its main en-

[81] Dresler, *Das braune Haus*, p. 5.
[82] Troost, *Bauen*, I, 20.
[83] Giessler, "Symbol des grossdeutschen Reiches," p. 10.
[84] Rosenberg thought they were "the first attempt to realize the ancient Greek ideal." (Rosenberg, *Portrait*, p. 274.)
[85] Dresler, *Das braune Haus*, p. 38. The Administration Building was partially gutted during the war but the *Führer* Building escaped serious damage. Today, the former houses an art museum, and the latter, the Munich Civic Archive and a music academy.
[86] See the photo of a model in Dresler, *Das braune Haus*, p. 44.

trance would have "monumental dimensions"; the outside stairs flanked by two lions were to be "imposing"; the reception hall was to be fifteen meters high.[87] Its style was similar to the "powerful monumental style" of the Führer Building but it echoed that of the Old Pinakothek (1826–1836), not far away.[88] Thus just as the buildings on Arcisstrasse were to blend with the Greek Revival structures on the Königsplatz, so this massive chancellery would be made to harmonize with the traditional appearance of Munich.

These buildings were built to impress both Germans and foreign visitors to the Reich. But the German government also went abroad with its representative architecture, to, for example, the Paris Exhibition of 1937. On the right bank of the Seine, in front of the Palais de Chaillot, Speer's German pavilion was built.[89] (See illustrations nos. 29 and 30.) Its large display hall was dominated by a square tower 65 meters high. The latter consisted of nine attached pillars backed by fluted stone slabs, recessed sections covered with gold mosaic marked by a stylized, bright red swastika pattern. On top, above a heavy cornice, stood the German eagle, holding the wreathed swastika.[90] Before one entered the pavilion, through doors at the base of this tower, one passed two sets of statues, each seven meters high, designed by Thorak; one set of three figures represented the family, on the right, and, on the left, three symbolized comradeship, reflecting the "community" values of the reborn Germany.[91] Through the entrance portal, the swastika appeared again on the door's grill and another eagle-with-swastika over the door. The exhibition hall itself [92] had no windows other than a large, long glass ceiling, recalling similar windows in Speer's Chancellery. The wallpaper, too, contained swastika patterns; the grilled railing around the

[87] Dresler, Das braune Haus, p. 43.
[88] Troost, Bauen, I, 20.
[89] This is described in Dupays, Voyages autour du monde, pp. 7–8.
[90] The tower was well illuminated at night by lights built into its base. See the photograph in Wolters, Albert Speer, p. 58.
[91] Rittich, Architektur und Bauplastik, p. 177.
[92] See the photograph of the interior in Teut, Architektur, p. 185.

platform of honor had a swastika pattern, and the stained-glass window at the rear of this platform contained another large eagle-with-swastika. (The interior decoration here was by Woldemar Brinkmann, of Munich.) Another symbol, that of strength — also seen in the Berlin Chancellery — appeared on the roof garden in the form of a bronze bison. Thus, at this international center, the German renaissance in the Nazi state was emphatically proclaimed.

As a symbol, the pavilion was designed to embody the "security, pride, self-consciousness, clarity, and discipline"[93] of the new Germany. Here, wrote Speer, "we must realize the ideas of the *Führer*."[94] Accordingly, there were no compromises in its construction, even though it was only a temporary structure, and no attempt was made to appeal to "international taste."[95] (The government planned to rebuild it in Munich as a theater museum.) The German pavilion was a contrast to the pavilions of Switzerland and Belgium across the Seine with their modern strip windows. Furthermore, Speer intended that the "cubic mass" of his pavilion seem to be checking the "onslaught" of the monumental striding figures on top of the nearby Soviet pavilion.[96] Despite the building's intense nationalism, and despite the strengths of its ideological statement, another writer maintained that "it was to bear peaceful testimony" to German civilization.[97]

The pavilion was more than a symbol of Germany, however. Its very materials and fixtures were brought from the Reich; more than 1000 railway cars carried 10,000 tons of building materials, including 3000 tons of steel and 3000 of stone. Like the Berlin Chancellery and the Munich party buildings, it was a piece of the "sacred" German earth. In spite of its classical appearance, the

[93] Rittich, *Architektur und Bauplastik*, p. 177.
[94] Cited in Hoffmann, *Deutschland in Paris*, p. 5.
[95] Rittich, *Architektur und Bauplastik*, p. 42.
[96] Speer, *Erinnerungen*, p. 95; *Inside*, p. 81.
[97] Cited in Hoffmann, *Deutschland in Paris*, p. 5. Paul Bonatz cites a conversation which he had with the French classicist, Auguste Perret, about the pavilion: "It is not architecture for an exposition," said Perret, "it's a monument, but one which fails [un monument faux]." (Paul Bonatz, *Leben und Bauen*, p. 171.)

structure had a steel skeleton; the traditional "natural" building material — stone — was attached to this frame.

Ironically, the pavilion least likely to resemble the German one, the Russian pavilion, stood directly across the street from Speer's tower and bore a striking resemblance to it. On top of this 33 meter high structure facing the German eagle stood steel figures of a young peasant holding aloft a sickle, which half-encircled a hammer held by a young worker, all symbolizing the strength of the Soviet movement.[98] Yet Wolters found the Russian pavilion's style "agitated and strident,"[99] and Speer himself maintains that the styles of the two buildings were quite different.[100] Although the sculpture on each was radically different, and although the Soviet building had less rigidly vertical lines and a more fluid appearance, in fact, photographs show no basic difference between the simplified neo-classicism of both structures. (See illustration no. 30.)

Throughout Germany, the Nazi government planned to construct representative buildings to serve as centers for the dissemination of Nazi "truths." Although few of these matched the monumentality of the aforementioned buildings, all were felt to play a role in communicating the proper ideas about Germany and its government to Germans.

Most ambitious were the *Gau* centers, or forums (again a word chosen to recall imperial Rome), large groupings of party buildings around parade squares, which were to be constructed in the capital of each *Gau* (the new administrative unit of Germany) and which would follow Dresler's ideas. Writing on Kreis'

[98] See Dupays, *Voyages autour du monde*, p. 221; or "Die Internationale Austellung Paris," *Moderne Bauformen*, XXXVI (1937), 372 (photo) and 497.

[99] Wolters, *Albert Speer*, p. 58.

[100] Interview with Speer, June 13, 1968, in Heidelberg-Schlierbach. "Two buildings, two philosophies of life!" commented Heinrich Hoffmann (*Deutschland in Paris*, p. 105). Stalin, however, did not detect anything specifically "Nazi" in this architecture, for he exhibited considerable interest in Speer's plans. (Speer, *Erinnerungen*, p. 183; *Inside*, p. 168.) Breker also reports that the Russian leader admired his monumental sculpture, which decorated several "Nazi" buildings. (Breker, *Paris, Hitler et moi*, p. 91.)

plans for a *Gau* forum in Dresden, one critic said that the government aimed "to give a number of significant German cities, as focii of the German living space, the face of our time in the shape of monumental buildings of the state and the *Volk*, buildings which in scale and execution dominate the cityscape . . ."[101] For example, Giessler's plan for Augsburg envisaged a parade square dominated by a tower surmounted by an eagle.[102] Four squat towers marked the corners of the main imposing building, from one side of which ran a Romanesque colonnade.

The forum, being very expensive, was built only in Weimar. On the other hand, every German city had its House of the NSDAP,[103] which was often a converted classical mansion from the early nineteenth century, exuding tradition and respectability. The smaller towns were more likely to have party offices in local styles. Aside from administrative centers of the party itself, most urban centers had the offices of large organizations such as the German Labor Front, which also converted older buildings, often embellishing their dignity with the party message. In Essen, for example, the Labor Front's local administration was housed in an older classical building renovated by Schulte-Frohlinde; a square had been created beside it for marches and demonstrations, and also to enhance the monumental dignity of the structure. A large *Führer* balcony was added with reliefs praising the virtues of work. Within, a ceremonial chamber served as a shrine to honor "Fallen Laborers."[104] In this way, an older building was given

[101] Hans Stephan, *Wilhelm Kreis*, p. 61.

[102] A photograph of a model of this is in Wolters, *Neue deutsche Baukunst* p. 67; see also p. 68 for Kreis' sketch of his planned *Gau* complex for Dresden.

[103] See Troost; *Bauen*, I, 90–91, for photographs of the small *Gau* house for Franken and the Kreishaus for Weimar, similar in style to the Munich *Führerbau*. From 1932 and 1933 on, Hitler well considered the impression party headquarters should make; at this time Speer felt that this architecture was treated by his *Führer* "with extraordinary seriousness." (*Erinnerungen*, pp. 41 and 38; *Inside*, pp. 28 and 24.)

[104] "Haus der D.A.F. — Gauverwaltung Essen," *Moderne Bauformen*, XXXVII (1938), 233–48. See also Schulte-Frohlinde, *Bauten der Bewegung*, pp. 62–68. On the oriel window, one of the inscriptions said: "Individuals come and indi-

many features necessary to communicate the Nazi message. In style, the Essen building differed from Kurt Tischer's large classical Labor Front office building in Berlin; yet the latter, with its balconies and huge swastika in the tympanum of the central section, still offered dignity, sense of tradition, and even greater representative monumentality than its Essen counterpart.[105] In the countryside, the Labor Front built in local styles, in timber or brick, with thatched or tiled roofs in the north or central Germany, or in white plaster in the south. (See illustration no. 74.) The buildings of the Reich Forest Service were also built in the *völkisch* manner.

Even the new post office buildings could be representive and monumental. The best example was in Karlsruhe, on Ettlingerstrasse. This massive, five-storey building with its campanile resembled a Renaissance palace; its windows, simply and heavily framed, were in neat rows, expressing that "clarity" the commentators loved; its ground floor was marked by an arcade running along the two street sides of the building.[106] In this type of building, the "holy grail" style of post offices in the "age of decay" was emphatically abandoned. The result is less "Nazi" than in most other structures, but writers found that it expressed the new *Zeitgeist.*

City and municipal halls were important to the Nazi commentators, as centers "representing" authority and as "community" buildings. The writers praised structures built both before and after 1933 as "buildings of the movement" although they are not unified in style. In the same book, Rittich includes both Schultze-Naumburg's Provincial Council Office in Parchim, a brick, Biedermeier structure, as well as Höger's City Hall in Rüstringen, also

viduals die, but the community, out of which the nation eternally renews itself, shall be immortal." (*Bauten der Bewegung*, p. 65.)

[105] See Troost, *Bauen*, I, 59, or Rittich, *Architektur und Bauplastik*, pp. 114–115.

[106] Troost, *Bauen*, I, 143 (photo). Five small balconies are provided on the Ettlingerstrasse facade, and a small arcade runs around the tower near its top.

brick, but very "modern" with its vertical lines, and large windows.[107] Gerdy Troost includes photos of smaller town halls in southern Germany, all built in the indigenous style.[108] As long as no frivolous, "egotistical" experiment was undertaken by the architect, considerable latitude was allowed for smaller local "representative" buildings. At all events, it was expensive to hire a nationally famous architect to design a representative center for small town, and, given the economic problems of the thirties, it is not surprising that local tradition-oriented architects produced simple, practical structures for their communities.[109] The commentators, of course, made a virtue of this necessity, citing the correspondence between these simple structures or the plain lines of larger monumental buildings and an allegedly native German sobriety. This was functionalism in the German fashion.

Hitler's Berghof, his large chalet near Berchtesgaden, could also be considered a "representative" building in that it supplemented the Berlin Chancellery and foreign diplomats and leaders were invited to visit the *Führer* there to be impressed by the scenery, if not by the comfortable building itself. (See illustration no. 31.) To reach the Eagle's Nest, a "teahouse" 150 meters higher up the mountain on the Kehlstein, the visitor passed through an entrance arched in the Roman fashion, built of heavy stone, and then walked through a long tunnel, which ended in a large elevator car of polished brass; if this did not impress him, the stone Eagles' Nest itself, perched fortresslike on its mountain crag with an air of watchful militancy, would surely impress one that here resided a man to be reckoned with.[110]

[107] Rittich, *Architektur und Bauplastik*, pp. 120 and 126 (photos).

[108] Like Rittich, she does not suggest whether these were constructed in the Third Reich. Troost implies these buildings were part of the patriotic movement which originated before 1933. She includes photos of the *Rathäuser* of Mittenwald and Garmisch-Partenkirchen. (*Bauen*, I, 134 and 136.) These had simple lines, but were decorated with traditional murals.

[109] See Teut on this nonpolitical necessity, *Architektur*, p. 236.

[110] On the construction and design of this retreat see Speer, *Erinnerungen*, pp. 99–100, and 102–104, *Inside*, pp. 85–86, or Breker, *Paris, Hitler et Moi*, pp. 128–131. Hitler designed the Berghof himself.

Other Nazi leaders sought to live and work in the representative splendor they felt was appropriate to their positions and to their country. Ribbentrop, for example, had the former presidential mansion in Berlin renovated in 1939–1940, in a style similar to the new Chancellery nearby, with marble door and window frames and many reliefs.[111] But the most interesting home of any Nazi leader was Karinhall, where Hermann Goering, head of the Luftwaffe and minister for forests and game, lived. Fifty miles north of Berlin, Goering had a small shooting lodge built, named after his late wife. Karinhall was expanded by Hitler into something resembling a summer palace for entertaining distinguished foreigners. By 1935 this expansion was completed and persons like the Duke of Windsor or the Japanese Foreign Minister, Matsuoko, were regally entertained in these "representative" surroundings. (See illustrations nos. 32–34.)

Karinhall's heavy thatched roof and walls of large stones were only partly visible through clumps of tall pines.[112] An overstatement in the *völkisch style*, it was one of the few large *völkisch* buildings constructed during the Third Reich. The visitor entered Karinhall through a large and deeply carpeted entrance hall with dark oak beams and heavy old furniture.[113] From here one passed into the main room of the complex, the German Hall with its large fireplace and its window doors looking out on the

---

[111] Hans-Georg von Studnitz, describes this "decor à la Third Reich" as "redolent of a clumsy neo-Biedermeier . . . Even the reception rooms have a homely air. The furniture arrangement is just like that in the home of a typical German *Hausfrau*." (*While Berlin Burns, The Diary of Hans-Georg von Studnitz 1943–45*, Englewood Cliffs, Prentice-Hall, 1963, p. 259.) This petty bourgeois respectability was probably important to most Nazis. For an illustration, see *Erste deutsche Architektur*, p. 23.

[112] See photographs of the exterior in Rittich, *Architektur und Bauplastik*, pp. 138–139. A typical laudatory *völkisch* article is by Richard Pfeiffer, "Jaghaus 'Karinhall,'" *Die völkische Kunst*, I (1935), 19–24 (This journal was an organ of Rosenberg's *Kultur* Society.)

[113] The German Hall is illustrated in Hermann Glasser, *Spiesser-Ideologie: Von der Zerstörung des deutschen Geistes im 19. und 20. Jahrhunderts*, Freiburg, Rombach, 1964, illustration 6.

lake; the high pointed ceiling sported heavy exposed beams, and the walls were decorated with antlers. The mood of this room and others such as the study and the cinema was comfortable but solemn.[114]

The commentators stressed the *völkisch* qualities of the building. Not only was Karinhall in harmony with the surrounding landscape, but all the possibilities of "pure construction in wood" were used with local building materials and the handworked details were "beautiful and healthy." The result was a "harmony of the house with the woods and the lake, a language of native materials and natural human handicrafts which everyone can understand."[115] Thus Karinhall, constructed in a style appropriate to the reviving "Aryan" *Kultur*, was a house which was not a "machine for living in" (LeCorbusier), but one which was held together organically, excluding "the world of the metropolis," and realizing "the new concepts of building and living."[116]

For entertaining and housing foreign dignitaries, older buildings were used as the Reich's representative monuments. These were often in a traditional style to show that the 1933 revolution was not isolating Germany from its glorious cultural past. For example, the Klesheim castle, near Salzburg, planned by Fischer von Erlach (1656–1723) in baroque splendor, appealed to Hitler's taste, and because it was also not far from Berchtesgaden, it was refurnished and became his guest house.[117]

Much more was built, renovated, and used in the drive to create suitable representative buildings for the reborn Germany. Even structures like kindergartens or holiday resorts had to correspond to the mood of the Berlin Chancellery or the Munich *Führer* Building; they had to be somehow "German," whether in their "Doric" classical style (for this was considered "Aryan") or

---

[114] For a description of life at Karinhall, see Emmy Goering, *An der Seite meines Mannes: Begebenheiten und Bekenntnisse*, Göttingen, Schütze, 1967.

[115] Pfeiffer, "Jagdhaus 'Karinhall,'" p. 19.

[116] *Ibid.*, p. 19.

[117] See Ciano's impressions of it in the *Ciano Diaries 1939–43*, p. 477.

in the use of local building materials and motifs (the *völkisch* styles). In this way, they were "community" buildings which represented Germany to the world, while reminding the *Volk* of their traditions and virtues. They stood also for authority, both of the party and of the state, and disturbed neither the landscape nor the mind with suggestions of revolution, technological change, or foreign ideas.

CHAPTER EIGHT

"Community" Architecture

THROUGHOUT MANY books and articles of the Third Reich, on architecture and other subjects, runs the concept of *Gemeinschaft*, or community. "Formation of the *Volk* community," said one writer typically, "is the task which we are continually challenged to accomplish."[1] Some believed that this had already been achieved in 1933, and that now the idea of the *Volk* community must become explicit in architecture.[2] Many representative buildings described in chapter seven were often called "community" architecture by commentators. These structures were, of course, designed to explicitly communicate the power and authority of the Nazi state. But they were "community" buildings in that they were to create the feeling of belonging to great and glorious community.

This concern for strengthening the bonds of the German national community was more than just a desire for a stronger sense of patriotism. It reflected the continued search for that elusive unity which German society had not achieved in 1871.[3] Class

[1] Schrade, *Bauten des dritten Reiches*, p. 28. Retrospectively (in 1964), Ziegler wrote that "a true *Volk* community" was the aim of all Hitler's buildings. (*Adolf Hitler*, p. 216.)

[2] Karl Vogel, "Nationalsozialistische Architektur," p. 325.

[3] On this problem, see Peter Gay, *Weimar Culture: The Outsider as Insider*, New York, Harper and Row, 1968, chapter IV, "The Hunger for Wholeness: Trials of Modernity." For a study of architecture, a typical example is Wolters' *Vom Beruf des Baumeisters*; see, for example, pp. 46 and 65.

hostilities were still strong in the twenties, not to mention particularism and religious differences. At the same time, the Weimar period saw more radical architects interested in another kind of "community" architecture; art and architecture, they felt, should be brought into greater contact with the needs of the working masses. Some even called for a new "community," not in the Nazi sense, but in a socialist context. A good deal was also done by local governments in this period to create closer community life through working class housing.[4] The Dessau *Bauhaus* conducted its own experiments in the unification of mass production and craftsmanship; in trying to make the worker's employment, his personality, and his home life more of a whole entity again, men like Gropius fought the decline of pride in work and the separation of the worker's place of work and his home.[5] However, the Nazi party and many of its sympathizers were seeking something less individualized for the German laborer.

They longed for a new order in which the individual would feel bound to the community's life, as in the Middle Ages; then, it was believed that the inhabitants of towns derived spiritual sustenance from the great cathedrals, the symbol of their union in a faith (Christianity), to which they could look every day.[6] Many writers saw the medieval German way of life as the result of the "organic structure of the *Volk*"[7] (a view which conflicted with the equally popular belief that medieval Germans were oppressed by an alien church). This ideal uniformity had been lost in the nineteenth century. No "buildings of the community" were produced at this time, because, said Frau Troost, such structures only "reach their perfection when they grow out of ideological faith."[8] Al-

[4] See Lane, *Architecture and Politics*, pp. 87–124.

[5] See Hans M. Wingler, *Das Bauhaus 1919–1933: Weimar, Dessau, Berlin und die Nachfolge in Chicago seit 1937*, Bramsche, Rasch, 1968.

[6] Rosenberg, *Mythus*, p. 360.

[7] Karl Neupert, "Die Gemeinschaft formt das Bild der deutschen Städte," *Heimatpflege – Heimatgestaltung*, supplement to *Der Deutsche Baumeister*, 1939, no. 6, cited in Wulf, *Die bildenden Künste*, p. 251.

[8] Troost, *Bauen*, I, 8.

though nineteenth and twentieth century materialism and communism had reduced Germans to cogs in a giant machine, fortunately, in the Third Reich, the "communal spirit" had revived, thanks to the alleged Nazi aim of creating a *Volk* community.[9]

The party's slogan, The Common Good before Individual Good, is well known. In the writings of this period, certain words and phrases recur, such as *Einheit* (unity or oneness), *Ganzheit* (the whole), *Allgemeinheit* (the general public), and of course, *Gemeinschaft* (the community), a word often linked with others, such as *Gemeinschaftsarbeit* (community work). Assuming the party and its state represented the *Volk* in a form of democracy, then the buildings commissioned by the government were commissioned by the people.[10] There were no longer any traditional political parties; consequently no tangle of conflicting political philosophies prevented the people from building. Their "will to build" could at last be felt.[11] This meant that the architect must be the "servant of the whole"; his architecture must have a form understandable to all Germans, and a living relationship with the individual German.[12] This, then, was the aim of the new community architecture, particularly of the new stadiums, *Volk* halls, and parade squares.

Perhaps the one building of the Third Reich that impressed the outside world more than any other was the Olympic Stadium in Berlin. (See illustrations nos. 34-40.) Just as Nuremberg's Zeppelin Field was more than a mere sports center, so the Berlin stadium was part of a large complex; the Reich Sport Grounds was designed to do much more than serve as the focal point for the 1936 Olympics. For Hitler and the commentators, the Olympic

[9] Schulte-Frohlinde, *Die landschaftlichen Grundlagen*, p. 330.

[10] This idea was expressed by the architectural expert Joseph Umlauf, in "Die Bauten der Gemeinschaft," *Raumforschung und Raumordnung*, 1941, H. ¾, cited in Teut, *Architektur*, pp. 330-32. (Umlauf was in charge of city planning in the Planning and Soil section of the S.S.)

[11] "The parties are swept away," said Goering, "The German civil war is transformed into the German *Volk* community." (*Reden und Aufsätze*, p. 178.)

[12] Karl Vogel, "Nationalsozialistische Architektur," p. 326.

Grounds were as symbolic as was the Chancellery, and their function, beyond "representing" particular German qualities to the
world in 1936, was that of a national center. The stadium, the
May Field, and the Dietrich-Eckart Open Air Theater were "community" architecture.

Some writers stressed that only the Nazi government had had
the courage and the imagination to build this large complex.[13] On
October 5, 1933, Hitler visited the grounds of the older Sport
Forum: "With one glance, he recognized the possibilities here for
a large scale plan, rejected the idea of converting the Grunewald
Stadium into an Olympic stadium, demanded the sacrifice of the
[older] stadium and outlined for the fields a truly monumental
building program."[14] According to the *Führer* himself, the Olympic Stadium and grounds were not to be built on a "niggardly
scale" as Germans had tended to build in the past. The Ministry of
the Interior submitted plans for a stadium to him, he said, which
would have cost one-and-a-half million marks. "None of the people
concerned seems to have taken into consideration the fact that the
Olympic games afforded us a unique opportunity to amass foreign
credits, and at the same time a splendid chance of enhancing our
prestige abroad." He therefore suggested that a preliminary grant
of twenty-eight million marks be set aside for the construction of
a stadium.[15] Hence, from the start, the Olympic Grounds were to

[13] Twice before the First World War, Germany had been invited to be host
to the games, but was forced to turn down the invitation because of lack of money
and facilities. Only through private initiative was the Grunewald Stadium built in
1913 for the 1916 games, a celebration which, of course, never occurred. Nevertheless, some groups continued to press the Olympic Committee to have the
games in Germany and to get an adequate setting for the celebration, the 1913
stadium being too small by the thirties. Despite continued financial problems, in
1925–28 the Sport Forum was designed and built by Walter and Werner March,
and included a gymnasium, a swimming pool, and other facilities, all in a modern-
ized neo-classical style.

[14] Werner March, *Bauwerk Reichssportfeld*, Berlin, Deutscher Kunstverlag,
1936, p. 10. Actually, according to Speer, March's original plan, which envisaged
a concrete building with much use of glass, was rejected by Hitler as too "modern." He maintains he altered March's plans, eliminating the glass walls, with
March's (and Hitler's) approval. (Speer, *Erinnerungen*, p. 94; *Inside*, p. 80.)

[15] S.C., p. 404 (April 12, 1942); *Tischgespräche*, pp. 272–3.

Hitler monumental, representative architecture as well as "community" buildings.[16]

The monumentality of the grounds is immediately apparent to one approaching the stadium from the city. One walks along a large rectangular square, lined with flag posts and divided into square motifs for parades and reviews, towards the Olympic Gate, consisting of two towers, the lefthand one formerly with a swastika and the righthand one, still with a clock; between them is suspended the Olympic symbol. These towers, with their narrow windows, slit into the stone masonry like lancets in a fortress, lend the grounds a sober militant air. Just inside the gate, the visitor sees an oak tree, symbol of Teutonic tradition. Behind the gate looms the great stadium, built of blocks of Franconian limestone, in a severely classical vein.

The stadium, with its 65,000 seats and 35,000 places for standing spectators, was considered by March, its creator, as more than a sports center. Although, at the Marathon Gate (built into the northern side of the stadium) the Olympic Flame burned in a shallow basin, the movable loudspeakers and lighting fixtures, the broad entrances (underground and at ground level), rendered it ideal, he said, for "great parades, choral festivals, nationalist [volkstümlich] concerts, military and equestrian contests and shows."[17] Approaching it from the exterior, one should be impressed by its apparent height, an effect March attained by using rows of pillars running up two storeys outside;[18] These strong vertical lines, however, were balanced by a heavy horizontal cornice, an element often seen in the architecture of the Third Reich. March tried to give the grounds a unified appearance;[19] ac-

[16] Werner March sympathized with many of the aims of Hitler and the commentators. Clarity, symmetry, order, simplicity, and monumentality were his own goals; whereas these goals do not identify him as a National Socialist architect, his own comments make him a link between the neo-classical and völkisch schools.

[17] March, Bauwerk, p. 12.

[18] Ibid., pp. 24–25. March maintains that he was imitating the work of Schinkel.

[19] A visual connection between tower and stadium had been "commanded" by Hitler, said March. (Bauwerk, p. 25.)

cordingly, once within the stadium, one notices through the Marathon Gate, the huge bell tower at the end of the adjacent May Field. From this Marathon Gate on August 1, 1936, Hitler entered at the head of the Olympic contestants,[20] stressing the architectural connection between the two structures.

The Langemarck Tower dominates the stands on three sides of the May Field, a parade ground for "patriotic demonstrations" west of the stadium.[21] Five small narrow windows on each side of the tower sustain the militant appearance of the whole complex. The two halves of the stadium of the May Field slope away symmetrically in several levels from the tower standing in the center. On the stadium promenade the square pattern reappears; here lines of grey stone divide squares of white stone into orderly sequences. The central section of the stands, the base for the bell tower, contained the Langemarck Hall, a memorial to the fallen in the Great War. Within the hall, twelve pillars bore seventy-six flags of the regiments which took part in the Battle of Langemarck in 1914 as well as ten steel shields with the names of divisions. Earth from the cemetery at Langemarck was also preserved here. The outer side of the hall presents a columned façade, "forceful" and primeval. The May Field, which Hitler had himself "demanded" for the grounds,[22] was bounded on the east, the stadium side, by four other towers, each thirty-five meters high, and named after ancient Germanic tribes (Frisian, Saxon, Franconian, and Swabian); these also have narrow windows in their sides. Two sculptural groups, of strong nudes leading powerful horses, stand between the pairs of towers.[23]

The grounds were planned around two main axes, continuing

---

[20] This stress on linking the stadium with the tower underlines the political character of the stadium; the tower had a semimilitary, ideological function, and its position, brooding over the stadium, was deliberate. (March, *Bauwerk*, p. 26.)

[21] March, *Bauwerk*, p. 12. The field itself is about the same size as the Luitpold Field in Nuremberg, 290-by-375 meters. It was here that on September 28, 1937 Mussolini addressed a crowd of 650,000 on his visit to Berlin.

[22] March, *Bauwerk*, p. 27.

[23] See the photograph, p. 52, in Rittich, *Architektur und Bauplastik*.

the orderly, disciplined sense of the complex. The east-west axis runs from the Olympic Square in the east, through the stadium and the May Field to the bell tower; and the north-south axis, from the swimming pool to the north of the stadium through the stadium itself, to another square in the south. Other buildings of the grounds include a grass hockey stadium, a center for equestrian competition, tennis courts, and the Sport Forum (constructed in the twenties). The open-air theater in the forest to the west was least sport-oriented building here, but with its semireligious connotations, it serves to underline the ideological significance of the whole complex.[24]

Much was written about this center. The stadium and the May Field were considered "community" architecture, a center for communal rituals wherein all were participants, rather than just spectators. The curving stands of the stadium's interior were to give "a living feeling of community to the crowds of the Volk gathered there." The whole complex was a site for commemorative ceremonies of a nationalist nature; with its theatre and its monuments, it was a national festival center.[25] A philosophy which valued Volk unity, a militant and disciplined way of life, and an ideal of body and spirit were living in the Volk today, Rittich declared. In these Olympic games it was not the sport that really mattered, he noted, but rather the desire to carry out the games as a contest and a festival.[26] Moreover, the complex was also considered proof of the creative energy and will of Germans. For ex-

[24] It is described below as a Thingplatz. No doubt because of the Sport Forum's use as a physical-health center and because of its classical design, it was included by Gerdy Troost in her collection of buildings; she does not explain how the "ideologically sick" Weimar Republic could have created the atmosphere for the building of such a structure. (Troost, Bauen, I, 99; Rittich offers even more illustrations of the Sport Forum; Architektur und Bauplastik, pp. 54–63.) Presumably Troost and Rittich would maintain that the national revival was already evident in the twenties or that the German "will to build" was never completely extinguished.

[25] March, Bauwerk, pp. 22 and 11. He described the Cupola Hall of his earlier Sport Forum as a center for community experiences, too, (Bauwerk, p. 39).

[26] Rittich, Architektur und Bauplastik, p. 67.

ample, Schrade wrote that sport was "the expression of the will to life"; [27] here, then, the German *Volk* gave proof of its vitality. March saw the Olympic grounds as a collective achievement; any doubts which its creators may have had about accomplishing such a great task in a short time, he said, were overcome by the initiative of all concerned.[28] The same was written about those who built the Chancellery in less than a year.

If the German *Volk* community was capable of building such impressive edifices as the Olympic complex, it was at least in part (said commentators) because of their "Aryan" blood. The ancient Greeks, who first initiated the Olympic Games, were also "Aryans," and thus it was natural for the Germans to build the new Olympia and to excel also in such games.[29] March deliberately sought to emphasize the links between his stadium and the ancient games. His book, *Bauwerk Reichsportfeld*, contains a plan of ancient Olympia, and many references to the Greek Olympiad.[30] Germany, with her humanist traditions, said March, had the task of renewing the ideals of ancient Aryan Greece; appropriately, the mission fell to Germany when she was rejecting "foreign" cultural influences and devoting herself to the preservation and cultivation of her "Aryan" racial character.[31] The Reich Sport Field arose from present German needs, uninfluenced by foreign or historical models; yet it was an organism which, as a place for national celebrations, was related to ancient Olympia. Beside the *stadion*, lay the May Field as a *forum* with the Langemarck Hall as a *templon*, the open-air stage as a *theatron*, the Reich Sport Academy as a *gymnasion* (an enclosed area), the House of German Sport as a

[27] Hubert Schrade, *Die Bauten des dritten Reiches*, Leipzig, Bibliographisches Institut, 1937, p. 26.

[28] March, *Bauwerk*, p. 10.

[29] Accordingly, Hitler planned for all future Olympic Games to take place in Germany. (Speer, *Erinnerungen*, p. 84; *Inside*, p. 70.)

[30] The plan is on p. 11 of March, *Bauwerk*, and the comparison with the Greek stadium, on pp. 13 and 24. This idea was repeated by Rittich, *Architektur und Bauplastik*, pp. 67–68.

[31] March, *Bauwerk*, p. 7.

pretaneion (meeting hall), and the other fields as a *palästra* (wrestling ground). "And even the sacred olive tree at the entrance to the temple of Zeus," noted March, ". . . reappears as the German oak, which greets the visitor at the Olympic Gate today."[32] In the same vein, another commentator felt that the center's monumentality, its beautiful grounds and statuary entailed a "penetrating avowal of classical Olympic ideals, expressed in German form."[33] A familiar idea reemerges: the closely knit *Volk* community which Hitler created would have as glorious a history and culture as its racial forebear, classical Greece.

Just as Hitler was the acknowledged creator of the Berlin Chancellery, so was he described as the inspirer of the Reich Sport Field. March stressed that Hitler had commanded all the grounds' facilities be architecturally unified into one complex.[34] Rittich presented the *Führer* as the genius who had cleared away all the difficulties which had earlier obstructed the construction of such a center.[35] Here, then appears the familiar idea of Hitler as architect-statesman.

Commentators showed how, both in its location and in its form, the Reich Sport Field was an integral part of its natural environment. March wrote that his buildings never obscured the view of the forested landscape to the north and west of the complex; the tribunes of his swimming pool opened "with a free view of the landscape"; the hockey stadium seemed "to grow out of the landscape." He noted that the view from the windows of the Langemarck Hall gave a "feeling of union . . . with the homeland." Indeed, it was March's aim to arrange the whole grounds so that they gave the "impression of being completely imbedded in nature."[36] Although never genuinely *völkisch*, Hitler sometimes praised the use of natural materials and so did the commentators

[32] *Ibid.*, p. 13.
[33] Troost, *Bauen*, I, 52.
[34] March, *Bauwerk*, p. 25.
[35] Rittich, *Architektur und Bauplastik*, p. 69.
[36] March, *Bauwerk*, p. 15. His hockey stadium also afforded "an open view of the landscape." (*Bauwerk*, p. 34.)

on the Chancellery and the Munich party headquarters. Commenting on his Olympic buildings, March, too, emphasized their "genuineness." Here no "foreign" or synthetic building materials were used; "the genuine material" of the stadium gave it its "solemn dignity."[37] More important than the esthetic qualities of real stone were the nationalistic connotations of "native" limestone, marble, and granite "brought from every part of Germany."[38] And although the architecture of the major buildings might recall Germany's racial links with ancient Greece, the lesser buildings, such as the riding stables or the tennis stadium, were in the half-timbered style of Brandenburg.[39] Thus the complex was quintessentially German in both setting and structure.

Through the shape and the very existence of its buildings, the Olympic grounds were supposed to strongly unify the German community and to remind it of its roots in the German landscape and German soil. This task was also accomplished quite explicitly, by means of the sculpture set up around the fields. Here were strong, athletic figures with stalwart, determined expressions, vaguely reminiscent of Greek statues. For example, Breker's *Decathlon* and his *Female Victor* flanked the entrance to the Sport Forum, and the works of Georg Kolbe, one of the few "healthy" sculptors of the preceding decade, also decorated the field. Joseph Wackerle's horsemen guarded the May Field.[40] March explained the sculpture wanted here, declaring that the style must be "free of all ambiguity," it must be "healthy" and the will of the artist must not dominate in the finished work.[41] These figures had to communicate to all, the Nazi message of German strength and patriotic readiness for battle.

[37] *Ibid.*, p. 26.

[38] *Ibid.*, p. 28. Green Westphalian dolomite was used for the Hockey stadium (p. 34).

[39] *Ibid.*, p. 34. See the photos, nos. 36, 37, and 40 (of the riding academy) and no. 39, of the small tennis stadium.

[40] Photographs of this sculpture are on pp. 60–61 in Rittich, *Architektur und Bauplastik*. Breker discusses his work in his memoirs. (*Paris, Hitler et moi*, pp. 14–18.)

[41] March, *Bauwerk*, p. 42.

In the above ways, then, the Olympic buildings were "community" architecture. Unlike, for example, the Berlin Chancellery, they were designed for public use, and were to both serve and educate the *Volk*. However, they had an added role, as "representative" architecture. Any country which plays host to the Olympics seeks to impress foreign visitors with the athletic abilities of its population and with its culture. This need to impress was understandably strong in Germany in 1936. It was hoped that the complex "spreads the fame of the new German architecture throughout the whole world."[42] March considered the games "a rare opportunity to present monumentally [Germany's] will to culture before the world."[43] They were thus to communicate the message of German greatness to humanity at large.

Every German city and town was to have a similar stadium, parade ground, and other "community" architecture, but it was the old city of Nuremberg, home of the party rallies, which was to have the most impressive "community" center. Southeast of the city, on its outskirts, lay a large park with a lake. Here in 1927, 1929, and 1933 the mass rallies were held.[44] Nuremberg, of course, had associations with a colourful period of Germany's past and was, until 1943, one of the best preserved, late medieval European cities; it therefore appealed to patriotism as well as to the popular myths about the medieval period, both of which were reflected by the ideology.[45] Hitler strongly felt the beauty of the city, and wanted to tear down the nineteenth-century imitations of medi-

[42] Troost, *Bauen*, I, 52.

[43] March, *Bauwerk*, p. 10. These writers, and Hitler, too, would have been pleased with at least some reactions to the great show on these grounds. Impressed by the "cathedral of light" effect used here, the American Ambassador William Dodd wrote, "I have never seen such an elaborate show." (William E. Dodd, *Ambassador Dodd's Diary 1933–38*, New York, Harcourt Brace, 1941, p. 343.)

[44] For a description of the rallies, see Hamilton T. Burden, *The Nuremberg Party Rallies: 1923–39*, New York, Praeger, 1967. A Center for German National Festivals was planned for this area before 1914.

[45] For a *völkisch* view of Nuremberg, see Roland Anheisser, *Das mittelalterliche Wohnhaus in deutschstämmigen Landen: Seine Schönheit in Aufbau und Einzelheit*, Stuttgart, Strecker und Schroeder, 1935, pp. xxvi–xxvii. (Anheisser was a painter and art teacher.)

eval buildings, "mere trash."[46] He wanted festive celebrations and parades in the old city streets (as Leni Riefenstahl's film *Triumph des Willens* documents), or in the old town's buildings, such as the state reception in the town hall on the party Day of Unity, 1934, when the ringing of church bells and a fanfare of bugles heralded his arrival. It was natural, therefore, that after 1933, first Troost, then Speer, should be given orders to plan a larger "park" on Dutzend Lake for those mighty rallies, which were to simultaneously symbolize and strengthen the new unity of the German community. (See illustration nos. 41–49.) Hitler had plans drawn up in 1934, and enlarged in 1935. To be completed (under normal conditions) by 1945, this huge complex of buildings was Germany's biggest construction project besides the building of the west wall. Work was stopped during the war, but much was completed. Those buildings executed and plans for those unfinished show how strongly some architects adhered to the concept of the communal experience, as well as national discipline and pride. (Many foreign visitors came to the rallies, which gave their architectural setting a representative function as well.)

The first project was Speer's renovation of Luitpold Arena and Hall.[47] The older hall was changed to give it a blocklike, massive appearance, from which banners were draped. But it was the Luitpold Arena (or Grove) that had most significance for the commentators. Designed to hold 120,000 people, it was bounded on its southern side by a nearly crescent-shaped tribune of classical design supporting three, high swastika banners; at each end rose a large stone eagle. Across the field stood a pre-1933 Great War memorial, basically an arcade with a stone forecourt. On these grounds, *Volk* unity could be created.[48] The memorial re-

[46] A press reception on September 10, 1938 in Nuremberg, cited in Burden, *Nuremberg Party Rallies*, p. 156.
[47] See the photos in Wolters, *Albert Speer*, nos. 17 and 18, or Rittich, *Architektur*, p. 27.
[48] See Hubert Schrade's description of the rally here, in "Der Sinn," pp. 510–512.

called the dead heroes who perished for the community while the mass rally symbolized the close-knit community which survived.[49]

From Luitpold Field, the northernmost structure on the grounds, ran the granite Parade Avenue as the axis for other buildings. This eighty-meter wide street was perfect for large parades to and from Luitpold Field or March Field at its southern terminus about two kilometers away. Just as on the field itself was copied in other German cities (such as Berlin), so was this wide avenue a model for streets planned elsewhere (such as Augsburg and Linz).

Yet Luitpold Field was not large enough, and so southeast of Dutzend Lake was built Albert Speer's Zeppelin Field, which could hold 240,000 participants.[50] A square field surrounded on all sides by stands, the Zeppelin Field was dominated by twin colonnades which ran along the top of its northern tribune; this, the main stand, was laid out symmetrically, with the low horizontal lines of both colonnades lending space and distance.[51] The pylons, at each end of this tribune, were each decorated with a wreathed swastika and a large brazier while the central section, which included the speaker's pulpit, was crowned by a large freestanding swastika. From the outside (on the north), the tribune, with its blank bastionlike pylons, had the appearance of a huge fortress.[52]

[49] For the art historian, Werner Hager, this rally itself was a form of architecture. Nazism had "grasped the whole" and "forced it into form. . . . A strong movement of the *Volk* becomes something visible again." (Hager, "Bauwerke im Dritten Reich," *Das Innere Reich*, 1937, I. Halbjahresband, cited in Wulf, *Die bildenden Künste*, p. 241.) Here again, the German people themselves were regarded as architectural elements.

[50] See photographs 19–25 in Wolters, *Albert Speer*.

[51] Hubert Schrade found these strict rows of columns an expression of order. (Schrade, *Die Bauten des dritten Reiches*, p. 19.) The colonnade was removed in 1967.

[52] The dimensions of the Zeppelin Field can be found in Burden, *The Nuremberg Party Rallies*, p. 60. In 1968 the field contained a parking lot, a cinder track, a baseball diamond, and a soccer field. One of Speer's models for the tribune of the Zeppelin Field was the Pergamon Altar, from the 2nd century B.C. (Speer, *Erinnerungen*, p. 68; *Inside*, p. 55.) He sought a "synthesis of Troost's classicism and Tessenow's simplicity." (*Erinnerungen*, p. 75; *Inside*, p. 62.)

The Zeppelin Field, said Lotz, should be not seen as simply the solution of a technical problem, but as the expression of an idea, "the living-space of a community."[53] Similarily, Schrade wrote that the shape and concept of the Zeppelin Field recreated the Tannenberg Memorial in East Prussia, which, in its fortress-like appearance, was a symbol of an all-inclusive community.[54] It was also a great military camp for the soldiers of a political army, as well as their parade ground before the *Führer*. Hartmann called the Zeppelin Field "a complete parade square in stone."[55] Here "the leadership principle" assumed living form. Writing on all the fields at Nuremberg, Lotz said:

> Leadership is present everywhere, for in each meeting space and on each parade square is the place on which the *Führer* stands, especially prominent architecturally . . . Each individual participant sees before him the great colorful picture of the tribunes, with the powerful backdrop of the stone columns, the rhythm and dimensions of which is given by the banners hanging between them. There stand the standards and the flags, and in the middle, thrust out towards the field is the place of the *Führer*.[56]

Thus the Zeppelin Field, as all such fields, served to strengthen the bonds between the community and its leader.

Speer believes that the Zeppelin Field (and the unfinished German Stadium) are his "best" buildings.[57] He is also proud of the "cathedral of light" effect, created by directing 150 searchlights fifteen kilometers into the night sky. This was an attempt to create an "architecture of light." Moreover, he maintains, the effect was for illumination, not necessarily to stun the participant. Nevertheless, Speer admits that when the beams of light came together through the clouds, it was a "fantastic thing, like being

[53] Lotz, "Die Reichsparteitaggelände in Nürnberg," *Die Kunst im dritten Reich*, 1938, cited in Teut, *Architektur*, p. 192.
[54] Schrade, *Bauten des dritten Reiches*, p. 21.
[55] Hartmann, *Werkhefte*, p. 122.
[56] Lotz, "Die Reichsparteitaggelände," p. 192.
[57] Interview with Speer, June 13, 1968, in Heidelberg-Schlierbach.

in a Gothic cathedral."[58] Speer also effectively used the lighting of the building itself for evening rallies, directing spotlights at the various symbols of the party erected on the tribunes. Given the music of singing and bands, as well as the speeches and marching, Speer's architecture must have contributed immensely to the "community experience."

Hitler wanted to hold military maneuvers on the Nuremberg Grounds, and for these the Zeppelin Field was not big enough; therefore construction began in 1938 on the March Field, which would hold 500,000 people in its stands, and which on its longest side was nearly a kilometer in length. Named after the 1935 rearmament, the March Field was used for the Day of the *Wehrmacht* celebration and other military shows. Nine (out of a planned twenty-four) square travertine watchtowers, each thirty-eight meters high, were constructed, as well as a central tribune, with Hitler's pulpit and the usual structure for swastika banners.[59] The towers were "militant" and granite was used "in order to symbolize militancy."[60]

As these three stadiums were all for outdoor meetings and shows, an indoor area was needed. The architect Ludwig Ruff had planned a congress hall for Nuremberg in 1927–1928. Hitler approved of this plan, but had it enlarged to hold 60,000 people,

[58] "Die Bürde werde ich nicht mehr los," p. 52. See also his *Erinnerungen*, p. 71; *Inside*, p. 59. The effect of the *Lichtdom* on ordinary Germans can be imagined, considering its impression on the more sophisticated Sir Neville Henderson: it was, he said, "like being inside a cathedral of ice," and "the blue-tinged light" was "solemn and beautiful." (Neville Henderson. *Failure of a Mission, Berlin, 1937–39*, Toronto, Musson, 1940, pp. 66–67.) Some of Speer's contemporaries, however, found a political significance in the *Lichtdom*. Schrade maintained that the Sudeten Germans in Czechoslovakia, about 113 kilometers away, could see these lights. (*Bauten dritten Reiches*, p. 20.) It has been suggested that Speer did not discover this method of illumination himself, but rather derived the idea from a 1929 light festival project of Naum Gabo (1890–   ). (John Elderfiield, "Total and Totalitarian Art," *Studio International*, (April 1970) p. 154.)

[59] See the photographs on pp. 26–27 in Wolters, *Albert Speer*.

[60] Schrade, *Bauten des dritten Reiches*, p. 21. The American army blew up these towers after the war.

and ordered construction to begin in 1935. Originally the plans called for the use of reinforced concrete, but Hitler, "as befitted his task to build for eternity," decided the walls would be built of "pure" granite blocks.[61] This sixty-meter-high building rose between Luitpold Field and Dutzend Lake, at the northern end of the parade avenue.[62] Its curving façade, which corresponds in shape to the horseshoe curve of the interior stands, has a "mighty" arcade running around its entire length. Above this, two rows of arched windows, set deep in heavy rectangular frames, give the impression of order and permanence.[63] Two smaller halls adjoin the main auditorium on the side of the lake. The main hall was to have a free-standing roof stretching 160 meters across the floor. Hitler's lectern would occupy an appropriately prominent position near the center of the projecting stage. This stage was to have 2400 seats, leaving space for 900 standards. The latest electronic technology was to be used for sound and light. Yet, inside, the large window in the ceiling would give the impression that meetings here took place "under the open sky."[64] Even at indoor rallies, the "Aryans" would enjoy the healthy proximity of nature.[65]

Another building which was never finished — indeed, of which only the excavations were begun — was the German Stadium, designed by Speer. This ninety-meter high horseshoe-shaped amphitheater was to hold 300,000 people on five banks of seats and was to have been the biggest stadium ever built.[66] (Hitler himself had again enlarged the original plans.) It would hold

[61] Fritz Todt, "Bauschaffen im Dritten Reich," Bauen, Siedeln, Wohnen, XVIII:8 (April 5, 1938), 228.

[62] See the photographs in Troost, Bauen, I, 30–31.

[63] Ibid., p. 30.

[64] Ibid.

[65] Although construction of this hall began in September 1935, the outbreak of war prevented it from ever being finished.

[66] See the photographs of models in Wolters, Albert Speer, nos. 28–31. Troost maintains that 500,000 people could be seated in the stadium (Bauen, I, 30), but Spear states only 300,000. ("Die Bürde werde ich nie mehr los," p. 50. See also the Erinnerungen, p. 81; Inside, p. 68.)

nearly four times as many spectators as Berlin's Olympic Stadium; its field would be three times as big, and its outer walls, five times as high.[67] The main entrance would be through a forecourt dominated by a templelike structure; the forecourt's floor would be divided into square patterns for orderly demonstrations. Between the courtyard and the field itself was to stand a giant statue by Thorak, eighteen meters high. To be constructed of red-gray granite, "building material to last centuries,"[68] the outer walls would be rusticated, and broken on the first level by a large arcade. Braziers would crown the "battlement."[69] German oaks were to be planted on the grounds outside. The German Stadium would be bigger than the Circus Maximus of ancient Rome, said Lotz, who noted also that it was designed for sporting contests between the best men of the *Volk*, "as in ancient Greece." In accordance with its "community" function, too, it would "fuse spectator and contestant into a unity."[70]

These buildings were a setting for the mass political experience of the German "community." Before the Nuremberg center was built, said Gerdy Troost, Germany lacked "a shrine for the whole nation" which could strengthen community bonds; previously, the *Volk* was a "formless mass without inner cohesion . . . without an idea, which it could experience in common."[71] But now, in these rally grounds, the "communal experience of the unity of *Führer* and *Volk* was possible."[72] Rittich wrote that, although

[67] Troost, *Bauen*, I, 30. It was "even more gigantic" than the Congress Hall, said Troost.

[68] *Ibid.*, 30.

[69] Rittich, *Architektur und Bauplastik*, p. 51.

[70] Wilhelm Lotz, "Das 'Deutsche Stadion' für Nürnberg," *Moderne Bauformen*, XXXVI (1937), 491–492. There is some doubt that this fusion could really occur, for, as Dehlinger conjectures, from the highest seats, ninety-two meters up, it would be impossible to see what was happening in the field below. (*Architektur der Superlative*, p. 70.)

[71] Troost, *Bauen*, I, 24. Here, observed Hans Stephan, "The importance of the individual yields to the importance of the group." (*Die Baukunst im dritten Reich*, p. 11.)

[72] Troost, *Bauen*, I, 30. For Lotz, too, the grounds were a "proof of German will and strength." ("Das Reichsparteitaggelände in Nürnberg," p. 194.

these buildings were designed to direct attention to the *Führer*, they were also to relate him to the "community."[73] The theme of unity and oneness extended to the materials of the building itself, as noted previously in writings on the Reich Chancellery, the Paris pavilion, and the Olympic Grounds. Lotz wrote that "the soil of all German *Gaue* offers its most beautiful stones, just as the German craftsmen from all regions have a part in this great and unique creation."[74]

Thus the Nuremberg Rally Grounds were a "community" achievement, the most explicit example of the Nazi drive to create through "community" architecture and communal experiences a new sense of unity in Germany. But there are many other examples of this effort, in particular, *Volk* halls and parade squares.

Every German town, even if it could not afford a large stadium, was to have a *Volk* hall. These new "community houses" would combat the efforts of Marxist architects to make the German environment "ugly" and the German people "unhappy, dissatisfied, and nihilist."[75] Such *Volk* halls would have an influential role in the smaller towns. Gottfried Feder thought the *Volk* hall should be built near the square at the center of the town.[76] More detailed instructions were given in an article called "Community Buildings." The *Volk* hall should be the most important building in a town, forming its core, and serving immediately and exclusively "the idea." The medieval cathedral or church was removed from the life of this world, said the writer, but the *Volk* hall stood in the midst of life as a meeting place under the open sky. Only in unusual circumstances, or when dictated by the landscape, should the hall be placed apart. Means for building it might be sparse, but it must stand out because of its "inner significance." A tower

[73] Rittich, *Architektur und Bauplastik*, p. 50.
[74] Lotz, "Reichsparteitaggelände in Nürnberg," p. 194.
[75] Kretschmer, "Uber die Aufgaben des Amtes für 'Schönheit der Arbeit,'" cited in Teut, *Architektur*, p. 282.
[76] Feder, *Die neue Stadt*, p. 113.

was useful, for "the expressive strength of the tower cannot be fixed too highly."[77]

Another critic gave even more precise directions. The *Volk* hall, he said, should be simple. This was unavoidable, because villages could not afford expensive structures, and also necessary, in order to avoid the excesses of the nineteenth century and the utopian aberrations in the plans of men like Taut. Later generations could always add decoration to the halls. Preferably built in the local style, each could have a simple lobby and consist of one large room, with a sculptured group at one end and stone tablets on the walls to commemorate the deceased and historical events. The best location for this community shrine was on the town square, so that it could function as a backdrop for outside celebrations.[78]

As with many party headquarters, older buildings were often used as *Volk* halls. Many new structures were built, however, and many planned, although few had the magnitude of Speer's plans for a domed *Volk* hall in Berlin.[79] (See illustration nos. 50–51.) Most were relatively modest structures like Franz Stadler's hall in Garmisch-Partenkirchen, with white plaster walls, a tiled pointed roof, and extensive use of decorated wood.[80]

In *Mein Kampf*, Hitler wrote about a mass demonstration of socialists in front of the Royal Palace in Berlin after the war;

[77] Josef Umlauf, "Die Bauten der Gemeinschaft," p. 33. Umlauf was concerned with building German settlements in the conquered eastern lands.

[78] Günther Martin, cited in Hubert Schrade, "Der Sinn der künstlerischen Aufgabe," pp. 512–513. Martin was an architect and sculptor. See also "Richtlinien für die Errichtung von Gemeinschaftshäusern," pp. 206–208. A *Volk* hall that could be built without the aid of modern technology and that resembled a simplified medieval town hall was described by Schrade. (*Das deutsche National-denkmal: Idee, Geschichte, Aufgabe*, Munich, Langen-Müller, 1934, pp. 113–114; ill. no. 26; this publisher was directly administered by the Nazi *Zentralverlag*.)

[79] Planned as part of a vast enclosed square, that would encorporate and dwarf the old Reichstag. (See Speer, *Erinnerungen*, pp. 160–175; *Inside*, pp. 151–160.) Hitler's sketch for a version of this *Volk* hall can be seen in Reel 3, Folder 64, Film 1004 of the NSDAP Hauptarchiv.

[80] See the photograph in Troost, *Bauen*, I, 135.

A sea of red flags, red scarves, and red flowers gave to this demonstration, in which an estimated 120,000 took part, an aspect that was gigantic from the purely external point of view. I myself could feel and understand how easily the man of the people succumbs to the suggestive magic of a spectacle so grandiose in effect.[81]

The Third Reich provided many stages for the Nazi variety of spectacle. In the parade or market square, more people could congregate than in the Volk hall, and the demonstration was open for nonparticipants to observe. Here, too, more so than in the hall, the crowd became an element of architecture. Finally, of course, the square gave the Volk a sense of "community," and did so better than the hall as it allowed for even more of the faithful to participate in the ritual. In a sense, the Nuremberg buildings and the Olympic Stadium fulfilled this function; on the local level, however, the square or even the field was the most practical way to achieve this goal. Aside from inculcating a sense of togetherness, mass political demonstrations, for domestic and foreign consumption, were staged here. Enemies of all sorts could be intimidated by these disciplined, marching, singing crowds. The mass assembly itself, wherein individuals were molded in groups to fit a larger pattern or whole, could be considered the more coercive aspect of patriotic architecture theory.[82]

The square was one of the most important forms in city building, Schultze-Naumburg had written in 1909, for it could have the appearance of a "great ceremonial hall under the open sky," as did the Old Market in Dresden, which was completely enclosed on four sides. Indeed, this enclosed quality was the most desirable attribute of any square.[83] Schultze-Naumburg was concerned more with the traditional appearance of old German cities, a feeling shared, by many Nazi sympathizers.

[81] Mein Kampf, p. 492.
[82] A nationalist writer noted that Mussolini had reformed the Piazza Venezia to give Rome a new center and to allow for demonstrations and displays of the Italian people's "will." (Sepp Schüller, Das Rom Mussolinis: Rom als moderne Hauptstadt, Düsseldorf, Mosella, 1943, p. 95.)
[83] Schultze-Naumburg, Städtebau, p. 80. (Illustrations 63–64a.)

But Feder, in *Die neue Stadt*, placed a more political meaning on the square. Every city of 20,000 needs one for party functions, he said, and as participant and spectator, every inhabitant should be able to find room in the municipal square. It was good if the city hall on the square had a balcony for speechmaking. Most older cities had such equipment, but for large demonstrations, "a *Volk* field" or square at least twice as big should be built with the sport field.[84] Another writer noted that outdoor meeting places should always be rectangular or square, because this was a genuinely "Aryan" form.[85]

One of the first notable ideological ceremonies of the Third Reich was held, not in an urban square, but on an open field, the Tempelhof Field in Berlin, previously the site of annual spring and autumn parades of the Berlin garrison with 50,000 troops. Here, on May 1, 1933, the party held a great celebration, the Day of National Labor, the backdrops of which were designed by Speer. The latter wrote that the old squares and stadiums were no longer large enough, implying that, because the *Volk* itself was now the "living base of the state," it needed places where, in mass meetings, it could become a visible force. Since the field was open on all sides, Speer tried to give the occasion a "visible focus," "so large and powerful . . . that it worked as a symbol of the event, as the expression of the will of the assembling masses of people." This focus was a flag tribune 100 meters long and ten meters high from which hundreds of flags and banners could be unfurled. The celebration was held at night, according to the best Hitlerian prescriptions,[86] and Speer described it as follows: "The mountain of flags made radiant by thousands of lights stood with

[84] Feder's new city was divided into sections, and this field was to be built in the western main part. (*Die neue Stadt*, p. 179.) On the importance of squares for marches and reviews in "German" cities of eastern Europe, see Hans Bernard Reichow, "Grundsätzliches zum Städtebau im Altreich und in den neuen deutschen Osten," *Raumforschung und Raumordnung*, H. 3–4, 1941, cited in Teut, *Architektur*, p. 336.

[85] "Deutsche Baukultur in Böhmen und Mähren," *Bauen, Siedeln, Wohnen*, 1939, 19. Jahrgang, p. 329.

[86] *Mein Kampf*, p. 475.

its glowing red in stark contrast to the dark blue of the evening sky, while all irrelevant and intrusive elements sank away into the evening twilight."[87] In his propaganda diary, Goebbels wrote that the occasion offered "a grandiose picture of National Socialist will to form . . . the whole *Volk* is to unify itself in one will and one readiness."[88] The party repeated this outdoor demonstration in its harvest festivals, 1933–1937, on the Bückeberg near Hamelin. Speer designed the first of these, for October 1, 1933,[89] but instead of an open field, he utilized a mountain slope and a natural depression to give the occasion a framework; in the evenings, the "cathedral of light" effect was used "to increase the sense of a great open space."[90] On other occasions already existing fields, such as the Theresienwiese in Munich, were used.

As for urban squares, the new government often remodeled and "improved" older ones. For example, the square in front of the Technical University in Berlin had its thick growth of trees removed because they prevented the monumental buildings from being "appreciated." The newly paved square became "simpler," better able to stress the monumental façade of the university. Here large stands were erected for "*Führer* parades." Across the street another monumental structure was planned.[91] Similar "im-

[87] Albert Speer, "Die Aufbauten auf dem Tempelhofer Feld in Berlin, zum 1. Mai 1933," *Baugilde*, Heft 13 (1933), cited in Teut, *Architektur*, pp. 187–188. See the photographs in Wolters, *Albert Speer*, pp. 8–9.

[88] Goebbels, *Vom Kaiserhof zur Reichskanzlei*, p. 304. Goebbels expressed here the desired effect. It is possible that it did not transpire on this occasion. Sigmund Graff reports that one if the officials told him Hitler was not pleased with the results and concluded that this sort of gigantic meeting needed an architectural framework: on an open field it looked "stupid and boring" and disorderly. (Sigmund Graff, *Von S.M. zu N.S. Erinnerungen eines Bühnenautors 1900–1945*, Munich-Wels, Welsermühl, 1963, p. 125. Graff was a playwright and an assistant to Rainer Schlösser, Reich Theater Chamber president.)

[80] See the photograph of a wooden model in Wolters, *Albert Speer*, p. 10.

[90] *Albert Speer*, p. 5. According to Speer himself (Correspondence, October 24, 1969), the attempt to create the *Lichtdom* effect failed here, because only movie lights were available. Apparently, Wolters' enthusiasm led him to exaggerate.

[91] Rittich, *Architektur und Bauplastik*, p. 103. See p. 360, illustration no. 537 in Schulte-Frohlinde, *Die landschaftlichen Grundlagen*. See also the plans

provements" were wrought by Speer on the *Lustgarten* for celebrations on May 1, 1936, Schinkel's Old Museum providing the
backdrop. Its templelike façade was decorated with long banners,
and at night illuminated with searchlights; stands were also built
on the side of the square, surmounted with more "flag walls." The
gardens were removed and replaced with square-motif pavement.[92] (See illustration no. 53.)

The most significant remodeling of a pre-existing square was
the paving of the Königsplatz in Munich, and the removal of sections of lawn there. (See illustration no. 52.) On one end of the
square Troost constructed the *Führer* Building and Administration
Building for the party headquarters as well as two temples of
honor. The Nazis had demonstrated here before 1933, so the
square had a special meaning for them. Hitler thought it was "the
most beautiful square in the Reich."[93] In 1935, therefore, 22,000
square meters of granite slabs were brought to Munich from the
Black Forest, the Odenwald and the Fichtelgebirge, for the surface of the Königsplatz. Apparently, this created a desirable organic connection between the new square and the soil of Germany.[94] The impression of inclusiveness was strengthened by the
low limestone sill built around the sides of the square. On the east
side, two steel flagpoles, each 33 meters high and topped by copper eagles, were erected; eighteen lampposts flanked the square,
giving "the giant space by night a further inclusive impression."
Loud-speakers were also installed. Thus, "the noblest architecture
of the past [the nearby Propylaen Gate] was united with the will

for Linz in *Linz, Stadt am Strom,* edited by Osterreich in Wort und Bild (Linz,
1962). (The pages are not numbered.)

[92] See the photographs on p. 13 of Wolters, *Albert Speer.* The Schlossplatz
in front of the Palace in Berlin was acceptable, even though it was not built as a
"community" meeting place, but rather to heighten the pomp surrounding Hohen-
zollern royalty. (Lindner, *Die Stadt,* p. 98; see illustration no. 182, on p. 99.)
There was praise for other older squares, such as the one designed by Frederick
Weinbrenner (1766–1826) for Karlsruhe.

[93] Cited in Hans Frank, *Im Angesicht des Galgens,* p. 92. See also *Mein
Kampf,* p. 547.

[94] Dresler, *Das braune Haus,* p. 24.

of the Third Reich to build monumentally." Since all vehicular
traffic was forbidden on the square, the "ceremonial character" of
the Königsplatz was increased further.[95]

Because this was one of the first architectural achievements of
the new Reich, much ink was used explaining its significance.
Dresler saw in it "the heroic character of the movement."[96] For
Troost, it was "a community space of the Volk."[97] The Königsplatz, Rittich added, for the first time met the demand for an
architecture that would express the feelings of the general public.
Here, the *Volk* could see a "stone symbol of the National Socialist
ideology, its greatness, its struggle, and its victory."[98] Another
writer was impressed with how the granite-covered square differed from the former lawn-covered one, and the difference lay,
for him, "not in the different material, but in the idea."[99] This
"idea" was the discipline that the Third Reich had restored to
Germany. Such at least was implied by Wolters, who wrote that
"every trivial chunk of lawn is gone from the square itself, yielding
to a grandiose expanse of stone slabs. With it, has been removed
from the new space everything accidental [and] natural and [the
square] has been given an austere form of stone."[100]

One of the few voices raised in dissent (albeit secretly) was
that of Rosenberg, who, as has been seen, was not always in tune
with the majority of approved opinion. It seemed to him that
Hitler was trying to "banish nature from architecture." The result
of "plastering" the Königsplatz with granite slabs, he thought,
was that it now looked like a barracks square. He was shocked
when he first saw the result of this "improvement," because all
the buildings around were "murdered" for the sake of a monu-

[95] *Ibid.*, p. 27. There is a photograph in Brenner, *Kunstpolitik* showing a
night rally on the square (no. 46).
[96] *Ibid.*, p. 10.
[97] Troost, *Bauen*, I, 12.
[98] Rittich, *Architektur und Bauplastik*, p. 32.
[99] Rolf Badenhausen, "Betrachtungen zum Bauwillen des Dritten Reiches,"
Zeitschrift für Deutschkunde (1937), cited in Wulf, *Die bildenden Künste*, p. 223.
[100] Wolters, *Neue Deutsche Baukunst*, p. 10.

mental effect.[101] Rosenberg's objection is a typical reaction of a man whose concept of the ideology differed from that of his *Führer*. Hitler was not seriously concerned about the sacred German soil or landscape, nor, although he had praised the original square, with expanses of lawns and gardens in cities. This sort of granite desert was planned for every German city.[102]

In the most grandiose of plans, the square was approached along a central parade avenue and was surrounded by monumental, representative buildings. Typical of these squares was the one planned for Augsburg, designed by Hermann Giessler. Wilhelm Kreis also planned a similar *Gau* center for Dresden with two temples of honor and a vast square before a large semiclassical *Gau* house. For Weimar, too, Giessler planned an Adolf Hitler Platz, surrounded by the *Gau* center with a large templelike structure and a tower.[103] These plans, of course, included *Volk* halls.

These types of "community" buildings — stadiums, *Volk* halls, and squares — were the simplest forms of unity-creating architecture. Despite their auxiliary functions, their purpose was primarily political and specifically nationalist. The square, for example, served as a site for military and political shows. It had few of the functions of the ancient Greek *agora* (although such connotations were intended by some writers) and was not designed to fulfill the social and cultural functions of the *piazza* or *campo* as they had developed in European urban history. Also coercively nationalist in function were the many other "community" structures erected, even when they were more traditional or less openly ideological.

[101] Rosenberg, *Portrait*, p. 274.
[102] Two other stone-paved squares were planned for Munich, on either side of the Old Pinakothek museum.
[103] See the photograph of a wooden model of this center in Troost, *Bauen*, I, 89.

CHAPTER NINE

Architecture for Social Order and Unity

THE HUGE stadiums at Berlin and Nuremberg, the *Volk* halls, and the parade squares were considered means for developing a greater sense of "community" in the German people, in accordance with the slogan, "the good of the community before the good of the individual." This ideal community of Germans would be well ordered and closely unified. Thus it was hoped that the new and planned military buildings, the monuments to soldiers and Party heroes, and the new highways would assure this disciplined order. The aim of unity would be achieved by more sophisticated structures.

Throughout the literature on architecture, there runs a concern for order (*Ordnung*) as a desirable quality in German society and as a feeling to be communicated by good German architecture. The writings on architecture, especially on military buildings, are filled with this concern for order, a concern which goes beyond the striving for good form. In the twenties, the German *Volk* was felt to have been "without order, without authority, without an ideology." But now, thanks to National Socialism, the Germans had an authoritative, disciplining principle of life. The new buildings served many purposes, but all were given their shape by this orderly *Weltanschauung*.[1] One writer maintained that order was synonymous with the *Volk* itself. A chaotic age, when the German people's instinct for order had been suppressed, had passed; the Third Reich would see the expression of this innate sense of order.[2] In a more specific, political sense, too, the new laws on building were for creating order. Laws which end indiscriminate "freedom to build" "give guidance and order."[3] These comments reflected the desire of millions of nationalist Germans both to see an end to the political disorders of the twenties and to return to the pre-1918 days when the class hierarchy was clear and the Kaiser on his throne. Architecture and ideology would provide a sense of national unity and strength; not only would the army itself be developed, but foreign incursions into German culture would be eliminated.

Furthermore, the love of order corresponds to the militarist aspect of the movement and its *Führerprinzip*. This principle, wrote Rosenberg, meant that a strong personality would be found for every task and would be given full powers with which to perform it.[4] The future Reich, said another writer, would be characterized by "inner militancy," by a "soldiery of the spirit."[5] Artists and architects should have this attitude, too; like the military commander, they also "must go through the toughest, hardest school of obedience."[6] The architect, then, should react to commands like a soldier.

[1] Troost, *Bauen*, I, 14.

[2] Schrade, "Der Sinn der künstlerische Aufgabe," p. 508. Wendland, too, wrote that architecture had an order-creating mission; a function of good "German" architecture was to remind all subjects of the authority of the state. (*Kunst und Nation*, p. 5.)

[3] Stephan, *Die Baukunst im dritten Reich*, p. 7. One of these laws was the Architects Laws, which required all architects who wished to practice to be members of the Reich Chamber. (See Teut, *Architektur*, pp. 99–100; for the laws on public housing, see pp. 105–106 in the same volume.)

[4] Rosenberg, *Portrait*, p. 322.

[5] Ernst Adolf Dreyer, ed., *Deutsche Kultur im neuen Reich*, Berlin, Schlieffen, 1935, p. 135. (Dreyer later became a publisher.)

[6] Richard Pfeiffer, "Die seelische Haltung," p. 29.

The government naturally considered the defense of Germany vital. As for the commentators, they believed that, since soldierly virtues were innate in the *Volk*, it was inevitable that Germans would provide well for their army and air force and would commemorate the exploits of fighters, both military and political. Such buildings and monuments would express German values and reflect the best qualities of the German community. They would also be representative architecture, teaching these attitudes and qualities. Much German architecture in this period therefore reflects the values of an orderly, regimented, militarist society; the severe lines of new buildings were echoed in the tough facial expressions of the sculpted figures which decorated them. Even as the architecture was hard edged, with few organic curves or "disorder," so the society was to be ordered and disciplined, allegedly according to its innate desires, and for the sake of its defence in a hostile world. To Fritz Todt (in charge of building the new highways), all the new monumental buildings were soldierly in spirit; they were "renderings in stone of the feelings and thoughts of the men who built them, masculine, robustly clean, truthful, serene of faith, every tower a sentinel, every wall a broad chest to be relied upon without misgiving."[7]

However, as Hitler said in a Reichstag speech on January 30, 1937, he wanted peace.[8] The commentators echoed this desire, and the whole building program of the Third Reich was supposedly witness to this pacific outlook.[9] Nevertheless, the government built as if it expected war.[10] Not only was every major building equipped with an air-raid shelter, but the appearance of much of the new architecture was warlike.

[7] Fritz Todt, introduction to Georg Fritz, *Strassen und Bauten*, p. 9.
[8] Domarus, *Reden*, p. 674.
[9] Rittich, *Architektur und Bauplastik*, p. 22. March called his Olympic grounds "a work of peace." (*Bauwerk*, p. 7. Troost uttered similar sentiments. (*Bauen*, II, 5.)
[10] In the catalog for the German Art Exhibition of 1938, of 113 models shown, 75 were of military buildings. (See *Erste Deutsche Architektur-und Kunsthandwerkaustellung.*)

The Third Reich built many new monuments to past military victories and many new buildings to house and serve the expanded armed forces. As for their appearance, they were to have the "heroic" style given to German architecture by Hitler.[11] In practice, this included towers, rusticated stone, and small windows. The militant towers of the March Field in Nuremberg and the Olympic Grounds in Berlin, as well as the many parade squares, covered with stone, have already been noted. The more specifically military buildings of the Third Reich include these features; their style was often *völkisch*, sometimes Romanesque, occasionally classical, but in the larger structures (especially monuments) it was most often a mixture of Germanic and Romanesque elements, favored by Schmitthenner and Bonatz, but also recalling the heroic days when the "first" German Reich covered much of central Europe.

In mood, these structures also echoed a more recent period. Pre-1914 Germany saw much building of monuments, the most significant being the Teutoburger Forest Monument (1875) to Hermann the Cheruscan (who, in A.D. 9 defeated the Romans), the Niederwald Germania Monument (1883), and the monument to the 1813 Battle of the Nations in Leipzig (1913).

Hubert Schrade devoted a whole book to the frustrating search for a truly "German" national monument. "With us Germans . . . ," he complained, "the idea of the national monument has been all too often connected with extremely vague if not actually contradictory, concepts, . . . and also burdened with memories, [and] forms, which are simply not worthy of the German *Volk*."[12] For example, in tracing the thwarted efforts of Germans through centuries to express their sense of nationality, he noted that too many memorials were "individualistic" in nature, reflecting the glory of one man rather than that of the nation.[13]

[11] Troost, *Bauen*, I, 14.
[12] Schrade, *Das deutsche Nationaldenkmal*, p. 5.
[13] See Schrade's chapter on "Das individualistische Denkmal des 19. Jahrhunderts," pp. 36–39.

None of the aforementioned monuments were really adequate; neither were the Valhalla (a German Hall of Fame constructed near Regensburg in 1830–1842) and the Hall of Liberation (built at Kelheim after 1842 commemorating the war against Napoleon), both in Bavaria. Schrade looked to the Third Reich for a solution to the dilemma.[14] After 1933, this concern for suitable monuments was expressed in works such as Will Decker's *Kreuze am Wege zur Freiheit*, which discussed, as part of one great national movement, monuments to the fallen of the Great War, the Freikorps battles, the Nazi Putsch of 1923, and the street battles with Communists.[15]

It is not surprising, then, that one of the most widespread building enterprises of the Third Reich was the construction of monuments to fallen patriots of all kinds. These were designed to remind Germans of the sacrifices made on their behalf, and to stand as symbols of German national identity; in the Third Reich, their form and style was particularly significant. Monuments constructed after 1933 were often in a different tone than those erected by the Weimar Republic (when "decadent" artists like Ernst Barlach [1870–1938] had been employed to execute memorials). In the Third Reich, the theme was more often that all soldiers had died heroes' deaths, and there was not the same element of sorrow expressed by earlier monuments (such as Barlach's

[14] Important for this study is Thomas Nipperdey's suggestion that, after many attempts to build a national monument which would truly represent the political and spiritual concensus of Germany, a type of monument was developed around 1900 which truly represented German feeling about the Reich, although not in the same sense that its builders meant. The Battle of the Nations Monument, with its heavy monumentality and seriousness, was to represent the *Volk* community and its strength, and was to be a reminder of the need for German national unity in a threatening Europe. Yet, far from being a statement of security and confidence, this monument symbolized the profound national insecurity of many Germans. For this reason, this memorial is the spiritual forebear of Nazi monuments and buildings of the Third Reich. ("Nationalidee und Nationaldenkmal in Deutschland im 19. Jahrhundert," *Historische Zeitschrift*, CCVI [1968], pp. 528–585).

[15] Will Decker, *Kreuze am Wege zur Freiheit: Ein Ehren- und Gedächtnisbuch*, Leipzig, Koehler, 1935. (Decker was an education official with the Labor Front.)

grieving mother on the Binnenalster in Hamburg), but rather a note of pride and joy in the sacrifice made for the *Volk* community. The construction of suitable monuments to battles and victories was important to Hitler. He sneered at the earlier "national" monuments.[16] Confident of his Germany's ultimate victory, he planned a giant victory gate, actually a double triumphal arch surmounting smaller arches and colonnades, for Berlin.[17] As stated, he also wished to make the Strasbourg cathedral a monument to Germany's unknown soldier. His desire to memorialize the great moments of his ascent to power initiated the building of the Temples of Honor in Munich.

The writers believed that there were suitable and unsuitable monuments. Wolfgang Willrich, a painter, labeled as Bolshevik and grotesque a monument executed by the sculptor Rübsam in Düsseldorf for the Fusilier Regiment General Ludendorff, and called Barlach's monument to the war dead in the Magdeburg cathedral the product of a "sick," "mentally disturbed" mind. On the other hand, Bernhard Bleeker's memorial in Munich showed the "great masterful expression of an artist whose senses are healthy."[18] Here, a statue of a dead soldier lying in state, his weapon at his side, was placed in a templelike shrine, constructed in a depressed basin below the surface of the ground; therefore, members of the *Volk* could actually enter the space of this monument, adding to its effectiveness.[19] For Rosenberg, it was also important to understand the symbolism of places such as the grave of Widukind, the Saxon leader who fought Charlemagne's forces. Proper monuments on these sites were often more useful, he said,

[16] *Mein Kampf*, p. 157.
[17] See the model in Brenner, *Kunstpolitik*, ill. no. 52.
[18] Wolfgang Willrich, *Säuberung des Kunsttempels; eine Kunstpolitische Kampfschrift zur Geseundung deutscher Kunst im Geist nordischer Art*, (2nd ed.) Munich, Lehmanns, 1938, pp. 55–56 and 146–147. Hitler was of the same opinion. (Correspondence with Albert Speer, February 22, 1970.) Bleeker (1881–) was an instructor at the Munich Academy.
[19] See illustration 23 in Schrade, *Das deutsche Nationaldenkmal*; and his great praise for it, pp. 107–112.

188   THE WORD IN STONE

than a lecture or a speech.[20] The mystical atmosphere of places
sacred to the Volk could definitely not be understood by a "non-
Aryan," who could easily desecrate both the memory of the dead
and a sacred site as well.

   Nevertheless, some pre-1933 monuments were praised in the
Third Reich. One earlier monument Hitler approved was the Victory Column in Berlin (1871–1873), which until 1933 stood in
front of the Reichstag building; after the fire of 1933, Hitler had
the column moved to the Great Star on the Charlottenburger
Chaussee, from which its golden Victoria figure could be seen
for several miles in either direction.[21] (This was to become the
east-west axis.) Another pre-Nazi monument which met with the
approval of Nazis and völkisch critics was the Tannenberg Memorial in East Prussia (see illustration no. 59.) designed by Walter and Johannes Krüger to commemorate the victorious Battle of
Tannenberg in 1914, which völkisch writers considered a revenge
for the defeat of the Teutonic Knights by the Poles near the same
site in 1415. Although it was executed in a period of "decadence"
(1924–1927), the writers found that, with its eight rectangular,
squat towers on a round, fortresslike structure of granite, it was
definitely "community" architecture. Allegedly, it revealed perfectly how Germans could construct a community building "in a
vividly völkisch landscape."[22] Schrade explained how Tannenberg
(which, after all, was only a memorial and not a stadium or Volk
hall) was indeed a community structure. The structure's round
fortress shape, he said, symbolized the united struggle of both the
living and the dead for the sake of the community.[23] Thus its
appearance was an appropriate symbol of the militant attitude
Germans should develop. With the burial in 1934 of the Volk

[20] Rosenberg, Tagebuch, pp. 33–34 (May 17, 1934).
   [21] Hitler valued the column as a monument to German victory over France
(see Speer, Erinnerungen, p. 154; Inside, p. 139) and wanted to use the square
in front of the old Reichstag as a parade ground and demonstration center.
   [22] See the photograph in Troost, Bauen, I, 40.
   [23] Stephan, Baukunst des dritten Reiches, p. 38. See also his Das deutsche
Nationaldenkmal, p. 105.

hero, Hindenburg, in the Tannenberg monument, Rosenberg envisaged the creation of other similar centers that would eventually replace churches as places of worship for Germans.[24]

One man who came in for special praise in this period was Wilhelm Kreis, an architect who had been designing monuments before 1914 and who received many commissions in the Third Reich. He had produced over fifty Bismarck monuments (usually massive columns), as well as monuments to legendary *Volk* heroes like Siegfried.[25] A patriot who believed he was serving his people, Kreis took much of his inspiration from the same sources as the *völkisch* movement. Believing that both Germanic and Greek culture derived from identical roots, he mixed Teutonic and classical motifs in his monuments.[26] His works express a militancy and solidity, which was supposed to symbolize the desired national identity of Germans.

Another architect active before 1933 in the field of monuments was Robert Tischler, whose work was also considered

[24] Rosenberg, *Tagebuch*, p. 55 (August 19, 1934). According to Nipperdey, certain pre-1914 monuments were already taking on a religious significance. (Nipperdey, "Nationalidee und Nationaldenkmal," p. 537.) The Tannenberg monument was blown up by retreating German armies in 1945, so that the advancing Russians should not have the pleasure of desecrating it (just as Goering's Karinhall was destroyed deliberately).

[25] From 1928 to 1933 he was president of the League of German Architects and after the Nazi takeover, honorary president. See his own comments on his work in Stephan, *Wilhelm Kreis*, pp. 93–94, and his essay "Kriegermale des Ruhmes und der Ehre im Altertum und in unserer Zeit," *Bauwelt* (1943), cited in Teut, *Architektur*, pp. 222–6. He is praised in Schrade's *Das deutsche Nationaldenkmal*, p. 100.

[26] One of his articles is a compendium of the *völkisch* views of German architecture and society in the twentieth century. He lamented the growth of materialism and foreign ideas in building and maintained that he tried to build "for the community" creating works which would be "an expression of inner unity and outward strength." ("Die Grossbauten der Partei und des Staates im Bilde der Stadt und der Landschaft," *Baugilde*, XLII:30 [October 25, 1938], 1035.) Like his contemporary, Theodor Fischer, Kreis was interested in developing the expressive qualities of stone, an undertaking which endeared him to the racists with their zeal for native materials taken from the sacred German earth. (*Baugilde* was the organ of the League of German Architects, one of the profession's major organizations, which became enthusiastically pro-Nazi in 1933.)

appropriate by Nazi writers. Tischler, like Kreis, had received several commissions from the *Volk* League for the Care of German War Graves. With their use of rough stone, monumentality, and simplicity, Tischler's fortresslike monuments seem quintessentially "Nazi"; yet they were produced before the Third Reich, another indication that Hitler's architects had a rich vein of peculiarly "German" architecture to use as models.[27] Troost considered Tischler's memorials "community" monuments, because they expressed the values appropriate for good Germans. For example, his Fortress of the Dead atop a barren hill, at Bitolj in Yugoslavia, consisted of a squat tower attached to a round fortress. Its "powerful mass," said Troost, towered above the landscape as a Teutonic "heroic ballad."[28]

Construction of monuments to the Great War heroes continued in the Third Reich. The Freikorps were also commemorated in a monument at Annaberg in Upper Silesia, built in 1936–1938. On this "frontier," significant as a battleground against the Slavs, the monument "rose like a gun turret on a tank."[29] It was also a round fortress, reminiscent of Bitolj, on top of a hill, beneath which was a *Thing* place. Here the dead *Volk* comrades were suitably honored and their heroic deaths glorified. Also in 1936, another round fortresslike tomb was erected on the Pordoijoch in Italy.[30] Monuments like these spoke "for all time of battle, sacrifice, and victory." As the prehistoric cairns of the Teutons and the tomb of the Gothic Emperor Theoderic, they were "great art, formed to express heroic spirit," and could serve as "models for the architecture of the Homeland itself."[31]

[27] The monuments described here are illustrated in Troost, *Bauen*, I, 40–45, and in Rittich, *Architektur und Bauplastik*, pp. 43–45.

[28] Troost, *Bauen*, I, 40. According to Tacitus, the early Germans had a different attitude to memorials: "They disdain to show honor by laboriously rearing high monuments of stone which would only lie heavily on the dead." (Tacitus, *Germania*, Stuttgart, Reclam, 1962, pp. 24–25.

[29] Troost, *Bauen*, I, 40.

[30] See the photograph in Hans Weigert, *Geschichte der deutschen Kunst*, Frankfurt, Umschau, 1963, II, 278.

[31] Troost, *Bauen*, I, 40 and 42.

On March 16, 1941, after a second war for the *Volk's* survival had broken out, and hence the need for more monuments to Germany's heroes arose, Hitler appointed Kreis general architectural advisor for the building of military cemeteries. Kreis had worked with Speer on the remodeling of Berlin, for which he planned a giant soldiers' hall.[32] In his new position, he was to plan and to supervise the building of a series of monuments which would dot the map of Europe from east to west, north to south, celebrating German sacrifice and victory. These were representative buildings, bearing a message for all Europeans. They would also be "more than places for honoring the dead," for they would embody on sites of crucial military decisions, "the meaning of a great historical turning point." Those on the Atlantic coast would be "eternal" monuments to "the liberation of the continent from dependence on Britain and to the unification of Europe under the leadership of its German heart *Volk*." The most significant of these was the giant pyramid to be constructed on the Dnieper River, "symbol of the defeat of the chaotic forces of the eastern steppes by the disciplined power of Germanic order-giving strength."[33] (See illustration no. 60.) The Romanesque design of most of these tombs was also symbolic of "the German inheritance of the spirit of ancient Hellenic culture."[34] Such monuments so pleased Hitler that he awarded Kreis the Eagle Shield of the German Reich in 1943.

Meanwhile, the party planned and built monuments to itself. A monument to Albert Leo Schlageter, a young Nazi shot by the occupying French forces in the Ruhr in 1923, was built on the

[32] He had also planned a large "freedom square" for a spot on the Rhine near Bingen to commemorate Germany's struggles since 1806, a structure resembling a huge acropolis. (See the model, ill. no. 41, in *Erste Deutsche Architektur und Kunsthandwerkaustellung*.)

[33] Troost, *Bauen* II, p. 7; for those planned for Norway and Sweden (also by Kreis), see pp. 12 and 15. Ironically, the largest monument in German-speaking Europe today is probably the Russian war memorial in Treptow Park, East Berlin (1949). In spirit and intent, it is closer to these Nazi monuments than any other European structure.

[34] Troost, *Bauen*, II, 7.

Golzheimer Heide near Düsseldorf. Circular in shape, and sunken into the earth, it combined the qualities of the Tannenberg Monument with those of Bleeker's Munich memorial; its shape enclosed "in a unit, in a community, the people gathered within."[35]

The most famous monuments, however, were the two Temples of Honor in Munich near the *Führer* and Administration buildings, part of the new Königsplatz. (See illustration no. 65.) Designed by Paul Troost, each consisted of twenty seven-meter-high fluted limestone pillars on a square platform. Braziers on ten-foot stands stood between the pillars. Within each roofless temple, on a depressed level, were eight coffins containing the remains of those killed in the *Putsch* of 1923. The architect's widow declared that these temples corresponded to "the greatness and living strength of the idea"; "no damp vault encloses the coffins of the fallen. Surrounded by towering pillars, they rest under the open sky of their Homeland, flooded with sunlight, [or] covered with snow." Nothing separated these heroes from the natural environment of the community for which they died.[36] "A dignity and clarity which reflects a soldierly, disciplined feeling for life" was expressed in the temples.[37] Thus they met the demands of many critics for German "community" architecture; a sense of disciplined order, respectable classical (in this case, "Doric") design, and a special relationship to the elements of nature.[38] Few writers noted that each temple had a framework

[35] Schrade, *Das deutsche Nationaldenkmal*, p. 10; see ill. no. 1. Comment on another monument to Schlageter is part of the cult of the German earth and of the sun. According to an article in *Das Bild*, this monument would be built near Schlageter's home town in the Black Forest, in harmony with its mountainous locale. "No cold stone" should be used here, the article said, but wooden (organic) materials. "Like a holy place, like a castle of the Holy Grail, it must crown the mountain and the land . . ." The Egyptian pyramids and medieval cathedrals were cited as models. ("Die Schlageter-Gedächtnishalle auf dem Belchen," *Das Bild* (1934), cited in Wulf, *Die bildenden Künste*, pp. 257–258.)

[36] Troost, *Bauen*, I, 20.

[37] Rittich, *Architektur und Bauplastik*, p. 36.

[38] Rosenberg found their effect "unfortunate"; the pillars were too thin for what they seemed to support and the "will to symmetry" had damaged the whole complex. He told Hitler that "sixteen men had fallen at the Feldherrnhalle, not

of steel beneath its stone, a structural element which might have clashed with the desire for pure classicism in natural stone.

Also planned for Munich was the Monument to the Movement, to be 99 meters high and to weigh 100 tons. This pillar, for which Hitler himself drew up the plans, and which would be surmounted by the symbolic eagle, would be built in 1947, on Munich's east-west axis. The finished monument would easily surpass in size and impressiveness the Second Reich's Victory Column in Berlin.[39]

All these plans, of course, assumed the ultimate victory of Germany and, needless to say, the continued rule of the Nazis in the Reich. To attain this end, a strong armed force as well as a powerful Nazi elite force were necessary. A movement with these aims and with such a stress on discipline and order provided well for its military forces. The buildings of the Reichswehr and the Luftwaffe, as well as the Ordensburgen, drew much comment from the writers who saw them as expressive of the ideology.

There was no one unified style for the military structures.[40] Their appearance ranged from Romanesque through *Biedermeier* and indigenous rural, to neo-classical; sometimes older appropriate buildings were taken over. (The Spielburg fortress in Brünn was renovated by the army as a barracks.) As well as monuments to, and an encouragement of, military virtues, the variety of styles in these buildings expressed all views on nationalist architecture.

eight multiplied by two." Rosenberg, who did not like the Königplatz either was again out of step with Hitler. (Rosenberg, *Portrait*, p. 274.) These temples were destroyed in 1947 by the American army and the coffins buried elsewhere.

[39] It would also be three times as high as Munich's famous Church of Our Lady, and would therefore dominate the skyline.

[40] Gerdy Troost was pleased to note the 'indigenous" form (yet "without romantic imitation") of many of these structures, and she was not disturbed to find many different styles reflected in military buildings. On the contrary, she wrote, "these buildings show that in an age of the most rigid political concentration of Reich unity, not only is any uniformity of cultural life avoided, but rather . . . the multiplicity of indigenous cultural development . . . has been fostered." (*Bauen*, II, 6.) Given the mentioned lack of a totalitarian approach to architecture, Troost must be considered correct in this manner.

Furthermore, the ultimate goal being to build a strong Germany, one finds army buildings described as "community" structures.[41]

In *Der Deutsche Baumeister*, an interesting article on ideal German barracks stated ideas that were not always followed in actual construction, but revealed facets of the broad theory of architecture. In any camp, each battalion should be given its own barracks, which should be about the same size as that of other battalions: after all, every *Volk* soldier was the equal of every other. Yet the clear subdivision of types of buildings would make possible effective discipline. In designing a barracks, then, the architect had to consider this ancient problem of order. Yet the individual barracks should stand on an equal level with every other barracks; they might even be aligned in ranks. The author opposed erecting monumental buildings in an army camp but also objected to flat roofs. Economies should be taken in building, he said, which should not, however, lead to primitiveness but to "healthy simplicity." Finally army camps should harmonize with the surrounding landscape. This necessitated the correct choice of building materials and styles. However, if timber were scarce, no fixtures should be of wood. The army should reject the current attempt to revive traditional, but expensive, forms of handicrafts. The writer may have been thinking of the air force's "eyries." He called such structures a manifestation of romanticism.[42] Some army architects seemed to share these views. In a barracks built in the Allgäu, for example, one finds general simplicity, pointed roofs, the traditional "onion tower" (*Zwiebelturm*) with clock.[43] (See illus-

[41] See, for example, Walter Deissner, "Die Kasernen, Adolf Hitlers," *Der deutsche Baumeister* (1939), cited in Teut, *Architektur*, p. 220. Dehlinger maintains that the buildings of the army and air force were largely uninfluenced by the ideology. (Dehlinger, *Architektur der Superlative*, p. 10.) However, if one considers the ideology in both its racial and its political aspects, the opposite seems to be true.

[42] Deissner, "Die Kasernen Adolf Hitlers," pp. 220–221. Teut speculates on possible tension between Goering and others in this matter (note, p. 221). Undoubtedly, Deissner would disapprove of Karinhall.

[43] Such structures are illustrated in Troost, *Bauen*, II, 28–29, and in Rittich, *Architektur und Bauplastik*, pp. 97 and 100. See also "Neue Kasernenbauten," *Kunst im deutschen Reich*, IV:5 (May 1940), 77–83.

tration no. 57.) The military architects did not try to build monumentally in these centers, which were usually sober and practical in appearance.

Nevertheless, in Berlin, Hitler planned a great monumental representative complex to both serve and honor his army. This was the Supreme Army Command (consisting of six major buildings) designed for the north-south axis and to become the "architectural zenith of Berlin."[44] (See illustration no. 64.) Planned by Kreis, it would contain a soldiers' hall to honor German military heroes and an eighteen-storey tower surmounted by a victory figure. The hall would have a huge granite vault, decked with flags, housing in an apse a statue of a soldier with sword and shield, flanked by eagles. Beneath this chamber was to be a burial crypt for great German soldiers. A large court of honor, opening to the Tiergarten, would have two temples of honor (as in Munich), and a huge obelisk supporting an eagle with outstretched wings. Nazi writers found such "rigidly articulated" (orderly) buildings appropriate.[45] Its "severe solemnity and soldierly rigidity" made the soldiers' hall a "symbol for eternity."[46]

The air force buildings covered a similar range of styles, from the severe classical headquarters in Berlin, to the luxurious *Horste* (eyries) in local styles; from some "modern" laboratories to Kransberg, an older castle in the Taunus Mountains. Overall unity of style was of no more concern here than it was in the army structures, yet nearly every building seemed to convey an ideological lesson.[47] Even the "functional" laboratories were didactic, teaching efficiency and sobriety.

[44] Troost, *Bauen*, I, 58.
[45] *Ibid.*
[46] Stephan, *Wilhelm Kreis*, p. 70. Another monumental army structure planned was a Danzig military school, a huge fortresslike building on a hilltop, five storeys high, with four square towers, "in harmony," said Frau Troost, "with the great historical tradition of the land of the Teutonic Knights." Troost, *Bauen*, II, 6).
[47] Lane finds air force architecture "free of the most striking features of the new [i.e. modern] architecture, [yet] usually executed in a very progressive manner which neither refers to tradition nor evokes military virtues." (*Architecture*

Perhaps the most well-known air force building was the Air Ministry in Berlin at the corner of Leipziger and Wilhelmstrassen, opened in 1935. (See illustration nos. 55–56.) The architect, Ernst Sagebiel, created a large, L-shaped structure in limestone with over 2000 rooms.[48] Panels of stone reliefs on the exterior portrayed German military heroes from Blücher to Hindenburg. The severe lines, relative absence of decoration, the disciplined rows of windows, as well as the iron fence and gate before the main courtyard give the Air Ministry that military bearing expected from "Nazi" architecture. Goering himself commented on the building in his speech at its opening in October 1935. For the first time, said the Luftwaffe chief, an impressive public building had been erected in "the spirit of Adolf Hitler and of National Socialism." It was also a sign of the new Reich's "joyful ability to create" that such a monument was constructed in eight short months. (Night and Sunday labor had been used.) In the Weimar period, he noted, political horsetrading would have extended the building time to twice that length. The Ministry was a "community" building, not the product of individual whims, but a building for everyone, something in which all Germans could take pride and consider their own. Constructing such an edifice provided work for the unemployed, too. The laborers were filled with "a will, a spirit, a drive forward," deriving from the *Führer's* inspiration.[49]

Goering expressed the main stream of official Nazi thinking about the major new buildings of the Third Reich: discipline, order, sacrifice, patriotism were shown in good "German" architecture. His words were echoed by those faithful writers, Gerdy

and Politics, p. 186.) Although this view seems correct, the patriotic commentators would disagree, finding these structures traditional.

[48] See the photographs in Troost, *Bauen*, I, 68–69. This building still exists in East Berlin; in 1968, its *völkisch* reliefs had been replaced with proletarian murals and a communist banner decorated one wall.

[49] It was a "symbol of a *Volk* community," he added, which would last for centuries because it was created by a unified people: a harmony of "workers of the fist with workers of the mind." (Goering, "Bauten des dritten Reiches," Rede beim Richtfest des Reichsluftfahrtministeriums, am 12. Oktober 1935, *Reden und Aufsätze*, Munich, Eher, 1938, pp. 194 and 196.)

Troost and Werner Rittich. The latter called the Air Ministry "large and mighty, soldierly in its layout and in the unity of all its parts."[50] It was executed in exactly the manner need to teach good German qualities to young people. Gerdy Troost believed the building had "grown out of the spirit of the Luftwaffe, tough, soldierly, disciplined."[51]

Whereas criticism of the new Reich Chancellery was rare, there was some discontent among Nazi leaders over the Air Ministry's grandiosity. Martin Bormann (Hitler's personal secretary) wrote that size alone could not take the place of hard work and that this opulent environment suggested too much high living in the air force.[52] Of course, this attitude was reflective of the rivalry among Hitler's cohorts. But the public attitude, too, was not always favorable. Berliners sneered that the Air Ministry was almost big enough to house all of Goebbels' propagandists.[53] In his speech on the occasion of the Ministry's opening, Goering denied that this was too luxurious a building.[54] But according to Speer, the Air Ministry was not big enough for Goering, who, after he had seen Hitler's plans for Berlin, wanted a huge new office building as a center for his work as *Reichsmarschall*.[55]

The air force seemed to differ from the main trends of thought on good "German" architecture by its technical buildings, particularly the experimental laboratories. The German Experimental Station for Air Travel (included in Troost's book) was a complex of buildings with many similarities to those *avante-garde* structures of the twenties that annoyed so many critics. (See illustra-

[50] Rittich, *Architektur und Bauplastik*, p. 122.

[51] Noting that the Air Ministry was surrounded by a nineteenth-century neighbourhood, Troost said, "our buildings become beacons"; "as a principle of order, they make painfully obvious the disaster of their surroundings." (*Bauen*, I, 52.)

[52] Bormann, *The Bormann Letters*, p. 131 [October 10, 1944].

[53] Stephen H. Roberts, *The House That Hitler Built*, New York, Harper, 1938, p. 132.

[54] Goering, "Bauten des dritten Reiches," p. 196.

[55] Speer, *Erinnerungen*, p. 151; illustrations following p. 160; *Inside*, pp. 136–137; illustrations following p. 286.

tion no. 58.) The red-brick montage hall, for example, had exposed structural members and much glass. Flat roofs and large surfaces of glass were repeated throughout.[56] As if unable to find a way to define these as typically German, Troost confines herself to a description of the manner in which the whole station was laid out.[57] Rittich also includes in his volume a photograph of a hangar in Brandenburg, a low, earth-hugging building of extremely fluid lines, a rounded roof, and long, large windows. He makes no comment.[58] However, the functional style of technological buildings was consonant with the ideology, not an indication that Goering or the Luftwaffe architects had found a loophole in any Nazi *Gleichschaltung* of style. Large windows, even entire walls of glass, were considered essential in a laboratory where as much light as possible was needed. Hitler knew the value of the air force and of its research. Neither from aesthetic conviction, ideological rigidity, nor lack of political sagacity would he prevent such buildings from being constructed. Besides, he was mainly concerned with the building of monumental, representative buildings. If it was felt necessary to justify their "modernity," their sober, efficient design could be called "German."

The ideology did influence air-force architecture in the smaller, local buildings, such as the air stations, called eyries, each designed in a style indigenous to its surroundings. These barracks, built in remote areas (which justified their having swimming pools and other recreational facilities), all had a *völkisch* character. Thus one finds here brick and stone widely used as well as thatched roofs, wall murals, and other indigenous touches.[59]

Elsewhere, too, the Luftwaffe's buildings had familiar qualities, considered ideologically appropriate by commentators. The local air-force center in Dresden (a neo-classical structure) was

---

[56] Troost, *Bauen*, I, 103–105 (photographs).

[57] *Bauen*, I, 87.

[58] Rittich, *Architektur und Bauplastik*, p. 168.

[59] See photographs in Rittich, *Architektur und Bauplastik*, pp. 92–99; and Troost, *Bauen*, I, 155, or Karl Gallwitz, "Fliegerhorste der Luftwaffe," *Die Kunst im deutschen Reich*, IV:6 (June 1940), 86–98.

considered "clear," "grandiose," yet also frugal" and "severe" in style.[60] With its tiled pointed roof and two obelisks, it also had two mottos carved beside the main entrance, Keep honor pure and muster weapons, and The German *Volk* must become a *Volk* of fliers.[61] In Munich, on Prince Regent Street, Bestelmeyer designed an office building for the Luftwaffe in a classical style, harmonizing with the other early nineteenth-century buildings of the neighbourhood. Creating typical Third Reich architecture, Bestelmeyer blended new structure with nearby traditional architecture and placed heavy statuary groups in forecourts.[62]

These military buildings are not the most significant structures erected in the thirties. Yet by avoiding experiments, stressing the indigenous, the classical, and the monumental, they represent the contemporary harmony between public opinion and the ruling clique.

Just as this "community" architecture was designed to strengthen the *Volk*'s unity and to aid in its defence, so the new Autobahnen were also to integrate all aspects of German life by providing easy and quick travel between the urban centers of Germany and between the cities and the rural areas. Of course, they also made national defence easier. The highways showed Germany's "new will to unification of the nation and of the German living space."[63] They were "the embodiment of the unity and authority of the new Reich," symbols of "extraordinary political significance." The new bridges, overcoming natural obstacles, expressed "a power binding the *Volk* together."[64]

The highways were "decorated" with the familiar symbols, mostly free-standing columns and eagles bearing swastikas. The

[60] It was designed by Kreis, whose plan had been chosen over nine others. (Stephan, *Wilhelm Kreis*, pp. 56–57.)

[61] See photograph in Rittich, *Architektur und Bauplastik*, p. 90.

[62] The main facade of the structure was recessed from the street, creating another parade square. (See Troost, *Bauen*, I, 80.)

[63] Stephan, *Baukunst im dritten Reich*, p. 8.

[64] Troost, *Bauen*, I, 98. The first of these highways, from Frankfurt to Darmstadt, was opened on May 19, 1935.

resting place near a bridge over the Saale River boasted a stone column surmounted by the eagle; the entry to the highway near Salzburg was to be flanked by two huge pillars each topped by eagles.[65] These trappings served to remind travelers of the national mission of this road network.

Highways were architecture, Rittich vigorously maintained. He wrote that their creator, Fritz Todt, had an understanding of form, a proper sense of structure and of the use of building material, as well as purely technical gifts. Hence the highways were "technology become architecture."[66] As for Todt himself, he found the building of the highways "an artistic commission."[67] Not only were they architecture, but they were "community" architecture as well. In the construction of the highways, he said, engineers and architects had learned to forget the follies of the liberal era and, as a team, to produce "genuine community work."[68] Rittich, too, considered their construction "a community accomplishment," because so many different experts were called in to advise on their design, from architects and engineers to landscape gardeners.[69]

Commentary on the highways coordinates with the general attitude to good architecture. According to Schönleben, because the concept of the highway network had allegedly originated with Hitler, it was fitting that the highways should be called The Roads of Adolf Hitler, structures built to "honor him."[70] For this writer, Hitler was the great architect-statesman who was personally remodeling the whole of Germany. As for Rittich, he typically

[65] See Fritz, *Strassen und Bauten*, p. 91, and Schulte-Frohlinde, *Bauten der Bewegung*, p. 76, respectively.

[66] Rittich, *Architektur und Bauplastik*, pp. 71 and 73.

[67] Cited in Eduard Schönleben, *Fritz Todt: der Mensch, der Ingenieur, der Nationalsozialist*, Oldenbourg, Stalling, 1943, p. 56.

[68] In fact, he considered the construction of parade squares for mass meetings, party schools, *Thing* places, and such buildings as an "architecture of the German landscape," a remodeling of the whole *Lebensraum*. Fritz Todt, ed., *Die Strassen Adolf Hitlers*, Berlin, Hillger, 1938, p. 228.

[69] Rittich, *Architektur und Bauplastik*, p. 73.

[70] Schönleben, *Fritz Todt*, pp. 64, 74, and 38.

described the highways and bridges as "grandiose" and "monumental."[71] The vocabulary here was the same as throughout this literature.

In themselves, the highways were remarkable achievements of modern technology, executed with respect for the value of natural beauty. Yet they also expressed the National Socialist ideology. "Our Nazi character corresponds to the new roads of Adolf Hitler," said Schönleben, "We want to see our goal far ahead of us, we want to strive directly and steadily toward the goal; intersections we cross, unnecessary delays are alien to us. We will not yield, we create for ourselves enough road on which to proceed, and we need a road which permits us to maintain a speed congenial to us."[72]

As for the "architect" Todt, he was praised for his ideological loyalty and faith. Although not trained as an architect, he was considered the correct breed of German builder. "The most attractive thing for him in his work was the close connection with the *Führer.*" Todt was the ideal "Aryan." He had a rigorous self-control and an indomitable will. Yet he also loved music and nature, feeling keenly the need to, in his own words, "protect Mother Earth." He was popular with young people, and was often asked to speak to youth groups which he willingly did, because he saw his work as "a legacy for future generations." Moreover, he apparently saw his architecture as didactic. This "unique engineer and artistic genius," who had belonged to the party since 1922, was also helping to bring German technology out of "a purely materialist and capitalist way of thinking."[73]

[71] Rittich, *Architektur und Bauplastik*, p. 76. Some of the bridges planned were, indeed, monumental, the most impressive being the bridge planned to span the Elbe River near Hamburg. This suspension bridge would have four pylons 178 meters high and each 20 meters wide, the whole structure being 1200 meters long: (*Architektur und Bauplastik*, p. 76) and this despite Todt's own warning that, in comparison to nature, an attempt to achieve more monumental effects would be out of place. (Cited in Schönleben, *Fritz Todt*, p. 72.)

[72] *Fritz Todt*, p. 13.

[73] *Fritz Todt*, pp. 12–21, and 55–58. Todt's background was, in fact, similar to Speer's. (See Speer, *Erinnerungen*, p. 209; *Inside*, p. 193.) The fact that, un-

The characteristic of the Autobahnen most often cited by the writers is their harmony with the German landscape. The effort to preserve the countryside from the destruction by modern engineering found praise throughout Europe, and this is what attracted non-Nazi architects (such as Paul Bonatz) to participate in the project.[74] Tight control was exercised on the design of all buildings near the highways, and only gas stations were permitted to stand close to the road. The new roads were justifiably praised by critics for their successful integration with the human and natural landscape and because they opened up new areas of the Fatherland for city dwellers.[75] For Bonatz, the highways led to a "rediscovery of Germany."[76] They were, in truth, one of the most praiseworthy and, with the passage of time, least "Nazi," architectural projects of the thirties.

Yet the commentators found the highways' harmony with the landscape and their human surroundings representative of a new *Weltanschauung* that had revived Germany. Writers, commenting on the buildings and bridges constructed for the highways, considered these structures as well as the Autobahnen themselves ideologically appropriate architecture. There was considerable latitude allowed in the style of buildings here, giving further evidence that a narrow concept of typical "Nazi" architecture is untenable.

Roderich Fick's small bridge over the Isar River near Tölz, Bavaria, was largely of wood, harmonizing with the local architecture and landscape.[77] In comparison, Bonatz built a huge

like Speer, he was not a professional architect, probably only made him more acceptable to Hitler.

[74] See Bonatz' article "Dr. Todt und seine Reichsautobahn," *Die Kunst im dritten Reich* (1942), cited in Teut, *Architektur* pp. 301–307; see also his chapter "Die Autobahnen," *Leben und Bauen*, pp. 158–70. The harmony between the German landscape and the new highways was the theme of a book of sketches published in 1939 by the Labor Front. (*Strassen und Bauten Adolf Hitlers*; the artist was Georg Fritz.)

[75] Rittich, *Architektur und Bauplastik*, p. 72.

[76] Bonatz, *Leben und Bauen*, p. 158.

[77] See the photograph in Troost, *Bauen*, I, 125.

bridge of stone over the Lahn River, with several monumental arches, reminiscent of a Roman aquaduct, but echoing the Romanesque lines of nearby Limburg cathedral. On the other hand, his steel suspension bridge across the Rhine at Cologne-Rodenkirchen seemed to grow from its urban location.[78] (See illustration nos. 68 and 69.) Yet each of these three bridges could be defended as appropriate to its own setting: a small village, a landscape with rolling hills with a rich medieval past, and an urban industrial locale. It was for writers like Troost, Rittich, and Schönleben to see the specifically National Socialist connotations in such structures. As for buildings, the same diversity is evident. The restaurant and hotel on the Chiemsee, near Munich, was a three storey low and heavy-eaved structure with picturesque shutters and much woodwork, white plaster, and an "oniontower." It showed, said Troost, how "indigenous beauty can be underlined and expanded" yet also serve practical ends.[79] The gas station at Chiemsee was in the indigenous style, but another service station, illustrated in Todt's own book, had horizontal lines, not in the Nazi "close-in-the-soil" sense, but in the "streamlined" trend popular in the thirties.[80] Nevertheless, these were approved by Troost and Todt, and in all likelihood by Hitler, who would not have allowed undesirable structures to be erected on a highway system named after and inaugurated by himself. Here again his own definition of "functionalism" came into play. *Völkisch* structures fulfilled a function which was essentially patriotic, but structures which ful-

---

[78] See the photographs in Bonatz, *Leben und Bauen*, opposite pp. 168 and 176. (Both of these bridges, at Limburg and Cologne, were destroyed in the war.)

[79] Troost, *Bauen*, I, 63; photographs on p. 101. This and the attached gas station were designed by Fritz Norkauer; see also Troost, *Bauen*, II, 101 and 102, for illustrations of two gas stations in a traditional style. For a typical example of this attitude, see Lindner's *Das Dorf*; he offered an illustration of a problematic gas station (no. 585); the sign was too large, but he approved of two large trees which stood close to the building. (*Die Stadt*, p. 226.) He also illustrated undesirable types of gas stations (nos. 130–132) and good designs (nos. 133 and 135). Directions for building good German gas stations are found on pp. 185–189; each structure, for example, should offer an opportunity for the use of craft skills.

[80] Troost, *Bauen*, I ,103; and Todt, *Die Strassen*, p. 29.

filled a purely technological function were acceptable. Hotels and restaurants were to provide mental and physical comfort; the gas stations were designed to serve machines — hence they could look like machines, while the building for serving humans had to have some human reference. Structures for maintenance or traffic service could be built with economy in mind without much concern for the materials used.[81] Rather than exceptions to any rule, the modern buildings and bridges on the Autobahnen (like those of the Luftwaffe) were typical examples of conformity to an official attitude which, however reactionary or petty bourgeois, was flexible and manysided. (See illustrations no. 66 and 67.)

When the new German army was adequately housed and when the new highways were finished, the German community might not necessarily become more closely knit. To create unity, structures of a more intensely psychological nature were needed. Monuments, military buildings and highways — as well as stadiums, fields, squares and halls — were the orthodox form of "community" architecture created by the Third Reich. But exotic structures, buildings which were considered more specifically ideological, and directly aimed at reflecting and stimulating community feeling, were built. These included the Ordensburgen, and above all, the *Thing* places.

Aside from the stadiums at Nuremberg and Berlin, few large buildings constructed in the Third Reich are as peculiarly nationalist in appearance and intent as the Ordensburgen, the largest in scale of all the monumental "community" buildings actually constructed. (See illustration nos. 61–63.) To call these elitist schools "community" centers may seem odd;[82] but Troost and others believed they were built to defend the community and in a style indigenous to Germany (with materials taken from the

[81] Stephan, *Baukunst im dritten Reich*, p. 9. Hartmann expressed the same idea when he wrote that glass walls might be suitable for the housing of machines, but young people and not engines lived in youth hostels. (*Werkhefte*, pp. 31–32.)
[82] This is Troost's word for them. (*Bauen*, I, 31.) See Harald Scholtz, "Die 'NS-Ordensburgen'," *Vierteljahreshefte für Zeitgeschichte*, XV:3 (July 1967), 269–298.

"sacred" German earth). Moreover, they consisted of a small community of men training together, learning the virtues of community living, recreating in microcosm the larger national community. The plans for each were supposedly developed from "the common experience and feelings" of future German leaders who were to inhabit them. These men wanted "a new form of community life."[83] The castles were to create an elite possessing "the strongest inner unity, clear uniformity of feeling, thought, and action."[84]

In 1933 Robert Ley, as Reich organization leader for the training of political leaders, gave out commissions to design Ordensburgen each capable of training one-thousand *Ordensjunker*.[85] As this term implies, these castles were to remind the trainees of the German crusades in the east and the military colonization of what is now Poland and Russia. As such, they expressed the militant racism of the Nazi ideology. Each was to be built on a new site, on hilltops, in remote areas, often on ancient Teutonic sacred places. In style, they hark back to the early Middle Ages, to that allegedly golden age of *völkisch* unity. Each castle was executed in a modified Romanesque, "serious, heavy, masculine," "like the castles of knights of an earlier age."[86] The layout of each was "austere." The materials used in construction, wood and stone, came from the surrounding area so that each castle complemented the landscape, indeed, seemed to grow out of it. Each has a tower, which, "as a sign of proud firm self-consciousness," looms above the complex. Yet these are water towers, not representative of a

[83] Rittich, *Architektur und Bauplastik*, pp. 65–66.
[84] Troost, *Bauen*, I, 31.
[85] Ley called the *Ordensburgen* "shrines." (Cited in Scholtz, "Die'NS-Ordensburgen,'" p. 274; this was not the generally held view, however, as Scholtz points out in his article.) The S.S. built what may have been the prototype *Ordensburg* near Paderborn in Westphalia, a town with historical roots going back to Charlemagne; it was constructed on the foundations of a medieval fortress.
[86] Rittich, *Architektur und Bauplastik*, p. 65. Yet more than with any other approved structures (except the factories), the *Ordensburgen* exhibited the influence of the *avant-garde*. Massive, simple forms are characteristic of all three: Crössinsee, Vogelsang, and Sonthofen. (See Schulte-Frohlinde, *Bauten der Bewegung*, pp. 11–26.)

romantic and pointless desire to decorate, but of good "German" functionalism. Rittich thought the Ordensburgen were impressive precisely because their function was expressed in their style.[87]

The Ordensburg at Vogelsang, near Gmuend, a hilly region south of Cologne in the Eiffel district, was designed by Clemens Klotz,[88] and seems to rise directly out of the mountainside, its four tiers of long low stone buildings (with pointed roofs), offering a view of a lake and hills. The largest of the castles, Vogelsang is still typical. One solitary tower rises above the central complex, which consisted of a hall of honor, a ceremonial hall, and a community house. The parade square was named Place of the Solstice, reflecting the cult of the sun and moon cycles in *völkisch* mythology. Planned, but never completed, was House of Wisdom, to crown the hill behind the main buildings, its massive tower and templelike façade giving the future complex the appearance of an acropolis or cult center. Klotz, the architect, was "totally involved" with the ideology, said one critic.[89] Like Speer and Todt, he evidently had the "correct" attitude for a German architect.

At Crössinsee, near Falkenburg in Pomerania, the Ordensburg, like Vogelsang, a complex of rusticated stone buildings, with a tall round tower, had most of the other facilities shared by these castles. Its stones were large; its woodwork, rough; its roofs, pointed. Throughout, there were the now familiar signs of the patriotic ideology: eagles, braziers, swastikas, exposed wooden roof beams, and here at Crössinsee, a *Thing* place (a theater shrine described below).[90] In the southern Allgäu, on Herman Giessler's plans, was built the third major Ordensburg, Sonthofen,

[87] Rittich, *Architektur und Bauplastik*, pp. 65–66.

[88] See the photographs in *Architektur und Bauplastik*, pp. 29–33. The best source of plans, photographs and side elevations of the *Ordensburgen* is Schulte-Frohlinde, *Bauten der Bewegung*, pp. 11–26.

[89] E. Bender, "Die Ordensburgen Vogelsang und Crössinsee," *Bauwelt* (August 1936), cited in Teut, *Architektur*, p. 210. Vogelsang suffered some damage during the war, but was repaired, and is now used by a Belgian contingent of NATO forces.

[90] See the photographs in Rittich, *Architektur und Bauplastik*, pp. 40–41.

with much the same fixtures, including a tower.[91] Troost's words are a good summary of the Nazi view of the castles: "the power and discipline" of these "representative community buildings," she said, "expresses the ideology and the age that created them."[92]

Relatively few Germans ever saw an Ordensburg, but many participated regularly in occasions of more intimate community feeling — in centers of orthodox worship and of entertainment. Whereas churches and theaters might be objectively considered community buildings they were not interesting as such to most Nazi and *völkisch* writers.

As for theaters, they were regarded by Hitler as representative monumental structures and his new Germany was going to be well supplied with them. Opera houses, in particular, had fascinated him from his evenings in Vienna at the Imperial Opera. He had the Nuremberg and Weimar opera houses renovated, and planned a magnificent new opera house for Munich. The enlarged Linz was to contain at least three new theaters, including a large opera house. "There are not enough theaters in Germany," said Hitler, "a lot of them were built in the seventies, it's true, but the number is no longer related to the importance of our population."[93] Of the several large theaters completed in the Third Reich, perhaps the most impressive were those in Saarbrücken and Dessau, both of which are severe, plain structures with neo-classical façades.[94] Yet these were not designed for the same "community"

[91] See photographs in Troost, *Bauen*, I, 36–37; Sonthofen is now used as an officer school by the German *Bundeswehr*.

[92] Troost, *Bauen*, I, 31. The official Nazi attitude to the *Ordensburgen* was expressed by the *Völkischer Beobachter* in 1936. See the articles "Ordensburgen der Bewegung: Auslesestätten der Besten der Nation" and "Verewigter Glaube: das Erlebnis Nationalsozialistischer Zukunftwillen und neuer deutschen Baukultur, die Ordensburgen Vogelsang, Sonthofen, und Crössinsee", Munich edition, April 24, 1936, no pagination.)

[93] S.C., p. 310 (February 19–20, 1942); *Tischgespräche*, p. 180. Gottfried Feder agreed with him. (*Die neue Stadt*, p. 204.)

[94] See Troost, *Bauen*, I, 85 and 86. In 1938, the Dessau theater was opened on May 29, and the Saarbrücken theater, on October 9. The former was built with private funds; the latter was a "gift" from Hitler on the occasion of the return of the Saar to the Reich; it became the official *Gau* theater of the Saar-Pfalz.

ends as were the aforementioned *Volk* halls and stadiums. Rather they seem to have been built to satisfy Hitler's desire to promote and to advertise German culture.[95] If they had any political purpose, it was more in this representative function than in any strictly "community" function.

Although Hitler had a special interest in theaters, he had none in churches. Hostile to the Christian Church, he rarely considered church buildings as "community" architecture, and to a great extent neither did his followers. Nevertheless, some *völkisch* writers did discuss the qualities of good German churches, apparently not understanding the fundamental antipathy of National Socialism to Christianity.

Indeed, in most Nazi planning, churches were to play a small role. Whereas the architectural centers of older settlements used to be churches, as symbols of a genuine, all-embracing community, this was not so in the twentieth century.[96] If churches were to be built in new communities, they must hold a more modest position than formerly. Few churches were deliberately destroyed by the new government (versus synagogues), but there were plans for tearing down certain ones. The Protestant St. Matthew Church was demolished when work on Munich's subway began, and in replanning the city many others were to be destroyed and not replaced, especially in the Schwabing district; the new North and South suburbs would have no churches at all.[97] Elsewhere, in the thirties, suggestions appeared for the use of churches as *Volk* halls, depriving them of their traditional Christian function. The Cathedral of Braunschweig, for example, was partially remodeled in 1935 for this purpose, the crypt being redesigned as a *völkisch*

[95] He inaugurated plans for the restoration of the bomb-damaged National and Prince Regent Theaters in Munich in November 1943, almost as soon as the damage occurred. (See Speer, *Erinnerungen*, p. 560.)

[96] Josef Umlauf, "Die Bauten der Gemeinschaft," *Raumforschung und Raumordnung*, 1941, H. 3–4, cited in Teut, *Architektur*, p. 330.

[97] Dehlinger, *Architektur der Superlative*, p. 117. On the other hand, two churches were planned for the Stadt der Hermann Goering Werke (Salzgitter).

monument to Henry the Lion, who was buried there.[98] "Now," commented one writer, the cathedral was "more than just an artistic medieval church; it is a sacred shrine of the German nation."[99] The same fate was to befall Strasbourg's cathedral. Nevertheless, Hitler was satisfied that, with his great outdoor ceremonies, especially those held at night, and with the *Volk* halls, he could eventually replace the church without using any of that hated institution's buildings. Several leading Nazis wanted to tear down churches whenever they could find an opportunity. There were disagreements on this issue between Speer, who was not anti-Christian and who valued Germany's churches as cultural monuments, and men like Martin Bormann, who wanted no churches in the new Berlin.[100] Anyway, the dominant feature of the new German city's skyline would no longer be church spires, but the hulking domes of the new *Volk* halls. Augsburg's new *Volk* hall, for example, would be more than twice as high as its cathedral.[101]

Yet such was the vagueness of both the government's church policy and the flexibility of its attitude to architecture, that far into the Third Reich books appeared illustrating and commenting on good German churches. The style of these buildings was *völkisch*; it seemed that as long as the *völkisch* advocates preached a German style, the government considered them politically harmless. For example, Rittich praised certain of the churches of Bestelmeyer and of Wendland, in his 1934 volume, and discussed several churches, all indigenous in style.[102] For some *völkisch* writers, the

[98] Henry the Lion began the work which Hitler was finishing, wrote Werner Flechsig; he was the "bold conqueror and farseeing colonizer of the wide German living space in the east" (Werner Flechsig, "Der Braunschweigische Staatsdom mit der Gruft Heinrich des Löwens: ein Vorbild gegenwartsnaher Denkmalspflege im neuen Deutschland," *Die Kunst im Deutschen Reich*, III:11 (November 1939),

[99] "Der Braunschweigische Staatsdom," p. 365.

[100] Speer, *Erinnerungen*, p. 192; *Inside*, p. 177. Speer also had difficulties with certain *Gauleiter*, who capitalized on damage from air raids to justify the demolition of churches hit by bombs. (*Erinnerungen*, p. 327; *Inside*, p. 314.)

[101] Dehlinger, *Architektur der Superlative*, p. 80.

[102] Rittich, *Architektur und Bauplastik*, pp. 122–124; Wendland, *Kunst und Nation*, pp. 65–69. An interesting study of German churches written at this time

German church was a community building wherein the *Volk* could worship a German God, but for Hitler and most Nazi leaders, the Church was an alien institution and its buildings would have only a restricted role in the new Reich. The time was not yet ripe for a full-scale persecution of Christianity, however, and thus in this field, any architectural policy (which would be largely destructive) was postponed.

The Nazis stimulated a lesser known, more sophisticated, but ultimately unsuccessful body of thought and building: the *Thing* place, a combination of theater and church. This architecture was quintessentially Nazi, as it expressed so many of the tenets of the ideology, from the concern for community feeling to the reverence for nature. Significantly, however, most of the forty *Thing* places built are rarely used today. The movement declined before 1939 and commentators like Troost had almost nothing to say about it. Yet the *Thingplätze* may well be the only original contribution of the Nazi state to architecture.[103]

The *Thingplätze* built in the thirties were basically outdoor theaters based on the Greek amphitheater, a resemblance which was to recall the alleged racial kinship between modern Germans and classical Greeks. But the word *Thing* also recalled the prehistoric Germans' tribal meetings and courts in an open space in the forest.[104] The *Thing* movement reflected that longing to return to a simpler age, characteristic of so much German thought in the late nineteenth and early twentieth centuries.

and one which has a *völkisch* theme is Wolfram Freiherr von Erffa's *Das Dorfkirche als Wehrbau*, Stuttgart, Kohlhammer, 1937. The early churches of Württemberg are shown to have a military as well as a spiritual function. Karl Willy Straub, in his *Architektur im Dritten Reich*, found room for churches in the Third Reich, but not in "modern" styles (p. 47).

[103] Lane makes no mention of *Thing* places in her *Architecture and Politics*, and hence misses an important element in the nationalist attitude to architecture. On the other hand, Teut has collected an interesting set of readings on the subject; *Architektur*, pp. 226–233. ("Die dritte Bühne".) The *Bausteine zum deutschen Nationaltheater* (the voice of the Nazi Kultur Society) was given over to the *Thing* movement in 1935 (III, 129–153).

[104] On the Germanic *Thing*, see Tacitus, *Germania*, p. 8 and pp. 12–13.

Nazi *Thing* productions were ceremonies with dramatic plots, key speakers, and choruses. There were processions, and the audience was encouraged to participate, particularly in the singing of well-known national songs.[105] The great Nuremberg spectacles, of course, were also theatrical in organization and intent, but the smaller *Thing* theater had a special significance, particularly for *völkisch* enthusiasts.[106] It was the "outward embodiment of the National Socialist ideology's concept of community." In the *Thing* place, the *Volk's* new experience of unity could be expressed in a form which their Teutonic forefathers had used and which was still deeply imbedded in their character.[107]

The case for *Thing* places was vigorously argued by Wilhelm von Schramm in a book on reform of German theater. "Sickened by individualism," German theatrical life had lost "community will," he wrote. But now the Nazi revolution had brought the opportunity to win back a national theater for the *Volk* community. And in "the great summer of 1934," the height of the *Thing* movement, a new theater form emerged which corresponded to the new "life style" of the Germans, a style determined by "landscape and light, nature and soil." Indeed, Schramm considered those *Thing* experiences best which "grow out of a German landscape"; he cited, as an example, the performance of a *Thing* play about the Battle of Teutoburger Forest in A.D. 9 (the triumph

[105] Neither the idea of an open-air theater nor the concept of audience participation was new in the thirties. There were many outdoor theaters in Germany before 1933, and Max Reinhardt's production of *Everyman* (1912), not to mention the Oberammergau Passion Plays, used popular participation. Furthermore, the *völkisch* movement inspired the construction of a outdoor theater in the Harz Mountains (1907) by Ernst Wachler. Many of these enthusiasts turned to the *Thing* movement in the thirties.

[106] The Nuremberg rallies were a "political *Thing*," said Wolf Braumüller, "the greatest *Thing* of our time." (*Freilicht- und Thingspiel: Rückschau und Forderungen*, Berlin, Volksschaft-Verlag für Buch, Bühne und Film, 1935, p. 42.) Braumüller was an advisor on *Thing* places with the theater division of the *Kultur* Society.

[107] *Freilicht- und Thingspiel*, pp. 20–21.

of Hermann the Cheruscan over the Romans) in Nettelstadt, a small town in Westphalia near the battle site.[108]

Schramm, like many others, linked architecture and ideology. Since the end of the Middle Ages, he wrote, theater had moved away from being "cult and community," and a conflict had arisen between the private and the political spheres. This tension was noticeable in the outward appearance of theaters, which like political meetings, should create a personal intimacy between actors and audience. However, the "peep-show theater" (*Guckkastenbühne*) was not suitable for "the representation of the cultic or heroic." The open-air theater movement was the first sign Schramm detected that the "humanist-individualist" theater was dying and a new form of theater was emerging, one which entailed the rebirth of old "Nordic-*völkisch*" custom.[109]

When the first *Thing* place opened on June 5, 1934 at Brandbergen near Halle, Schramm rejoiced, because here, he said, "a new period of community experience and community form" began. At Halle, the audience "was near the greatness and expanse of the German landscape and felt the breath of the earth," which was not covered with stones, but which was "molded into an artistic shell of lawn." For Schramm, nature itself was part of community architecture. He thought that the best *Thing* plays were produced, not in a "neutral stadium or amphitheater," but in an "open camping ground" where the occasion became "a living symbol" of the *Volk* community. In the latter situation, architecture and nature were in harmony, especially if a sacred stone or tree were part of the celebration.[110]

As few other structures, the *Thingplatz* seemed to combine all the necessary attributes of good "German" architecture; possibly monumentality and representation were less emphasized, but

---

[108] Wilhelm von Schramm, *Neubau des deutschen Theaters: Ergebnisse und Förderungen*, Berlin, Schlieffen, 1934, pp. 16, 28, and 29. Schramm was a novelist and poet.

[109] Schramm, *Neubau*, pp. 35–36.

[110] *Ibid.*, p. 49.

the spectacle itself often took on grandiose proportions and certainly "represented" German values and strengths. Above all, the *Thing* place was community architecture and the *Thing* play was to produce a communal experience. "The basic concept of the *Thing* play," said Braumüller, "is political"; [111] "the deepest meaning of the Idea, . . . community experience and experienced community." [112] This was "the theater for the *Volk* as community," said another writer, in which the theater was "at one with the masses of spectators — no longer cut off in levels or 'rows', . . . [It] is at one with the actors . . . who are no longer cut off by visible curtains dividing the dark auditorium from the brightly lit stage." [113] Similarly, Braumüller warned against the overuse of technology; Germans must get away from "the theater of illusion," he said, because the *Thing* experience was a real one, not vicarious. [114]

The *Thingplatz* was supposed to revive the ancient Teutonic worship of nature. Therefore, it should always be in the form of a circle, said Felix Emmel, because the Teutonic sacrificial site on mountains or in sacred groves was round. Nature should not be used simply as a panoramic backdrop, he wrote, but, if it had some sacred function (such as a sacred tree or a runic stone), it should be drawn into the theater area itself. [115] As if following Emmel's advice, the designer of the Koblenz *Thing* place set a "pow-

[111] Wolf Braumüller, "Thingspiel-Beginn 1935," *Bausteine zum deutschen Nationaltheater*, III:5 (May 1935), 129. (Braumüller was editor of this periodical, an organ of Rosenberg's *Kultur* Society.)

[112] Braumüller, *Freilicht- und Thingspiel*, pp. 44 and 45. The aim of the *Thing* was "the education of the German through the mass meeting." (Rainer Schlösser, *Das Volk und seine Bühne: Bemerkungen zum Aufbau des deutschen Theaters*, Berlin Theater Verlag Albert Langen — Georg Müller, 1935, p. 40; Schlösser was president of the Reich Theater Chamber.)

[113] Josef Buchhorn, "Sinn und Sendung des Theaters," *Deutscher Kulturwacht* (September 1935), cited in Josef Wulf, ed., *Theater und Film im Dritten Reich*, Hamburg, Rowohlt, 1966, p. 181. Buchhorn was advisor to the state *Kultur* supervisor in the Gau of Berlin.

[114] Braumüller, *Freilicht- und Thingspiel*, pp. 38 and 42.

[115] Felix, Emmel, *Theater aus deutschem Wesen*, Berlin, Stilke, 1937, p. 92. Emmel, a theater critic, was director of the Düsseldorf state theater.

erful" boulder in its midst, a stone which, said one journalist, "once arose from the glowing lava of a volcano in the Laacher Sea, and which . . . shall be a symbol of [the theater's] indigenous bonds with nature."[116] Other architects planned a stream to flow through their structures or trees or hedges to grow in the audience area.[117]

As we have seen, the *Thing* theater was to also communicate a sense of the German past and to embody the mystical significance of a place. Prehistoric graves, historic battlefields, ruins, fords, and princely seats were appropriate sites.[118] Furthermore, in this sort of theater, the auditorium and the stage were close, one writer noted, "as in ancient Greece.[119] Thus for most writers, the *Thing* place represented the "blood-and-soil," "Aryan"-Greek aspects of the ideology. Through it, Schramm summarized, a new type of German would develop: "the nature-German, loving sunshine, delighting in physical activity, and oriented toward community and comradeship, [living] in the open air and in sunlight."[120]

In 1934 and 1935 the enthusiasm of some critics ran high. These theaters were not only designed for plays, one writer noted, but also as settings "for great national celebrations."[121] The *Thing* place should become the "center of the whole ceremonial, national-political, and artistic life of each city."[122] The champions of the *Thingplatz* saw a great future for the *Thing* movement, and were encouraged by government support for a while.

A Reich League for German Open Air and *Volk* Plays was

[116] From the *Deutsche Allgemeine Zeitung*, March 26, 1935, cited in Brenner, *Kunstpolitik*, pp. 201–202.
[117] See illustration no. 13 in Brenner, *Kunstpolitik*.
[118] Emmel, *Theater*, p. 92. Feder thought it a good idea to build the *Thingplatz* near a historical building, a castle, or an abbey. (*Die neue Stadt*, p. 204.)
[119] Carl Niessen, director of the Cologne university theater institute, cited in Buchhorn, "Sinn und Sendung," p. 166.
[120] Schramm, *Neubau*, p. 45.
[121] Ludwig Moshamer, "Die Thingstätte und ihre Bedeutung für das kommende deutsche Theater," *Bauwelt* (1935), cited in Teut, *Architektur*, p. 232.
[122] Schlösser, *Das Volk*, p. 61.

founded in 1934 in collaboration with the Propaganda Ministry, which also regulated permissions to build *Thing* places. Most of these centers were built under the supervision of the Labor Front. As many as 1200 were envisaged: for every 50,000 Germans, one such structure, seating a thousand people.[123] Rosenberg and his *Kampfbund*, meanwhile, tried to encourage the writing of *Thing* plays. These dramas, such as Wilhelm Matthiessen's *Sacred Earth*, had suitable themes.

The first *Thing* place to be completed was at Brandbergen near Halle. The site chosen was a prehistoric cult area and many mass meetings had been held there after 1933. Perhaps the best example, however, is the Dietrich Eckart Stage on the Reich Sport Field in Berlin. (See illustration no. 54.) Designed by Werner March to fit into a dry depression to the west of the Olympic complex, behind the Langemarck Tower, it could seat 20,000 people. The approaches to the stage led directly through the rows of seats. The stage itself was divided into three levels. Hedges marked off the seating areas, and the tree-covered Murellen Hill provided a natural backdrop. Thirty-nine splotlights illuminated the stage from towers, which also provided space for the bells and trumpets, which were often used. March stressed the natural environment and the "curtain" of trees surrounding it.[124] Hedges also marked off parts of the stage, while much of the stage itself, particularly the forepart, was of lawn. The whole theater seemed sunken into the forest. March said, that, in designing it, he rejected any idea of "competing with nature," for the natural surroundings as well as the quality of the natural limestone used in building forbade any decoration or intrusive use of "over-refined technology." But not only is March's *Thingplatz* a reflection of the current obsession with nature; it is also part of "community" architecture. He described the "inclusiveness" of its space, a quality which should heighten the "feeling of a community."[125] Braumüller appropri-

[123] Graff, *Vom S.M. zur N.S.*, p. 145.
[124] March, *Bauwerk*, p. 15.
[125] *Ibid.*, p. 32.

ately concluded that this theater perfected the ideological concept of architecture.[126]

Despite the primitive forebears of the *Thingplatz*, the accoutrements of the Nazi variety were anything but simple. Special effects were used to heighten the impact of the play being performed: loudspeakers, colored lights, as well as special sound effects. The main difficulties with the *Thing* places, however, were also their essential characteristics: they were open-air theaters, usually remote from urban life. This meant that there were acoustical problems, difficulties with the weather, and the problem of getting people to come out to participate in the spectacle. (Hence the need for special effects to attract viewers.) As it turned out, many Germans were bored and uncomfortable in the *Thing* places; even a zealous Goethe devotee might quail at seeing *Faust* outdoors on a cool north-German evening, and it took a very dedicated patriot to participate in the new *Thing* plays written for this new form of *Volk* theater.[127]

Thus the *Thing* movement failed, and, in 1937, the Propaganda Ministry ceased to support the Reich League. Goebbels was never a devout "blood-and-soil" advocate, but he saw the propaganda possibilities of the *Thing* places. Hitler, disliking the *völkisch* cult, was never a supporter. The major commentators,

[126] Wolf Braumüller, "Die Dietrich-Eckart-Bühne: Grundlage einer neuen dramatischer Architektur," *Bausteine zum deutschen Nationaltheater* (June 1936), cited in Wulf, *Theater und Film*, p. 187. Another example of this type of building is the Heidelberg *Thingplatz*, on the top of the forested Heiligen Berg (sacred mountain) across the Neckar River from the city. Here, a round forestage has rounded platforms for speakers and five acting levels; two sets of stairs (one on each side of a rear platform) provide areas for a large flag-bearing choruses. Again, the woods are the real backdrop of the theater. A ruined abbey nearby gives romantic historical atmosphere.

[127] In order to overcome the difficulties of outdoor stage and retain the ideological qualities of the *Thing* place, Emmel planned a German Festival House, a sextagonal building with sextagonal towers and a flat roof. This was to combine the best qualities of the *Thing* place with the traditional aspects of the older theater form; that is, to increase national awareness in the *Volk* by celebrating "the eternal values of German *Volkstum*," while avoiding the cold night air and uncertain weather conditions. (Emmel, *Theater*, pp. 92–96. A plan is on p. 93.)

Troost and Rittich, make little reference to the amphitheaters,[128] a silence which probably reflects Hitler's disapproval. The *Führer* wished to concentrate all Nazi ceremonial in the middle of cities, where it was easier to reach more people and to develop a crowd.[129] Some commentators were openly critical of the movement. Emmel wrote that, although the *Thing* theaters were a "bold experiment," they resisted stubbornly all forms of poetic drama; moreover, the individual actors appeared small and foreshortened, and only the massing of crowds on stage worked. The result was that technology (loudspeakers and lights) came "between art and the *Volk*, between the landscape and the community." Emmel thus criticized the movement for failing to achieve its own goals.[130] Ironically, this architecture was closer than any other form to the racial and "community" aspects of the ideology, at least in creating a mood of national unity.

Some students of German history have stressed the similarity between these Nazi rituals and orthodox religious ceremonies.[131] If National Socialism ever came close to being an *ersatz* religion, it was in its *Thing* places. Although German writers did not usually refer to the *Thingstätte* as cult centers, they regarded them as somehow sacred. Braumüller, for example, wanted a protective zone around every *Thing* place, to separate it from "the materialistic business and tourist traffic."[132] Feder, however, stated bluntly that the *Thing* place was "a kind of shrine" (*Kultstätte*).[133] "The business of the *Thing* place," wrote an author of *Thing* plays, "is

[128] Troost makes only one reference. (*Bauen*, I, pp. 52–53.) Rittich offers only a few photographs without comment. (*Architektur und Bauplastik*, pp. 64–67.)

[129] Correspondence with Albert Speer, March 9, 1969.

[130] Emmel, *Theater*, p. 23.

[131] See Hans-Jochem Gamm, *Der braune Kult: das dritte Reich und seine Ersatzreligion*, Hamburg, Rütten und Loening, 1962; Dehlinger, *Architektur der Superlative*, pp. 176–177; or Brenner, *Kunstpolitik*, p. 102.

[132] Braumüller, *Freilicht- und Thingspiel*, p. 37.

[133] Feder, *Die neue Stadt*, p. 204. Schramm was pleased to see a general tendency to reject the concept of a sterile amphitheater for that of "the Nordic cult place." (*Neubau*, p. 49.)

the cult of the dead. The fallen arise, and from the stones strides the spirit." "Cult, not art," he said, "is the business of the *Thing* place."[134] Eugène Wernert, a French observer, described best this *Thing* experience:

> In the audience, one is drowned in the anonymous mass, rubbing elbows with one's neighbour; one sings with the others familiar songs, one reacts together and violently to the simple but marvellous episodes in the action [on stage]: the appearance of the dead soldier, etc. . . . Then one becomes aware of an inchoate but omnipresent mass of Germans, in the audience, on the stage, and beyond the *Thing* place, one is reassured, happy in the certainly that all Germany is marching, that Germany is both its present and its ancient self: the old and romantic, tough Teutonic joy in [the] tribe runs through each of the spectators in the crowd; the miracle occurs; for several seconds, the *Volk* community is a living reality.[135]

This, of course, was the desired effect of all the celebrations carried on in Nazi "community" architecture. Buildings, whether monumental or barely more than manipulated landscape, were to help restore that sense of community which Germans had lost. Nowhere else, however, was the effort more concentrated than in the *Thingplatz*.

[134] Richard Euringer, "Thingspiel-Thesen I," *Völkischer Beobachter*, June 20, 1934, cited in Wulf, ed., *Theater und Film*, p. 183.

[135] Eugène Wernert, *L'art dans le IIIeme Reich: une tentative d'esthètique dirigée*, Paris, Centre d'études de politique étrangers, 1936, p. 100. Wernert is one of the few non-Germans to study the *Thing* places.

CHAPTER TEN

Architecture for *Völkisch* Health

ONLY THROUGH public housing projects, youth hostels, schools, and factories was the Nazi concept of "community" architecture directed at Germany's social problems, such as the need for improved working and living conditions, or for better mental and physical health. The commentators, often racists, believed that it was imperative to preserve and to improve the spiritual health of the "Aryan" *Volk* through, for example, the construction of apartment complexes in a style expressing the appropriate values. As spiritual health was considered dependent on physical health (healthy "blood"), the hygiene of the home itself had to be improved. A similar attitude prevailed for youth and labor facilities. In these fields, the well being of the "Aryan" community as an aggregate of Germans (rather than simply "community feeling") was the main concern.

The *Volk* itself was quite capable of building its homes or schools correctly. "The German," wrote Schulte-Frohlinde, has "always had a natural feeling for beauty" and "an unerring sense for the healthy, the clear, the German."[1] Another Nazi said that "the healthy, pure instinct of the German *Volk* has continually rejected the products of sick and un-Aryan decadent art . . ."[2]

[1] Schulte-Frohlinde, *Die landschaftlichen Grundlagen*, pp. 7 and 9.
[2] Walter Hansen, *Judenkunst in Deutschland*, Berlin, Nordland, 1942, p. 12. Writers on the history of the German peasant and his architecture marveled over

"The people have a healthy feeling for authentic accomplishment," said Goebbels, "its taste derives from a solid predisposition, but," he added significantly, "it must be correctly and systematically guided."[3]

Concern for the survival of a healthy "Aryan" race led to an interest in living conditions in cities and on the land. The theme of health and the healthy race, of hygiene and purification, appears often in Nazi writing and in works sympathetic to the Nazi cause. The years prior to 1933 were considered decadent and unhealthy, but the Third Reich would see Germany cleansed. Comments on the purpose of the Berlin Olympic Stadium and the cult of sunshine and fresh air (although similar to other non-Nazi urban reform projects) were in this racial vein. March noted that the location of his Olympic Stadium was "healthy," with westerly winds driving away urban smog, and that the swimming pool gave a "beautiful feeling of cleanliness."[4] Hitler wanted no gloomy cathedrals but brightly lit *Volk* halls. There was much talk about pure and healthy art and architecture.[5] Pinder announced: "We want to create a high-quality human being, without an overrefined brain, without excessive prudence, but with a healthy body, a healthy mind, and a healthy soul." Architecture would help to do this.[6]

his alleged sense of hygiene and his general health. (See Walther Darré, *Neuadel aus Blut und Boden*, Munich, Lehmann, 1935, p. 88.)

[3] From his speech at the annual congress of the Reich Chamber of Culture and the Strength Through Joy Organization, Berlin, November 26, 1937. (Cited in Mosse, *Nazi Culture*, p. 156.) In *Mein Kampf*, Hitler explained why the "Aryan" feeling for culture was so important: "Human culture and civilization on this continent is inseparably bound up with the presence of the Aryan. If he dies out or declines, the dark veils of an age without culture will again descend on this globe." (*Mein Kampf*, p. 383. See also Kiener's article, "Germanische Tektonik," p. 186: "The clarity of the constructive elements which reveals the Aryan spirit is in contrast everywhere to the dull, vague massive buildings of non-Aryan peoples.")

[4] March, *Bauwerk*, pp. 15 and 31.
[5] See, for example, Wolfgang Willrich, *Die Säuberung des Kunsttempels: Eine Kunstpolitische Kampfschrift zur Gesundung deutscher Kunst im Geiste nordischer Art*, 2nd ed., Munich, Lehmanns, 1938.
[6] Pinder, "Architektur als Moral," pp. 210–211

Much public housing was built during the Weimar period.[7] The *völkisch* anti-Marxist critics maintained that too many left-wing architects were at work then, and condemned the latter's projects because of their flat roofs, their "cold" appearance, or their alleged expense.[8] These critics reserved their praise for those traditional architects who continued to build row houses or apartments in familiar "German" styles. When Hitler came to power in 1933, they expected his government to provide many more and larger homes for the *Volk*, and to provide these in suitable *völkisch* or "German" styles.

Some of the commentary is not explicitly ideological. Indeed, the simple desire to preserve folk arts or the visual unity of a village cannot be labeled "Nazi" or nationalist. However, the peculiarity of this literature is that many writers linked esthetics with racism — and had done so even before 1933. For example: "We want the German house to be a home, in which we can think, feel, and dwell according to our racial instinct. This house must also grow organically out of the landscape and the urban environment."[9] This writer went on to say that considering the new appreciation of peasant life, the character of this home would not be urban, but *völkisch*.[10] For Wendland, the small house was "the seed core of the *Volk*"; therefore, "everyone who builds a house," he wrote, "must feel the duty to do a small service for art, something to give a house a more beautiful character. It does not always have to be figures for the garden or a painting. A pair of

[7] See Lane, *Architecture and Politics*, pp. 87–124. On the Stuttgart Weissenhof settlement see Deutscher Werkbund, ed., *Bau und Wohnung: Die Bauten der Weissenhofsiedlung in Stuttgart errichtet 1927 nach Vorschlägen des Deutschen Werkbundes im Auftrag der Stadt Stuttgart und im Rahmen der Werkbundausstellung "Die Wohnung,"* Stuttgart, Wedekind, 1927. A concern for sunshine and fresh air in buildings was not restricted to the *völkisch* or the Nazi critics. The Siemenstadt settlement in Berlin, built in 1929 by Gropius and others, was geographically aligned to obtain maximum sunshine.

[8] For "incorrect" public housing, see the description of the Stuttgart Weissenhof Settlement in Feistel-Rohmeder, *Im Terror*, p. 16; or in Hansen, *Judenkunst*, ill. no. 14.

[9] Ziegler, *Wende und Weg*, p. 11.

[10] Schrade, *Baukunst des dritten Reiches*, p. 33.

carved beams or a carved door will do."[11] Building homes for the
people was just as important as constructing representative edifices, Rittich reminded his readers, for the development of a
"healthy family life" was fundamental to the success of the Third
Reich.[12]

What was Hitler's attitude? In his Vienna days, he developed
a brief interest in working-class housing, which was later over-
shadowed by monumental "community" buildings for the state
and his movement.[13] However, in 1940 he astutely noted that the
soldiers who would return after the end of the victorious war
would not want to go on living in old tenements side by side with
the magnificent new buildings in Berlin, Munich, and Nuremberg.[14] In 1941 he privately admitted that his government had not
created enough homes for the workers; public housing, he said,
was "a sphere in which we are terribly behind."[15] Aerial bombardment of German cities during the war added a special urgency to
this problem. A few months later, however, he outlined some
rather utopian plans for postwar housing: "To put an end to the
housing crisis, we shall build . . . a million dwellings a year, and
that for five consecutive years."[16] Yet the *Führer's* later plans for

[11] Wendland, *Kunst und Nation*, pp. 55 and 61.

[12] He wanted lawns and gardens included in housing developments, with
buildings so situated that "community feeling" would emerge. (*Architektur und
Bauplastik*, p. 121.) See also Feder, *Die neue Stadt*, pp. 315–344, which links the
European urban-reform movement to German nationalism.

[13] Schacht reports that in December 1930 Hitler mentioned to the industrialist
Fritz Thyssen the importance of rearmament over housing. (Hjalmar Schacht,
Account Settled, London, Weidenfeld and Nicolson, 1949, pp. 29–30.) This remained his attitude. Any interest in public housing which he later developed was
a facet of his anti-Marxism. He seemed to want to make every German a property
owner, and favored the building of single-family residences over apartments. He
was cited as saying that "the day when every German worker possessed a house
and a plot of his own, Communism will disappear from the land." (Roberts, *The
House that Hitler Built*, p. 171.) Poor living conditions made good Communists,
in Hitler's view.

[14] Cited in Rosenberg, *Tagebuch*, p. 149 (October 12, 1940).

[15] Hitler, *S.C.*, p. 97 (October 19, 1941).

[16] *Ibid.*, p. 334 (February 28, 1942). Every house would be equipped with
a garage.

sheltering the "Aryan" *Volk* after the war reveals the true extent of his interest in their health and well being. For refugees and the homeless, any sort of building material was acceptable; communal facilities would replace private bathrooms; there would be no need for gas, electricity, or water in the flatroofed settlements envisaged.[17] If the *völkisch* housing enthusiasts had known the *Führer's* attitude, they would have been disillusioned, to say the least.[18]

These, then, were some of the attitudes behind the public housing created during the Third Reich. For the writers, the program's most important undertaking was the building of rural settlements. Most agreed that "Aryan" culture bloomed when "Aryans" lived close to the soil, for the healthy peasant had a strong innate sense of beauty.[19] Walther Darré, head of the party's Agricultural Department, was perhaps the most enthusiastic supporter of the "blood-and-soil" aspect of the ideology. "Whoever would create a nobility in the genuine and peculiarly German sense of the word," he maintained, "must extract selected families for this purpose out of the city, transplant them into the land, and above all in conditions under which the race can strike roots."[20] When this program was undertaken, and a healthy race emerged, then a great "Aryan"-German culture could flourish.[21]

[17] Conversation of August 20, 1943 between Hitler, Speer, Giessler, and Ley, from a document cited in Dehlinger, *Architektur der Superlative*, p. 42. See also *Wohnungsbau nach dem Kriege*; microfilm, NSDAP Hauptarchiv, Reel 54, Folder 1305, Frame 110, Film 1004.

[18] At all events they must have been disappointed with the relatively small amount of public housing constructed. The Nazi state actually reduced its spending on housing as early as 1938, whereas the need for new dwellings increased from 900,000 in 1933 to 1.5 million in 1938. (See Franz Neumann, *Behemoth; The Structure and Practice of National Socialism 1933–1944*, New York, Harper, 1966, p. 250; or Teut, "Der soziale Wohnungsbau," *Architektur*, pp. 251–253.

[19] See Hitler, *Mein Kampf*, p. 138, on the importance of preserving a healthy peasant class; and Schulte-Frohlinde, *Die landschaftlichen Grundlagen*, p. 9.

[20] Darré, *Neuadel*, p. 89.

[21] Throughout *völkisch* and Nazi propaganda runs the image of the idealized peasant, particularly in painting and related arts. See Eberlein, *Was ist deutsch in der deutschen Kunst?* p. 13.

The *völkisch* and Nazi writers developed a rather idealized view of peasant life, especially of its past. No peasant class ever lived in such freedom as did the "Nordic," it was maintained; the "Aryan" never suffered under despotism or serfdom, and therefore he developed a proud feeling of liberty and, since he lived together under the same roof with his servants, a sense of democracy.[22] Thus the actual structure of the farmhouse corresponded to the peasant's sense of equality. Moreover this peasant took his building materials directly from the German earth (wood, stone, brick, clay, thatch) and hence, his home, barns, and community buildings were "rooted firmly in the soil."[23]

The indigenous architecture of rural Germany was examined. Before 1933, not only had a few *völkisch* specialists fostered a movement to have "community" and representative buildings constructed in this style, but they wanted to preserve and expand it in its native environment. This work continued after 1933, often becoming more racist in tone. The peasant's house, said Schultze-Naumburg, was "reservoir of all genuine *Volk*-ish qualities," and its form was fundamentally "bound to the blood."[24] The one idea which united two apparently disparate streams of thought on architecture, the *völkisch* and the neo-classical, was the belief that both streams had "Aryan" blood roots in ancient Greece.[25] Thus it was argued that German farm buildings were related in form to the temples of ancient Greece, the ground plans of some row houses in the bronze-age village of Buch, near Berlin, being similar to buildings in Troy, Mycenae, and Olympia. "The Greek temple and the Indo-German wooden buildings of the east are the product of one and the same racial laws of structure. In both types the harmonious balance of all dimensions, width, depth, and

[22] Hans Henniger, "Das Erbe germanischer Baukunst," *Bauen, Siedeln, Wohnen*, 1937, p. 199.
[23] Troost, *Bauen*, I, 5.
[24] Schultze-Naumburg, *Kunst der Deutschen*, p. 61.
[25] Lane is, therefore, not wholly correct to suggest that the two streams were always "incompatible" and "conflicting." (*Architecture and Politics*, p. 215.) For these writers, at least, there was a way of reconciling them.

height is perfect"; "in wood and in stone, [is embodied] the same earthbound, self-contained soul, which rises mysteriously from the depth of the *Volkstum*."[26]

In the writing on peasant architecture, concern for the landscape also emerges strongly. Preserving the natural beauties of Germany was important for the highway builders; although this attitude does not stamp a person as a racist or Nazi, in the Germany of the thirties, it was another point at which ideology and architecture met. Many believed not only that buildings should harmonize with the surrounding landscape for aesthetic purposes, but that the landscape itself was somehow German and had helped to form the "German soul." Hence it must be protected from buildings that distracted from its purity or were not German in style.[27]

Interest in the golden age of the race led to a concern for German settlements elsewhere in Europe, particularly in areas where the German population was considered oppressed. It was held that there was no Slavic influence on "Aryan" building in the East.[28] The peasant houses in the Sudetenland were considered witnesses to the far-flung superior Germanic culture which once dominated the east.[29] Everywhere in the east where German culture met Slavic, it had a refining effect on the Slavs, improving the general level of life, and, "despite all the opposition of the present, [it] will continue to fulfill its mission in central Europe."[30] The early Teutons had taught the Slavs a more orderly plan for

[26] Franke, *Ostgermanische Holzbaukultur*, pp. 144–147. In a similar vein Lindner wrote that it was important for house plans to be rectilinear (a more "Aryan" form). (*Die Stadt*, p. 134.) See Troost's *Bauen*, I, 6, for her approval of the rectilinear ground plan.

[27] Schultze-Naumburg, of course, had been denouncing the destruction of the landscape around cities since 1900, in his *Städtebau*.

[28] Gustav Wolf, a painter, cited in Schulte-Frohlinde, *Die Landschaftlichen Grundlagen*, pp. 15–23 (ill. nos. 1–17).

[29] Franke, *Ostgermanische Holzbaukultur*, p. 147. Klaus Thiede maintained the same thing. (*Das Erbe germanischer Baukunst im bäuerlichen Hausbau*, Hamburg, Hanseatische Verlagsanstalt, 1936, pp. 87–88.)

[30] Bruno Schier, "Der deutsche Einfluss auf der Hausbau Osteuropas," *Nationalsozialistische Monatshefte*, VIII, 409.

their houses, for thatching roofs, for erecting farm buildings, as well as for the use of fences and the separation of cattle from humans in living quarters.[31] All this concern for *Ordnung* was proof of their "Aryan" nature. A volume focusing on this problem, *Städtebild und Landschaft*, was published in 1939 by the Labor Front. "The human abode, . . . gives man, in its union with soil and landscape, the experience of his homeland," said the editors; "house and homeland . . . create the foundations of all *Kultur*."[32]

There was also interest in Teutonic architectural monuments in the territories lost in the West. A good example of this trend was Roland Anheisser's study of medieval homes, although the author disclaimed any political bias. Alsace, a "lost German territory," was "completely German" as its architecture showed. The German inscriptions on houses revealed an "understandable loyalty to the German Reich." The "lovely painted glass" of the Metz cathedral (thirteenth to sixteenth centuries) was almost completely created by German masters. Indeed, Anheisser found the entire architecture of Alsace "purely German." "*This land is definitely German,* its *Volk,* its speech, its architecture is German," he wrote.[33] As for Holland, its architecture was "also Teutonic-German." Bohemia and Moravia, he added, were German lands, and it was German blood which made Prague "one of the most beautiful and splendid cities of the world." Cracow, too, was a "German city," as were Eger and Tabor. In Hungary, at Odenburg and Pressburg, and in the Siebenbürgen, German blood was a

[31] Schrade, *Bauten des dritten Reiches*, pp. 400, 404, 406, and 409.

[32] Reichsheimstättenamt der Deutschen Arbeitsfront, Planungsabteilung, *Städtebild und Landschaft*, Berlin, Verlag der Deutschen Arbeitsfront, 1939, p. 94. Despite the concern of the *völkisch* Nazi supporters for the landscape and for nature, Hitler insisted on covering vast expanses in German cities with granite paving blocks. The Munich Königplatz, the Berlin Lustgarten, and other squares have already been noted as examples of the *Führer's* lack of sympathy with the *völkisch* viewpoint. This holds true despite Hitler's short disquisition on rural architecture in his *Secret Conversations* (p. 641 [September 4, 1942]).

[33] Anheisser, *Das mittelalterliche Wohnhaus*, p. 202. The italics are Anheisser's.

"distant bulwark of our *Volk* ways against the Rumanians."[34] Anheisser was concerned mainly with past urban architecture, when Germans living in cities had not lost their bonds with their rural roots or with *völkisch* styles. He warned that "no *Volk* disappears too easily in foreign customs as does the German or allows itself to be overgrown with them, as does the German." Modern Germans had "a sacred duty" to preserve old German houses wherever they were to be found.[35] This attitude was typical *völkisch* Pan-Germanism applied to architecture.

To maintain that this was all Nazi political propaganda, or that these writers all supported Hitler's foreign policy, would be an oversimplification. These comments reveal what *völkisch* writers felt toward German architecture and the German peasantry in Europe. In defending these entities, they buttressed, knowingly or not, the political propaganda of the government agencies.

Critics examined the causes of the architectural "decay" of German farms and villages in the Reich itself. In the nineteenth century, "false" urban styles had crept into the rural landscape, so that the German architectural heritage had been "senselessly disfigured."[36] The peasant home, "mirror of the racial character," said another commentator, was endangered by the same international trend, a movement that sought to render "everything even, the same, and spiritually poor."[37] All too often buildings had been added to older farms in cement, lead, and other artificial "dead" materials detrimental to the organic unity of beautiful old farms and landscapes.[38]

[34] *Ibid.*, x–xviii, and p. 330.

[35] *Ibid.*, xvii and xix. See also Lotz, "So baut Europa," and Straub, *Architektur im Dritten Reich*, for a similar theme. In 1935 a five hundred page catalog on the art and architecture of Eupen and Malmedy in Belgium appeared, although with no explicit political intent. (Herbert Reiners, *Die Kunstdenkmäler Eupen-Malmedy*, Düsseldorf, Schwann, 1935). The *völkisch* writer, Thiede, was interested in the Teutonic traces supposedly noticeable in Swiss building. (*Das Erbe*, p. 131.)

[36] E. Kulke, an architect, cited in Werner Lindner, et al., *Das Dorf: seine Pflege und Gestaltung*, p. 11.

[37] Eberlein, *Was ist deutsch in der deutschen Kunst?* p. 57.

[38] Lindner, *Das Dorf*, p. 59. *The avant-garde* architect, Hugo Häring, had

Although Hitler was not particularly interested in this aspect of the emergent theory of architecture, his government embarked on a program to save rural architecture. Robert Ley, the *Reichsorganisationsleiter* of the party, with the assistance of the Labor Front and the *Deutscher Heimatbund,* formed the *Arbeitsgemeinschaft Heimat und Haus* which published a series of books, *Die landschaftlichen Grundlagen des deutschen Bauschaffens.* Volume one of these series concerned the village and gave some precise recommendations.[39] One of the articles, on the role of the *Kraft durch Freude* organization in beautifying small towns, declared that "the village, the home of millions of Germans, must be clean, orderly, and beautiful, an ideological, social-political, economic, and cultural model." Indeed the first necessity for each village, was cleanliness, which meant not only conventional hygiene, but also "no urban architectural *Kitsch.*" Typically, the center of every village should be the square, where festivals and ceremonies could take place.[40] The square should be the site of the *Volk* hall, the "spiritual center of the village."[41]

Another volume in this series, *Der Osten,* concerned the conquered Slavic lands with further recommendations for German

designed farm buildings at Garkau near Lübeck in 1923; this was one of the worst examples of the "desecration" these writers feared. (See Wolfgang Pehnt, ed., *Encyclopedia of Modern Architecture,* New York, Abrams, 1964, p. 146.) Walther Darré, as head of the party's Agricultural Section, decreed on April 9, 1935 that the building materials unapproved by his ministry were not to be used in the building of peasant homes or barns. (See Lindner, *Das Dorf,* p. 37.)

[39] This book was a response to the decree of July 14, 1933, for the reform of the German peasantry, which introduced subsidies for the renovation of farms and general assistance to farmers, and to a law of April 9, 1935 which established an architect as advisor on rural building in each province and which decreed that "the harmonious fusion of the new farms and villages into the German living space is the goal." Another law decreed that all "formalism" was to be avoided while indigenous building materials were to be used. ("Runderlass des Reichs- und Preussischen Ministers für Ernährung und Landwirtschaft vom 9.4.1935," *Bauwelt,* 1935, Heft 21, cited in Teut, *Architektur,* pp. 273–276.)

[40] Franz Gutsmiedl, "Kraft durch Freude gestaltet das schöne Dorf," in Lindner, *Das Dorf,* pp. 111–114. Gutsmiedl was an official of the Beauty of Labor organization.

[41] Herbert Frank, "Grundgedanken zu unserem ländlichen Bauschaffen," Lindner, *Das Dorf,* p. 220. Frank was an architect.

peasant architecture in this crucial area of *Volk* development. Here, perhaps more than in any other geographical area, architecture was a political weapon. Sounding a note of missionary zeal, Schulte-Frohlinde hoped that "the will to teamwork" (community spirit) would develop among architects concerned with the East, for this quality would make clearer "the direction in which we must march." He urged builders to follow Frederick the Great's example in founding new rural settlements; that is, to use local materials and styles, and to give buildings a "Prussian appearance."[42] This included those allegedly "German" qualities of orderly layout, clear indication of building parts, neat arrangement of windows, and stylistic unity throughout.[42] He cited examples from the past, such as the city of Neu-Rüppin, built near the end of the eighteenth century, and his own works in Brandenburg.[43] As for the builders themselves, Ley extended Schulte-Frohlinde's pleas: "extraordinary willingness for self-sacrifice" would be necessary for this enterprise: "the preservation and expansion of a unified architecture corresponding to the National Socialist ideology."[44] The correct architecture, therefore, would help to re-establish the German image in eastern Europe.

Der Osten was devoted to rural German architecture and its propagation in eastern Europe. Many other writers devoted a few pages in their works to this problem. Often they centered discussion on the roof, and attacked *avant-garde* architecture of the twenties for its use of the flat roof. The writers would substitute the "Nuremberg roof," (very high, pointed and steep), "a work of art of the first order;"[45] "a symbol of the strong, protective strength of the Nordic feeling for the home."[46] Troost's examples of good German farmhouses, built in the traditional manner, all have steep, usually thatched roofs, and boast ancient decorative

[42] Schulte-Frohlinde, *Die landschaftlichen Grundlagen*, p. 9.
[43] See, for example, p. 107 (ill. no. 158, Neu-Rüppin), and pp. 75 and 83 in *Die landschaftlichen Grundlagen*.
[44] Robert Ley, "Zum Geleit," *Die landschaftlichen Grundlagen*, p. 5.
[45] Anheisser, *Das mittelalterliche Wohnhaus*, p. 304.
[46] Lindner, *Das Dorf*, p. 18.

motifs such as horses' heads carved on crossed end beams.[47] Not all her examples, of course, were farmhouses; some were homes for rural laborers. In addition, Rittich described buildings of the Forest Service, built from local materials, "boulders, rocks, pine, rushes." For these writers this style, embodying "a harmony of the building with the environment . . . and the close union of the builder and inhabitant with the forest,"[48] was to remind the viewer, whether peasant or urbanite, of his geographic roots. Roof covering should be "derived from the earth, quarries, or from the fields of the landscape," thus binding the building "with its soil."[49] Precise instructions as to the slant of the ideal roof — from 45 to 48 degrees — were given by another writer in *Das Dorf*.[50]

Nevertheless, it would be incorrect to conclude from these comments and from the other anti-Marxist propaganda that the Nazi era would see the demise of all flat roofs in Germany. Specific recommendations offered by the Labor Front for proper German farm buildings recommended the flat roof, for animal sheds behind row houses.[51] Lindner, while recommending "the warm red and red-brown of baked tiles," also admitted that a flat roof might be used in storehouses or milksheds.[52]

Some writers tried to keep a sense of perspective. The architect Erich Böckler, for example, approved in general of the *völkisch* school's efforts, but he objected to the building of essentially rural structures in an urban setting, such as the half-timbered, thatched-roof subway station in Dahlem (Berlin).[53] At all events,

---

[47] Troost, *Bauen*, I, 156–163; II, 162.

[48] Rittich, *Architektur und Bauplastik*, p. 140.

[49] Hartmann, *Werkhefte*, pp. 42–43.

[50] Wilhelm Grebe, "Sonderfragen des ländlichen Bauens," *Das Dorf*, pp. 174–175. Grebe was an official in the Ministry of Food and Agriculture.

[51] "Das Haus in der Landschaft," *Städtebild und Landschaft*, p. 101.

[52] Lindner, "Heimatpflege," *Das Dorf*, pp. 37 and 69. For more on the importance of roof lines, see Lindner, *Die Stadt*, pp. 133 and 139–40; or Hartmann, *Werkhefte*, p. 58.

[53] Böckler, *Landschaftsgemäss bauen?*, p. 55. The Berlin Olympic Grounds had rural styles for the equestrian center (which was supposed to look "like a rural farm" with half-timbered buildings and thatched roofs; the same design was

the zeal of the *völkisch* enthusiasts might have been tempered by the advice of Wilhelm Grebe, who noted that there were at least seventy different types of indigenous architecture in Germany, and that in the future it would be impossible to preserve all of them; standardization throughout Germany might be necessary in the future. Furthermore, he warned, it might prove impossible to use local materials in every case: "We shall have to move ahead towards a healthy standardization."[54] Here was a suggestion for mass production of material for indigenous peasant architecture which surely ran counter to everything *völkisch* writers sought. This project, however, never materialized, and the plans of government branches and of other reformers for the preservation of the rural home and landscape were the guide for much that was actually accomplished in the Third Reich.

Although the visions of the writers outran achievements, real attempts were made between 1933 and 1939 to develop a "blood-and-soil" architecture. Even though public housing took second place to the monumental program, commentaries on public housing, particularly rural settlements, reveal an attempt to unite ideology and architecture. If much that was built was plain, it was still *völkisch* in style, and this, said many writers, was the way it should be.

Several hundred rural settlements were built by the Labor Front, each with about 150 houses, to be inhabited by workers employed in factories within or outside cities. Most of these single-family homes were high gabled, with pointed rooms, and separate yards. There were no flat roofs or large window areas.[55] (See illustration no. 74.) Although these homes might seem as monotonous

extended to the tennis stadium. March, *Bauwerk*, pp. 12 and 34, ill. nos. 36–37 and 39–40.)

[54] Wilhelm Grebe, "Wiedergesundung und Neuausrichtung des ländlichen Bauwesens," *Bauwelt*, cited in Teut, *Architektur*, pp. 278–279. See Hitler's remarks in the *Secret Conversations* on the necessity of standardizing building parts in the future (p. 97, October 19, 1941; and p. 335, February 28, 1942).

[55] See Teut, *Architektur*, pp. 250–270; and Lane, *Architecture and Politics*, pp. 206–211.

as the lamented modern architecture, to Frau Troost, they possessed, as did all the great works of the movement, "clarity, beauty, and harmony."[56] Near Munich, in 1934, Ramersdorf was opened, a model settlement of 150 single-family homes, well landscaped with the appearance of a village. According to one writer, this settlement revealed how the *Volk's* "joy in life" could be increased, here where "mother nature" offered the chance to breath fresh air freely. The settlement, he noted, was not rigidly laid out, but pre-existant trees were left where they grew, and the streets curved through lawns and gardens.[57] Another example is the Schottenheim settlement near Regensburg, which contained the essential community house, kindergarten, and even a church.[58] Where rural settlements could not mitigate the disadvantages of urban living, the Third Reich continued the Weimar Republic's program of slum clearance and building of apartment houses in major cities, although there had been much criticism of the modern experiments in this fashion.[59] In the thirties fewer apartments were built than rural settlements, and little was written on the former. Expansion of Munich and Berlin was planned, but the war prevented completion of the projects. In the capital, a large apartment suburb was planned for the Charlottenburg district, with tree-lined streets laid out in geometric patterns, the flats traditionally designed.[60] Troost offered examples of the type of apartment which she, reflecting both government and *völkisch* opinion, approved; one of these, built in Munich, was a four-storey

[56] Troost, *Bauen*, I, 157.
[57] Guido Harbers, "Randbemerkungen zur Deutschen Siedlungsausstellung München 1934," *Das schöne Heim*, Munich 1934, cited in Teut, *Architektur*, pp. 236–237. Harbers was a member of the Nuremberg board of works, and editor of *Baukunst*. Another model settlement was built in Düsseldorf in 1937. ("Gemeinschaftssiedlung auf der Ausstellung 'Schaffendes Volk' in Düseldorf," *Deutsche Bauhütte*, XIV:18 (August 25, 1937), 236–237.)
[58] See the photograph on p. 166; also p. 156 of Troost, *Bauen*, I; Troost also carried illustrations of new rural settlements, such as the Adolf Hitler Koog in Schleswig-Holstein (photo on p. 162).
[59] See for example, Rittich's comments, *Architektur und Bauplastik*, pp. 5–6.
[60] Wolters, *Neue deutsche Baukunst*, p. 86.

building with tiled roof, picturesque shutters, a false arcade on the street front, and an oriel window.[61] (See, for example, illustration no. 75.) A touch of traditional, smalltown, or rural life was thus introduced into the metropolis.

Although the government of the Third Reich took little interest in the privately built home as potentially influential architecture, some writers nonetheless expressed concern for this sector of architecture. Schultze-Naumburg had been writing on the private home, mansion, or villa for many years, noting that although the homes of princes had changed style with international fashion, the German *Bürgerhaus* had shown "clearly a national character."[62] The privately constructed building, said Troost, must be planned as a unit and be in keeping with the natural beauty of the landscape. Clarity and functionalism was important in the smallest house, which must fit organically into the "great harmony of our new Reich."[63] Larger individual homes were not important in the overall scheme of the Nazi building program; only in a limited way could they be considered "community" architecture. Hence, however many private homes were built with private means, the commentators were not interested in writing on them.[64]

[61] Troost, *Bauen*, I, 144–145. These would also have satisfied Lindner, who gave an example of an undesirable apartment, a four storey, flat-roofed structure in Neissen, which he called "an attack on artistic city planning." (*Die Stadt*, p. 19, ill. no. 13). Despite the relatively small number of urban apartments built, time was found to replace the flat roofs of the controversial Weissenhof settlement in Stuttgart with sloping ones, allegedly because the flat ones were not thick enough. (Correspondence with Albert Speer, December 14, 1968). Similar alterations were made to the *Bauhaus* buildings in Dessau. (Correspondence with the civic authorities of Dessau, May 12, 1969.)

[62] Schultze-Naumburg, *Kunst der Deutschen*, p. 66.

[63] Troost, *Bauen*, I, 132–133. In their books both Troost and Rittich had illustrations of several larger homes, all in a *Biedermeier* or *völkisch* style. See *Bauen*, I, 138–140, 148–153; and Rittich, *Architektur und Bauplastik*, pp. 150–153.

[64] In the realm of private, domestic building, as Anna Teut indicates, *Gleichschaltung* was slow to penetrate. Flat roofed homes with large ceiling-to-floor windows of solid panes of glass were constructed by the modern Hans Scharoun in Potsdam (1934), Rudolf Schwarz in Offenbach-Main (1934), and by Egon Eiermann in Berlin-Dahlem (1935) (Teut, *Architektur*, pp. 143, 151, and 161.)

Nevertheless, one aspect of private homes — and public
housing, too — seems central to the Nazi ideology as well as to
the *völkisch* movement: the role of the garden. Nature-loving
"Aryans" would want to be surrounded by gardens, if not by
natural landscape. The Reich Garden Exhibitions in Essen in
1938 and in Stuttgart in 1939 were held for this reason.[65] Günther
noted that there were two styles of garden: the "Nordic" type
based on an understanding of nature, and the Western type, based
on a sterile, purely architectural concept. The ancient Greeks
had possessed the former concept, as did the English, with their
landscape gardens; the French, who developed ordered "rational"
Renaissance and baroque gardens, on the other hand, were "non-
Aryan."[66] Other writers also stressed the need for gardens and
parks in German towns and cities. Quite sensibly, one writer
noted that hedges and trees would help bind a house to its surrounding landscape,[67] but, in *Das Dorf* another commentator went
so far as to cite appropriate examples of "shrubs and creepers on
the house," and "flowers at the window,"[68] a good example of the
prevalent concern for order and control.

Interest in gardens, however, did not penetrate thinking at
the top. In the German urban centers, gardens were often torn up,
and replaced with stone expanses — the example of Munich's
Königsplatz comes immediately to mind. Thus, in its love for
nature, as well as in its concern for a healthy race, the *völkisch*
movement had a restricted effect on the building program. The
government and the *völkisch* writers meant different things by
"community architecture." Government practice and contemporary theory remained far apart in this area.

[65] See "Reichsgartenschau Stuttgart 1939," *Moderne Bauformen*, XXXVIII
(1939), special supplement after p. 120; and Troost, *Bauen*, II, 139 (this is a
photograph of the stark, glass-walled exhibition hall in Stuttgart).
[66] Citing the painter and writer Willy Lange, whose *Gartenbilder* had appeared in 1922; Günther used the English Garden in Munich as an example of
the appropriate German garden, and the Herrenhausen gardens in Hannover as
an example of the inappropriate "Western" sort. (*Rasse und Stil*, pp. 62–63.)
[67] Hartmann, *Werkhefte*, p. 56.
[68] Lindner, *Das Dorf*, pp. 141 and 149.

However, the government was interested in the spiritual health, or the "political-mental hygiene," of the German *Volk*. If Hitler himself took little real interest in rural settlements and less in urban housing, he was concerned with facilities for training and housing German youth. If the race was to continue healthy physically, then the minds of youth must be trained in a suitable manner.[69] Architecture had a role to play here. "Among the educative powers, which influence young people's development," wrote the Hitler Youth Leader, Baldur von Schirach, "[architectural] space takes a leading role."[70] When this space took the form of suitable buildings, it would not be difficult, he continued, "to train the young person into a conscious bearer of national values."[71] These are the familiar nationalist tenets. Hans Stephan, Speer's advisor, wrote that the aim of the new German architecture was "to train the *Volk* to an appreciation of the community, to give it political schooling, to raise its joy in life and its strength for life, to reflect its strength and accomplishments."[72] Obviously, young people were the most accessible and, for the future, most important groups within the *Volk*. Realizing this, a Berlin Hitler Youth architect wrote of the necessity of an "artistic-soldierly education of the younger generation": "Our homes and buildings will above all embody the soldierly, disciplined feeling for life of our youth, and are therefore constructed in simplicity, clarity, and Prussian austerity."[73] It was both to reflect and to propagate specific values, therefore, that the hostels and the youth centers were built. Thus

[69] Hitler wrote that "the crown of the *völkisch* state's entire work of education and training must be to burn the racial sense and racial feeling into the instinct and the intellect, the heart and brain of the youth entrusted to it. No boy and no girl must leave school without having been led to an ultimate realization of the necessity and essence of blood purity." (*Mein Kampf*, p. 427.) Therefore, all the youth of Germany were made members of the Hitler Youth in December 1936 (on paper, at least).

[70] Baldur von Schirach, *Revolution der Erziehung: Reden aus den Jahren des Aufbaus*, Munich, Eher, 1942, p. 84.

[71] *Ibid.*, p. 12.

[72] Stephan, *Baukunst im dritten Reich*, p. 9.

[73] Hans Dustmann, "Vom Bauen der Hitlerjugend," *Der Deutsche Baumeister*, 1940, Heft 1, cited in Teut, *Architektur*, pp. 213–217. See also the descrip-

the writing on architecture for youth is more directly political
and propagandistic than the previously discussed works on settlements and flats. And, as with the representative monumental
architecture, the Hitler Youth structures (although much smaller)
were didactic in purpose.

The writers on German youth centers naturally regarded
them as devices for teaching the tenets of the ideology. For one
Hitler Youth *Oberbannführer*, the Hitler Youth *Heim* (or clubhouse, as distinct from hostel) was an integral part of the training
of young Nazis. The smallest *Heim*, he wrote, was a "building of
the movement" and must in every detail embody the attitude and
dignity of that movement.[74] Particularly important was the degree
to which the *Heim* taught the concept of "community" in all its
forms.[75] For example, von Schirach noted that, because the public had allegedly contributed generously to the construction of
hostels, the *Volk* itself was the patron, and was wealthier and
more powerful than any capitalist. Thus the youth centers were
"community buildings," devoted, at the same time, to "training
for the *Volk* community."[76] The Hitler Youth, said von Schirach
elsewhere, had always found the *Heim* to be an "important pre-
requisite for their community work."[77] The *HJ* group was advised
by another Nazi to take a hand in building its own clubhouse, an
undertaking which would strengthen their sense of group achievement.[78] The youth group was described as a "closed community"[79]
in which the young German would best learn the virtues necessary
for Germany's survival. One of these virtues, of course, was the

tion of a planned *Heim* for Gleiwitz in Hartmann, *Werkhefte*, p. 99, wherein the
lines of the home are praised for their "clear and soldierly appearance." This book
was prefaced with remarks by Goebbels and Bernhard Rust (minister of education).

[74] Hartmann, *Werkhefte*, p. 32.
[75] *Ibid.*, pp. 21, 51, and 91.
[76] Von Schirach, *Revolution*, pp. 83 and 84.
[77] Cited in Hartmann, *Werkhefte*, p. 17.
[78] *Ibid.*, p. 128.
[79] Heinrich Hartmann, "Der Feierraum," *Musik in Jugend und Volk*, 1937–
1938, cited in Wulf, *Bildenden Künste*, p. 197.

readiness to subordinate individual will to the will of the large group. When an old *Wandervogel* (a member of the prewar youth movement) complained that the large new hostels were not youth homes, but rather hotels, von Schirach allowed that this exaggeration was partially justified; the old *Wandervogel* individualism was dead, he implied, and the day of the mass *Volk* community had dawned. "We built the new youth hostels on the scale which we considered correct," he said in his memoirs.[80]

The function of the *Heim* was slightly different from that of the hostel; in fact, said Gottfried Feder, the hostel and the home should not ordinarily be united in one building, since the hostel was used partly by foreign young people traveling through Germany. The *HJ Heim* must be more quintessentially German than the hostel. At least three *Heime* must be built in each city of over 20,000 inhabitants; one of these must have a special ceremonial building (as a kind of *Volk* hall) attached, and must be centrally located as well as near a park or sports field.[81]

What was to differentiate the Hitler Youth home from the hostel was its greater dimensions and its representative function. Each home, according to the approved view, should have "a bright and wide entrance hall," which could serve the "dignified preservation of banners." There should be no "trivial porch." Inside, the *Heim* must have much light, space, and a "unified fresh atmosphere," as well as "clarity and spatial order in the layout of rooms."[82] As with many other "community" buildings, its color and material was important; recommended were "natural coloring with the grey marbling of broken stone, [and] the friendly white of a whitewashed wall." These homes must obviously appear as "buildings of the movement," and with the "mighty" body of the ceremonial room, "the richer entrance, the proud window-

---

[80] Kitchens large enough to serve three or four hundred guests were in order. (von Schirach, *Ich glaubte an Hitler*, p. 180.)

[81] Feder, *Die neue Stadt*, p. 194; similar suggestions were made by Toni Maier, an architect, in "HJ-Heim und altes Stadtbild," in Lindner, *Die Stadt*, pp. 274-284.

[82] Hartmann, "Der HJ-Heimbau im Dorf," in Lindner, *Das Dorf*, p. 208.

doors, flag, symbols" must show a "different face" from the other buildings in the neighbourhood. Considering specific styles, von Schirach felt that Hitler's "architect's will" rejected stone squares or "Doric" façades in the villages of Germany; on the contrary the Hitler Youth homes and hostels were to "sing the song of their landscape."[83]

In 1937 the office of the Reich youth leader produced what was to be the first in a series of manuals, edited by Hartmann, who gave explicit instructions for those architectural features that would give the home its suitably didactic character. The roof must be slanted, he said, for the *Heim* must blend with the appearance of old villages.[84] As the doorway to the *Heim* was more than just an opening in a wall, it should be built larger and wider than functionally necessary, because, said Hartmann: "Our entry [to the *Heim*] is more than just an incidental 'function,' it is a first encounter and reception, which particularly in a community building should be joyful and proud."[85] The entrance hall, too, should create the atmosphere of the *Heim*; "it should liberate through light and breadth," also revealing the general layout of the rooms.[86] The most important room in the home, of course, was the *Feierraum*, or ceremonial room, the appropriate form of which was a rectangle with an altarlike fixture at one end, containing a bust of the *Führer*, flags, or the eagle with wreathed swastika. The shape of the room determined the form of the ceremony, said Hartmann: "An honest confrontation of community and symbol, of followers and *Führer*. We want no loose crowds there, no community divided by oriel windows and niches, by ranks, reserved seats, or places of honor, but rather united blocks of boys and girls, who are arranged in place in the room, where a symbol announces in clean, worthy shape the power and greatness of the

[83] Cited in Hartmann, "Der HJ-Heimbau im Dorf," p. 210.
[84] Hartmann, *Werkhefte*, p. 42.
[85] *Ibid.*, p. 51.
[86] "We prefer not to enter by a side door and through tiny porches, tube-like passages, and winding corridors . . ." Hartmann, *Werkhefte*, p. 24.

movement."[87] If ceremonies were not held in the *Feierraum,* they were to be held in the courtyards and terraces in some *Heime,* fixtures which served the same function as the urban parade square.[88]

New buildings independent of other institutions were necessary, said Hartmann. In a city of ten-thousand inhabitants, a large *Heim* costing as much as thirty-thousand marks should be built and constructed so that it was obviously a "community building."[89] In the small towns, money for an adequate *Heim* might be lacking, but, said Hartmann, "mass-produced barracks" of substitute building materials were as much to be avoided as was "gazebo architecture."[90]

Not only did the writers believe that the *Heim* should represent the ideology, but they also wanted it to reflect the supposed virtues of Nazi youth itself, "simple, clean, honest, and loyal."[91] In this vein, the new youth was praised for their "willingness to sacrifice for the whole, to subordinate themselves to the great idea, to discipline themselves";[92] those not yet converted would learn these virtues in and through the hostels, homes, and schools, if, as Hartmann implied, the lines of the buildings were clear, upright, and uncomplicated.[93]

[87] *Werkhefte,* p. 122. See p. 100 for the plan for a home at Plettenberg which has a *Feier und Fahnen Halle* with one end set apart for a bust of Hitler.

[88] See the plan for the Melle home with its stone-flagged terrace (*Werkhefte,* p. 92) or the plan for the home at Herringen (pp. 86 and 87) with its enclosed courtyard; the ceremony described by Hartmann as appropriate for this court with its choruses, speakers, and banners resembles a *Thing* play. (The ceremonial room of the center functioned as a small *Volk* hall.)

[89] Hartmann, *Werkhefte,* p. 29.

[90] *Ibid.,* p. 28. He also fully described the quantity and quality of the rooms and equipment of the home, (p. 21.) Rooms included showers, toilets, and bicycle rooms (pp. 22–27). A community of nine-hundred needed a structure of only two rooms, whereas a city of three to ten thousand needed ten rooms (pp. 28–30). As if these details were not sufficient, Hartmann and the *Reichsjugendführung* planned another volume devoted to the individual rooms of the *Heim.*

[91] *Werkhefte,* p. 21.

[92] Pfeiffer, "Die seelische Haltung," p. 29.

[93] Hartmann, *Werkhefte,* p. 30.

As distinct from the *Heime*, the hostels were usually built in the countryside rather than in cities, but also in *völkisch* styles. The Reich League for German Youth Hostels envisaged a network of 50,000 of them, each no more than sixteen miles apart (about one day's hiking distance). Commentary on them was similar to that of the *HJ* homes; as architecture they were to reflect and teach Nazi values.

The commentators on the hostels explained how and why this was necessary. Since young people were in the process of having their characters formed, they must not be housed in structures built for another purpose; the hostel must itself become an "educator, the daily acquaintance with which awakens the feeling for the *Volk*, handicrafts, and *Kultur* . . ."[94] The hostels were not simply overnight shelters, but "cultural centers of the young nation," said another writer. Therefore, they must embody externally the spirit which inspired, or should inspire, youth, and must be "true to life, simple, and solid." Flat roofs were forbidden because they were "un-German" as well as weak in construction; sheet-metal, pasteboard, and cement were also prohibited.[95]

According to Feder, the hostel, as well as the Labor Front, should be built in the countryside in beautiful landscape.[96] Not only do young people need sunshine and fresh air, but they must develop a love of the German landscape. Lindner maintained that Hitler, in his parent's house at Leonding, had developed a "deep experience of nature [which] is of decisive significance in the development of great personalities."[97]

As for the style of the hostel, it must be *völkisch*, said Gerdy Troost; "architectural forms foreign to the *Volk*" were to be

[94] Rittich, *Architektur und Bauplastik*, pp. 136–137.
[95] Otto Schairer, "Uber das Deutsche Jugendherbergswerk und die Planung von Herbergen und Heimen," *Moderne Bauformen*, XXXVI (1937), 121–122. (Schairer was a local Nazi leader in Stuttgart.)
[96] Feder, *Die neue Stadt*, p. 197; *Städtebild und Landschaft*, p. 14; Hartmann, *Werkhefte*, pp. 54–60.
[97] Lindner, *Die Stadt*, p. 40; photographs of Leonding, and of Hitler's parents' house there, ill. nos. 46 and 47.

avoided.[98] Thus ideal hostels would be copies of Bavarian farmhouses, Black Forest chalets, Frankish half-timbered houses, lower Saxon homes, or Prussian country seats. (See illustrations no. 70–72.) Yet in a field where paradoxes are common, it is no surprise to find von Schirach declaring in a speech that the Hitler Youth could build in a "youthful" style using steel and glass and concrete.[99] Nevertheless, his recommendation was not followed and the illustrated examples in the approved volumes are all indigenous in style.

Public schools were less important as architecture to the government and the commentators. Yet, an article in *Bauwelt* summed up the approved attitude to the style of these buildings. The National Socialist school administration, it said, wanted no expensive frills, no flat roofs or glass walls, but simple, pleasing "functional" buildings.[100] Two architects who designed schools in this period were the tradition-oriented Schulte-Frohlinde and Schmitthenner. The "function" of their buildings was to communicate good German values. If they did so, they could justifiably be called "functional," but not, of course, in the *Bauhaus* sense. Most of these schools are dignified and simple structures, unimaginative, but inoffensive to right-wing nationalist taste.[101]

Apart from public schools, other schools were planned and built, institutions with a purely political aim. The architecture of these structures was important to the propagandists and commentators. Of course the Ordensburgen were, strictly speaking, schools. In a similar vein, the Nazi government planned to build a university of the National Socialist party (*Hohe Schule der NSDAP*),

[98] Troost, *Bauen*, I, 42 and 61.
[99] Baldur von Schirach, "Baustil für die Jugend," *Frankfurter Zeitung*, March 6, 1936, cited in Lane, *Architecture and Politics*, p. 190; see also Teut, *Architektur*, pp. 49–54; Rittich, *Architektur und Bauplastik*, pp. 118–119, and 132–133. See also Hartmann, *Werkhefte*. This speech by von Schirach, significantly, does not appear in the edition of his collected speeches, *Revolution der Erziehung*.
[100] Karl Bonatz, "Schulneubauten im Verwaltungsbezirk Berlin-Neukölln," *Bauwelt*, 1936, cited in Teut, *Architektur*, p. 239.
[101] Troost, *Bauen*, II, 116–125.

which was to train a more exclusively intellectual elite, experts in the ideology. (See illustration no. 73.) To be built on the shores of the Chiemsee (near Seebruck), the university was designed by Herman Giessler. Its main building, a monolithic twelve-storey tower with small narrow windows and four huge eagles on the roof, would surmount a promontory jutting out into the lake. Its severely rectilinear plan included four large courtyards, several playing fields, and a large archway entrance. Its symmetrical lines were vaguely Egypto-Grecian, as in much of Giessler's other work.[102]

Another series of schools, also serving ideological ends, were the Reich Training Castles of the Labor Front, at Erwitte, in Westphalia, and Sassnitz, on the island of Rügen. The latter school was a hotel converted by Schulte-Frohlinde, of *Biedermeier* classical design, equipped its Nazi planners with a parade square in front. The Erwitte structure was a seventeenth-century castle, again renovated by Schulte-Frohlinde. In this case, the Labor Front took over — as was its habit — older buildings with an aura of respectability, tradition, and dignity.[103] Similarly the Hitler Youth took over the Marienwerder Castle (1233) of the Teutonic Order in East Prussia as a Leadership School.[104] On the other hand, the planned Adolf Hitler Schools (also leadership institutions) were to be new buildings; for Hesselberg, Schulte-Frohlinde planned a massive four-storey structure with a thick squat tower in a simplified Italian Renaissance classical style; Hans Dustmann and Robert Braun planned a neo-classical "Doric" structure for Potsdam.[105]

[102] This university was one of Rosenberg's favorite projects, a center for both research and indoctrination. (See I.M.T., *Trial*, IV, 82; and Rosenberg, *Tagebuch*, pp. 79–133, and 135.)

[103] The Sassnitz school is well described in Schulte-Frohlinde, *Bauten der Bewegung*, pp. 27–38. The Erwitte structure can be seen in the same volume; plans, photographs, and sketches, pp. 39–47. On page 43 is a photograph of a large classroom, decorated typically with flags and with a quotation from Hitler carved on the wall.

[104] Schulte-Frohlinde, *Bauten der Bewegung*, pp. 109–113.

[105] For the Hesselberg and Potsdam schools, see Troost, *Bauen*, I, 57 and 56.

Just as government agencies tried to improve the education and training of youth, so they also tried to raise the general standard of German working conditions, an end to be achieved in part through improving the architectural surroundings of the laborer; of course, these surroundings were to express acceptable values. Thus these buildings were planned, remodeled, or constructed in the same spirit as the *HJ* clubhouses, the hostels, and the schools. Nazi propaganda tried to idealize the worker.[106] A half-hearted effort was made to reintegrate the worker into the life of the countryside, ostensibly for the sake of his physical health and spiritual well-being. Hitler liked to present himself as a "worker," and, when the new Chancellery was completed, he welcomed the construction workers into the new building first.[107] Optimistically, Wilhelm Lotz predicted that, in Hitler's Reich, new production centers would arise which the worker would not regard as a mere place of labor, but as "a living space, the architectural mood of which corresponds to the great values which are created there."[108]

Given all the *völkisch* and Nazi propaganda condemning the expansion of industry in the nineteenth century, it was to be expected that the new government would change urban working conditions. But how could architecture increase the well-being of the German as a worker? Many model Houses of Labor were

Others were planned for Koblenz, Waldbröl, and Heiligendamm on the Baltic. (See Schulte-Frohlinde, *Bauten der Bewegung*, pp. 125–126. For the plans of the Reich Academy for the Leadership of German Youth in Braunschweig, see Hartmann, *Werkhefte*, p. 37. Another completely new structure for German youth was the House of German Education at Bayreuth, designed by Hans C. Reissinger of that city. This large complex included a narrow high-ceilinged ceremonial hall, with pillars of limestone, a marble floor, and a large statue, *The German Mother*; Its style was "Nazi classical," complete with pillared portico. (See Schulte-Frohlinde, *Bauten der Bewegung*, pp. 94–101.)

[106] See, for example, James H. McRandle, *Track of the Wolf*, Evanston, Ill., Northwestern University Press, 1965, pp. 80–120.

[107] "I, too, am a son of the people," he said on May 1, 1937 (Domarus, *Reden*, p. 690; Baynes, *Speeches*, p. 620); and in 1938 he told the Reichstag that "for the past five years, I too have been a worker" (Domarus, *Reden*, p. 794; Baynes, *Speeches*, p. 1382; February 20, 1938).

[108] Lotz, "So baut Europa," p. 177.

planned, but few actually executed. Like the Strength through Joy City in Berlin (1936), they contained game rooms, sport halls, theaters, rooms for transient workers. This Berlin settlement contained five large halls — the Berlin Hall, Saar-Pfalz Hall, Bavaria Hall, Hanseatic Hall, Rhineland Hall — all in *völkisch* styles.[109] According to Ley, leader of the Labor Front, these centers must become the "center of comradely cultural life . . . the most beautiful type of building that the city has to offer."[110]

As for the factories where the workers spent most of their days, much building occurred during the thirties, most of it private of course. But the Beauty of Labor organization encouraged employers to beautify their factories. Thus by 1940 many workshops had been redecorated, with dressing rooms, canteens and restrooms. Gardens and sports grounds on factory property became more common.[111] The new factories were not built in a neoclassical or *völkisch* style; although they avoided experimental and radical designs, almost all were in a "modern functional" style, with large expanses of glass, exposed building members, and flat roofs. (See illustration no. 76.) Therefore, although some larger factories erected "chapels" whose main aisle led to a bust of Hitler beneath the symbol of the *Labor Front*, flanked by heroic statues of workers, the new industrial buildings seemed remote from the main architectural streams of the ideology. Hitler, believing that a factory should not look like a state building, was willing to praise functional design when it was in the right place. According to Speer, "Hitler was even more impressed by factory buildings . . . if they were built only of steel or glass."[112] The Labor Front, too, for economy, encouraged its architects to employ efficient styles.[113]

[109] See Schulte-Frohlinde, *Bauten der Bewegung*, for photographs, plans, and elevations, pp. 48–59.
[110] Cited in Teut, *Architektur*, p. 281, note.
[111] See Mason, "Labor in the Third Reich," p. 120.
[112] Correspondence with Albert Speer, March 9, 1969.
[113] Lane, *Architecture and Politics*, p. 190. It was proper, wrote Heinrich Hartmann, to build railway stations of steel and glass, as well as factories, but not the "houses of living communities." (*Werkhefte*, 106.)

Similarly, an article of 1943 stressed the need for "absolute thrift" and "limitation to the most essential" materials in factory buildings erected during the war.[114] Thus, functionalism, which was considered dangerous elsewhere, was rationalized. Not "architectural Bolshevism," but "German" sobriety would teach the worker.

Gerdy Troost expressed the official attitude. Good German technical buildings and factories would be structures "of proportion and order, examples of thrifty and clear lines, symbols of precise, clean work . . ." She approved of the new, modern factories: "How rich in ideas, how noble are these technical buildings!" Such structures of cement, steel, and glass were conducive to "joy in labor, pride in work, as well as bold and disciplined creativity." Despite their "modern" lines, she believed that they were not "foreign bodies in the landscape, because they are the essence of the spirit of the *Volk*." Even when the factory was constructed by private funds, the building was a "community building," because of the great influence exerted by the Labor Front and the Beauty of Labor organization.[115] These remarks suggest that whether a building was called "un-German," or "Bolshevik," or "decadent" depended ultimately on the intentions of the writer and not on the style.

Werner Rittich offered some details to support Troost's point of view. Obviously, much light was necessary in a factory and large windows should therefore be constructed. Here was "true functionalism," he said, "true" because it grew out of the necessities of the building and not from an alien philosophy.[116] The factories which Troost, Rittich, and others illustrate as examples of good German technical architecture are all in a functional style.[117]

Factory production, however, was not to be the exclusive

[114] "Kriegsgemässer Industriebau," *Bauwelt*, 1943, cited in Teut, *Architektur*, pp. 245–249.

[115] Troost, *Bauen*, I, 87–91; see the photos in II, 66–87.

[116] Rittich, *Architektur und Bauplastik*, p. 82.

[117] Troost, *Bauen*, I, 106–114; Rittich, *Architektur und Bauplastik*, pp. 66–67; "Bauten für Industrie," *Moderne Bauformen*, XXXVII (1938), 585–587.

form of labor in the Third Reich. Conservative *völkisch* writers were interested in the craft tradition of Germany. Many commentators and not only those in the party, considered industrialism destructive of the old skills in decoration of buildings, along with old social values, which buildings might represent. Granted the valuable contributions which skilled craftsmen might make to architecture, this attitude in the thirties in Germany was part of the desire to return to a simpler age, such as the medieval period, when crafts flourished and architecture seemed more familiar, more understandable, and more German.

The Austrian *avant-garde* architect, Adolf Loos (1870–1933) had earlier written that "the true greatness of our age [is] that it can no longer bring forth ornament. We have vanquished ornament, and broken through to an ornamentless world."[118] This is exactly what annoyed and frightened Nazis and *völkisch* writers who supported them. To these men, ornamental decoration was a sign of racial strength; lack of ornament was "architectural Bolshevism." Eugen Hönig looked back wistfully to ages when the unity of all the arts was symbolic of community oneness: "Egypt with its colossal and decorated temples and sphinxes, its obelisks decorated with hieroglyphs, Greece in the age of Pericles, with the acropolis, the apotheosis of all art, the Rome of Hadrian . . ."[119]

Throughout these writings runs the idea of defending traditional German values and activities (such as the crafts) from foreign and revolutionary incursions. Architecture had a role to play:

[118] Cited in James Marston Fitch, *Walter Gropius*, New York, Braziller, 1960, p. 14.

[119] Eugen Hönig, "Die Reichskulturkammer und die bildende Kunst im Neuen Reich," in Dreyer, ed., *Deutsche Kultur im neuen Reich*, p. 60. Schmitthenner similarly predicted that, in the future, Germans would "again paint in their halls and carve stone saints and kings, heroes and mythical animals." (*Baukunst im dritten Reich*, p. 34.) The *avant-garde* Gropius was also seeking unity of the arts at the *Bauhaus*, but not, of course, with the traditional and nationalist outlook of Hönig and Schmitthenner. The somewhat radical Working Council for Art (*Arbeitsrat für Kunst*) in 1919 also sought this aim, seeking to preserve the craft tradition and the apprentice system. This attitude's background helps to explain why so many professionals looked hopefully to the Nazi government for realization of their ideals.

schools, such as Stuttgart and Munich, which tended to teach in a traditional manner, were praised. An article in 1935 praised the Darmstadt Technical University's architecture division for maintaining and supporting "indigenous architecture" even in an age in which this was called old fashioned.[120] Lotz remarked that the new chancellery showed the "high quality of German handicraft *Kultur*," and Wolters, too, proudly noted that the furniture in the Chancellery was not imported, but made "in German workshops."[121] Thus Hitler's government seemed to be defending traditional crafts. The *Führer* supported German crafts, and a large House of German Crafts was planned by Clemens Klotz for Frankfurt.[122]

Schmitthenner's attitude was typical: "architecture declines with the development of technology."[123] The "architectural Bolsheviks" were possessed of a "technoid madness," said another commentator.[124] Too great a respect for technology was tantamount to materialism.[125] Gropius and Le Corbusier were condemned for their "oriental-Bolshevik-unartistic" attitude which led to the production of "sitting machines for chairs, eating machines for tables, and sleeping machines for beds."[126] Here, in

[120] H. R. Rosemann, "Erziehung zum Bauen an der Darmstadter Hochschule," *Moderne Bauformen*, XXXIV (1935), 325–328. Rosemann was a professor of art history in Darmstadt.

[121] Lotz, "Die Innenräume," p. 80; Wolters, *Albert Speer*, p. 61.

[122] See Schulte-Frohlinde, *Bauten der Bewegung*, pp. 92–93. Many writers concerned themselves with sculpture and decoration in wood. See, for example Wendland, *Kunst und Nation*, p. 23; Schultze-Naumburg, *Kunst der Deutschen*, p. 41; Herbert Hoffman, "Holzbauten aus Deutschland, Osterreich, und dei Schweiz," *Moderne Bauformen*, XXXII (1933), 223–252. See particularly Carl Shäfer, *Deutsche Holzbaukunst: die Grundlagen den deutschen Holzbauweisen in ihrer konstruktiven und formalen Lage*, Dresden, Jess, 1937. These are mainly in the *völkisch* stream, but Hoffman's early article contains some examples of furniture which is "functional" in style.

[123] Schmitthenner, "Tradition und neues Bauen," cited in Teut, *Architektur*, p. 121. Wendland made a similar statement. (*Kunst und Nation*, p. 28.)

[124] Kiener, "Germanische Tektonik," p. 186.

[125] Wendland, *Kunst und Nation*, p. 28.

[126] Ziegler, *Wende und Weg*, p. 11. These comments are based on Le Corbusier's suggestion that a house was merely a "machine for living in."

furniture, as well as in doors and staircases, were areas where German wood carvers and stone cutters should be allowed to develop their crafts.

But if wood or stone carving and similar crafts were to play a greater role in German architecture, how should the new state deal with the craft-destroying powers of technology? None of the commentators suggested that Germans should abandon modern means, for it was agreed that technology had its uses, if controlled. Toward the end of the Third Reich, ideas emerged which suggest that some government departments were changing their earlier position and were about to abandon support of the older crafts, but this never developed into policy. The critics were not opposed to technology correctly used any more than was Hitler absolutely opposed to flat roofs and glass walls for factories. Technology was a "tool for art." The architect, in particular, could use machines to solve his technical problems, just as the builders of the Parthenon used their building machines.[127] In a speech of 1935, Rosenberg found a role for technology in good German architecture, noting that it was perhaps even good that architectural technology with its stark bare "machines for living," had destroyed the pomp of nineteenth-century architecture because now the way was open for a new start.[128] Schmitthenner approved of the new iron and concrete construction methods and of the flat roof, too, where necessary; but technology, he said, should just "serve *Kultur*," and, to do so, must be controlled.[129]

The wartime movement for standardization of building parts provides another irony.[130] The trend to "neo-functionalism" inaugurated by the government during and because of the war used technology, but surely not in the way which the critics wished. Prefabrication of houses by mass production would leave less

[127] Wendland, *Kunst und Nation*, p. 29.
[128] Alfred Rosenberg, "Kultur und Technik," *Gestaltung der Idee: Blut und Ehre*, Vol. II: *Reden und Aufsätze von 1933–35*, Munich, Eher, 1942, p. 326.
[129] Schmitthenner, *Baukunst im neuen Reich*, pp. 5, 35, and 36.
[130] See Teut, *Architektur*, pp. 120–121.

room for the work of, for example, woodcarvers, for in all likelihood something resembling their products could be produced by a machine. Factory-produced *völkisch* houses or hostels, in cities or in the countryside, would be shabby counterfeits of what was wanted. Yet whatever the sincerity of the commentators, the leadership of the Third Reich was fundamentally cynical about the *Volk* and the glories of *völkisch* culture.

CHAPTER ELEVEN

The New German City

THE TECHNOLOGICAL threat to German crafts, plus many of the other dangers to German architectural traditions were believed to emanate from the expanded urban centers of the Reich. Right-wing nationalist critics consequently considered the problems of the modern city. Although German literature on this subject in the thirties had much in common with foreign contemporary studies, German reform plans were often in line with other Nazi ideological concerns.

To discuss the approved attitudes to city reform is to summarize much that has already been considered, because, in the replanning of the larger German cities, "community" architecture in most of its forms — with the significant exception of *völkisch* styles — played an important role. However, the commentary on most of the great monumental and representative "community" structures built and planned for Berlin, Munich, Nuremberg, Linz, and smaller cities includes additional important aspects of the nationalist attitude to architecture.

The one fact underlying all German thinking on city planning in the twentieth century is that, whereas in 1871 approximately two-thirds of the German population lived in communities of less than 2000 inhabitants, by 1933 only one-third lived in the countryside and the rest lived in cities in an industrial environment. For example, Berlin, which in 1871 had 800,000 inhabitants, had by 1937 over four million.[1] To broad strata of the German community, this sudden urbanization was a social shock. Such a swift change in the environment and living conditions, whether it involved poverty or not, was difficult for the average German to understand. Adjustments were needed for all the peculiarities of city life, as well as for the twentieth-century phenomena of industrialization, socialism, communism, strikes, and political demonstrations: hence the longing to return to a simpler age, and hence the dislike of the *Grosstadt*, or metropolis, expressed by *völkisch* critics and also many ordinary Germans.

Writings on Nazi city planning stressed that the metropolis was evil, a source of communism, Jewish capitalism, and general pollution of healthy German life. Hitler's own attitude, however, was typically ambivalent. His unpleasant experiences in Vienna made him hate the big city as a hotbed of social democracy, Jews, and miscegenation; for relaxation, he retreated to his mountain chalet in Berchtesgaden. He planned to restrict the number of large cities in Germany: Berlin would have five million people, but that was the upper limit for the capial and no other town should be so large. Two cities, Vienna and Hamburg, would be allowed to have two million inhabitants each.[2] Although antipathetic to large cities, he did not support indigenous architecture, the *Thing* movement, or *völkisch* zealots like Schultze-Naumburg. He would not carry condemnation of city life to the point that every city must be a center of racial and cultural decay. Naturally it was advantageous to the movement and the state to have grandiose urban centers with monumental architecture; the impressionable masses of the city were easily gathered into crowds for demonstrations and rallies. Thus he disagreed with the attempt of some critics to dismantle the urban centers of the Third Reich.

[1] Figures cited by Stephan, in *Baukunst im dritten Reich*, p. 12. They can be corroborated in Gerhard Masur, *Imperial Berlin*, New York, Basic Books, 1970, pp. 62 and 133.

[2] S.C., p. 432 (May 3, 1942); *Tischgespräche*, p. 311. He preferred Weimar or Bayreuth to larger towns, he said. S.C., p. 311 (February 19–20), p. 180.

Some of Hitler's ideas are familiar; he believed that German cities had become no longer "culural sites," but "mere human settlements," "masses of apartments and tenements." There were no "community monuments" in these cities which could give a "special bond" or sense of community; nothing, too, which could "reflect . . . the greatness and wealth of the community." But in the "Germanic middle ages," with urban cathedrals, German cities had such a focus. Contemporary German cities, therefore, needed "an outstanding symbol of the national community."[3]

Hitler was only one among many Germans who had long been critical of the metropolis. Adolf Bartels, a *völkisch* novelist (1862–1945), had reminded his readers that the ancient Teutons could not bear to live in cities.[4] In 1909, Schultze-Naumburg had called the metropolis "the Moloch of our time."[5] The widespread view that modern architecture and the large city were "civilization" expressed the equally widespread concept that German *Kultur* was superior to the "unspiritual," "materialist" *Zivilisation* of western Europe.[6] The party philosopher, Rosenberg, wrote that the metropolis tended to "annihilate" "Aryans" and create "racial chaos"; like Hitler, he recommended that the growth of certain cities be limited.[7] "The decadent metropolis is the death of the nation!" cried Feder.[8] Günther expressed the same idea, and recommended that through new rural settlements, the great German cities could be reduced to size.[9]

These were typical aspects of the contemporary rejection of the city. But the metropolis was also considered deleterious to architecture. The large city, "hostile to the arts," "herded" artists to-

[3] *Mein Kampf*, pp. 263–266.
[4] Cited in Brenner, *Kunstpolitik*, p. 124. Günther cited Tacitus on this matter. (*Die Verstädterung*, p. 1.) Darré, the peasant "expert," wrote on how the ancient Teutons had hated the city. (*Neuadel*, p. 52.)
[5] "The child of the big city no longer knows the soil," he wrote, "only asphalt." (*Städtebau*, p. 15.)
[6] Wendland, *Kunst der Nation*, p. 48.
[7] Rosenberg, *Mythus*, p. 298 and 554.
[8] Feder, *Die neue Stadt*, p. 14.
[9] Günther, *Die Verstädterung*, p. 48ff.

gether, "proletarianized" them, and "uprooted" them from "healthy nature and from a healthy way of life."[10] "The metropolis is always the enemy of a true culture," said an art critic. "This, too, is a question of soil. Out of asphalt and tenements only pipes grow."[11]

Writers looked back to a time when industrial pipes and "asphalt wastes" did not characterize German cities. Most had an idealized view of the medieval town community. Well-preserved towns like Danzig, Rothenburg, and, Nuremberg were taken as models of the typical medieval German urban center. Troost praised the practicality of their market places and town halls and wrote that the act of creating these fixtures for the economy and administration was an example of the "will to self-representation of the community." The "harmonious picture" and the "unified architectural image" of medieval cities was a community accomplishment, the mirror of "an acknowledged *Volk* order."[12] (See illustration no. 2.) For the editors of *Städtebild*, the Middle Ages saw the "full bloom of the German *Volk*," which, in its towns, expressed the organizational structure of its life. A common political experience developed the *Volk*'s sense of community and strengthened the whole organism for great accomplishments. This community, said the editors, demanded the subordination of the individual and limited the bounds of his private life. Whereas the very construction of the city reflected this "rigid order," the city hall mirrored the community's self-awareness; despite its impressive dignity, it stood in "healthy" relationship to other buildings. The homes of craftsmen revealed a "clean craft sense," while the homes of the merchants had a more individualistic tone, yet restrained themselves continually within the limits acceptable to the community. The city was incorporated into the surrounding landscape and did not sprawl in an inorganic fashion over neighbouring valleys and hills.[13] Thus the approved view of the medie-

[10] Willrich, *Die Säuberung*, pp. 103–104.
[11] Eberlein, *Was ist deutsch in der deutschen Kunst?* p. 21.
[12] Troost, *Bauen*, I, 6–7.
[13] *Städtebild und Landschaft*, pp. 5–7.

val city was that it was ordered, regulated, clean, natural, and healthy. This was the type of society the Nazis and *völkisch* critics wished to see revived in Germany.

In the eighteenth century, some German cities, notably Mannheim and Karlsruhe, were constructed (according to the official view) with a "clean overall plan."[14] The decline of German cities began in the nineteenth century, other writers agreed. The age could not think "in great contexts,"[15] and hence, lacking an ideology of building, the community allowed private buildings to overshadow monumental "community structures." This "overemphasis on the individual's building," together with urban sprawl, was lamented by others too.[16] When city walls were torn down in this "decadent" century, the suburbs began their apparently limitless growth. The architectural styles of these suburbs used "masquerades" and slavish following of foreign building fashions. After 1871, said a Labor Front writer, the city centers were decorated by granite war memorials "in wedding-cake style," and by imperial post offices with "neo-Gothic fake-stone façades." Although the worst excesses occurred in northeast Germany and in Berlin, he singled out the late nineteenth-century city hall of Munich for special criticism.[17] (See illustration no. 11.) *Städtebild* also criticized the "uncoordinated expansion" of Dresden, which destroyed the surrounding landscape.[18] Imitative architecture, lack of true monumentality, and uncontrolled growth, then, were the main sins of nineteenth-century German builders.

As the twentieth century approached, another problem developed to vex the critics: industrial filth and unhealthy living conditions. Going beyond the Europe-wide concern for slum living, the official view expressed *völkisch* anti-urban attitudes. *Die Stadt* described Germans living in "an unplanned, disorderly maze" of

[14] *Ibid.*, p. 10.
[15] Dresler, *Das braune Haus*, pp. 9–10.
[16] *Städtebild und Landschaft*, p. 10.
[17] Lindner, *Die Stadt*, pp. 50, 65, 126, and 245.
[18] *Städtebild und Landschaft*, p. 166.

"dirty factory walls . . . and oily garages," behind the metropolis' "pompous overblown mask." And in this "swampy soil" grew the "projecting façades," the "cubistic paintings," "cinema kitsch," the "jazz music with nigger dancing."[19] Rosenberg linked this to the "planned destructive activity of the Jew" who found his natural home in the metropolis.[20] But as if this situation were not bad enough, the smaller cities of Germany were now affected by the same bacillus. Here were "ruined inadequate houses, badly paved streets, poor lighting, cramped, unclear city plans . . ."[21] All this must change, and the official Nazi criticism of big capitalism and foreign cultural elements made it seem likely that after 1933 changes would be inaugurated.

The government plan to transform the face of Germany included a far-reaching reform of cities. For example, a 1936 decree outlined the responsibility of architects for the "architectural beauty and cleanliness of the cityscape and the landscape." Another law of 1937 covered regulations for "the reconstruction of cities."[22] In a speech to the Reichstag in 1937, Hitler said that the aim of the Four Year Plan was to "make life healthier and pleasanter for the German *Volk* . . . The planned improvement of several large cities of the Reich is outward proof of this great epoch of our *Volk*'s resurrection."[23] While the government did not seriously consider the dismantling of the metropolis, growth of urban centers (especially of their industrial areas) was to be controlled. Even more imporant, the major German cities were to be given impressive architectural centers and orderly street plans. Public housing was — some day — also to be improved.

Wolters wrote that, while things like traffic regulation, slum

[19] Lindner, *Die Stadt*, p. 18.
[20] Rosenberg, *Mythus*, p. 302.
[21] Lindner, *Die Stadt*, p. 57.
[22] For a description of the terms of these decrees (of July 28, 1936, and October 4, 1937), see J. Elfinger, "Kampf für eine gesunde Baukultur," p. 1034; and Gregor Janssen, *Das Ministerium Speer: Deutschlands Rüstung im Krieg*, Berlin, Ullstein, 1968, p. 349.
[23] Domarus, *Reden*, p. 674 (January 30, 1937).

clearance, and creation of parks were important, Germany's vital task was the creation of new city centers, "new architectural focii of a size which will outshadow any private buildings."[24] These centers, usually to be located where two great axes crossed, included the construction of representative buildings — Volk halls, Gau houses, and squares. Speer's plan for Berlin was often imitated in smaller centers, where the Gauleiters tried to outdo each other in urban replanning.[25]

Three important contemporary works on this theme, two by the Labor Front, and one by Feder, expressed the widespread belief that architecture could foster physical health, love of nature, sense of order, community feeling, and other approved qualities. In Der Stadt, Lindner wrote that buildings in the reformed urban areas would not be too high because, as building height increased, so did the inhabitants' "alienation from nature." "Shady crowns of trees" should rise above the roofs of houses, as in small cities, the models for Germany's urban revival. He believed that the metropolis should not be allowed to grow further. The new city would be small, full of natural parks, and resplendent with "air, light, and sunshine."[26] These views, although not purely "Nazi," appeared in this literature with the nationalist "community" idea and other ideological themes. For example, Feder opened his book with the statement: "These new cities of a new ideology will be the most visible and permanent expression of a new community will."[27]

Because the small city was the ideal urban form, the writers of Städtebild devoted much attention to plans for its reform, and to discussion of actual accomplishments. Few other sources are

[24] Wolters, Neue deutsche Baukunst, p. 13. Rittich insisted that these representative buildings must dominate all others. (Architektur und Bauplastik, p. 86.) The same idea, was expressed as one of the "fundamental rules of city building," by the editors of Städtebild und Landschaft, p. 14.

[25] Speer, Erinnerungen, p. 157; Inside, p. 143.

[26] Lindner, Die Stadt, pp. 98, 86–87, 49, and 58.

[27] Feder, Die neue Stadt, p. 1; the new cities would be another community accomplishment, said the editors of Städtebild und Landschaft, p. 18.

as complete a compendium of Nazi-approved thinking on architecture as is this volume. In the discussion of the planned expansion of Mittweida in Saxony, the land under consideration was divided into three "clearly recognizable sections."[28] Order reigned. A *Jugendburg* (youth fortress) was constructed. There were plans for a *Volk* hall on an enlarged market square, and for a hostel on the edge of town. Original forests were preserved and incorporated into the plans. All the new buildings here expressed the "rediscovered community consciousness": none revealed the hand of an individualistic architect.[29]

Most significant was the need for order, a principle which was often contradicted. In describing the plans for the town of Klingenthal, the editors wrote that even the smallest details of a house followed laws applicable elsewhere. Yet in describing the plans for the town of Meerane, they were critical of the "schematic" plans of earlier designers. Moreover, illustrations on consecutive pages show the rambling old streets and uniquely differentiated houses in old villages, contrasting sharply with rigid row housing of the new settlements.[30] The need for order led the Nazi planners into excesses, too.[31]

Plans for larger German cities were more grandiose, but the same rigid concepts applied. Representative, monumental buildings were planned for wide avenues and large squares,[32] in sharp

[28] Particularly in industrial Saxony, said the editors, there was a need for "order-giving action." (*Städtebild und Landschaft*, p. 41.)

[29] *Städtebild*, pp. 148–153.

[30] Wolters, too, was critical of such "artistically crooked streets, too quaint squares, and 'romantically' varied houses." (*Neue deutsche Baukunst*, p. 13.)

[31] See *Städtebild und Landschaft*, p. 88 (on Klingenthal), p. 62 (on Meerane), and pp. 136–137 (photographs). In plans for single-family homes, every tree in the garden was labeled as to its type; every section of the garden was given a function (for peas and beans, potatoes, strawberries, etc.). (*Städtebild und Landschaft*, pp. 144–146.)

[32] On October 4, 1937, a law on the reform of German cities was decreed; on November 30 of the same year, the law on the reform of Berlin was issued. Similar laws were decreed for Munich in 1937; for Nuremberg, Hamburg, and the Volkswagen City in 1938; for Augsburg, Bayreuth, Dresden, Graz, Breslau, Würzburg, Linz, and Salzburg in 1939; and for Königsberg, Oldenburg, Posen, and Saarbrücken in 1940.

contrast to the aforementioned green suburbs. These major urban centers would be linked by an all-encompassing transportation system. On these new "community" highways, Hitler intended to take official guests on a north-south axis from Berlin through Weimar to Nuremberg and Munich. German cities were also politicized by their new titles: for example, Berlin was the Capital of the Reich, later to be called Germania; Munich, the Capital of the Movement; Nuremberg, the City of the Party Rallies; Stuttgart, the City of Germans Abroad; Hamburg, the City of Foreign Trade; Graz, the City of the People's Revolution. There was also the City of the Strength Through Joy (Volkswagen) Cars, Wolfsburg, and the City of the Hermann-Goering-Works in the Harz Mountains.[33] (See illustration no. 77.) Plans for rebuilding Berlin and Munich were particularly important.

The center of Berlin contained the works of Schinkel and other renowned architects of the late eighteenth and early nineteenth centuries, plus the impressive avenue, Unter den Linden. But although it had historical associations with Frederick the Great and Bismarck, the German capital had none of the antiquity of other European cities, such as Paris, Rome, London, or even some Slavic centers. It was, in effect, a modern city.[34] Urban industrial expansion had unfortunate effects on Berlin's appearance; although the city contained many examples of the historicist taste in architecture (such as the Protestant cathedral) and a ring of factories and tenements, it had no Haussmann (as had Paris) and

[33] On the latter two cities, see Neue deutsche Baukunst, pp. 66 and 85.

[34] Madame de Stael wrote that "Berlin is a big city, with very broad streets that are perfectly straight, beautiful houses, and a general appearance of orderliness," a comment that would have pleased Speer and others; but, given their respect for the "Prussian style," they would disagree with her note that "this entirely modern city . . . shows no imprint of the country's history or the character of its inhabitants . . ." (Madame de Stael on Politics, Literature, and National Character, ed., trans. by Morroe Berger, New York, Doubleday Anchor, 1965, p. 272.) That very orderliness as well as the classicism of the Brandenburg Gate or the Opera House (which she could have seen on her visits between 1803 and 1808) could be considered emblematic of Prussian character or history.

no Ringstrasse (as had Vienna).[35] Even some non-German critics agree that the *Siegesallee* (Victory Avenue), constructed in 1898–1901, could not compete with anything Paris or Vienna had to offer. By the nineteen-thirties, aside from its objectionable — to Nazi and *völkisch* critics — Jewish and cosmopolitan quality, it had a number of modern buildings made "unacceptable" by their international or experimental style, such as the Siemensstadt settlement and works by Taut, Gropius, and Mendelsohn. It was believed, therefore, that Berlin was in a state of decline. An architect noted that although Goethe had called old Berlin a beautiful city, and although the early Hohenzollerns had built well there, later generations had ruined the capital.[36] The problem was that Berlin had become "intolerably remote from the *Volk's* way of life."[37]

In 1937 Speer was appointed General Building Inspector for the city. The following spring, he revealed his plans for rebuilding it.[38] On June 14, 1938, work began simultaneously on sixteen large structures in the city; the chancellery was, of course, already under construction. Eventually this new Berlin was to be not only the capital of Third Reich but the center of a new Europe.

Troost saw the new plans for Berlin as a product of the "farsighted genius" of Hitler and his "order-giving hands."[39] Although Hitler occasionally contributed ideas, it was Albert Speer who planned the new capital. After construction stopped in September 1939, he asked Hitler in January 1941 to free him from other architectural tasks in order that he could concentrate on his plans for the city; this he was able to do until 1942, when he was put in charge of munitions and war production. The control

[35] Prefect of the Seine under Napoleon III, Baron Haussmann (1809–1891) was responsible for the creation of Paris' wide boulevards. The Ringstrasse in Vienna was built after the city's fortifications were removed in the eighteen-sixties.
[36] Wendland, *Kunst und Nation*, p. 7.
[37] Troost, *Bauen*, I, 53.
[38] On the Berlin plans, see Speer, *Erinnerungen*, pp. 87–93 and 148–165; *Inside*, pp. 73–80 and 132–145.
[39] Troost, *Bauen*, I, 53.

of one architect, Speer (whose powers extended even beyond
those of the city council), meant that the new city would be
rebuilt in an orderly fashion, with new buildings following a unified line.

A new chancellery was to be built to replace the one Speer
was already building.[40] This huge new palace would stand on a
large Adolf Hitler Platz and would be linked to a new *Volk* hall
and the old Reichstag, also on the great square at the city center.
With over five million people, the new Berlin would be the largest
city in Europe, having a diameter of fifty kilometers. Yet it would
have the appearance of a large suburb or garden city. The Spree
River would be widened; a new subway and other tunnels would
guide much pedestrian and automobile traffic underground. The
capital would be a cultural center, with a theater quarter and a
large artists' colony.

The most remarkable thing about the new city, was the sense
of order to be communicated by two monumental avenues running north and south, and east and west, plus four concentric
ring roads and an Autobahn ring. (The remaining street system
was also to be simplified.) This concept was originally Hitler's and
no doubt satisfied his political desire for triumphal avenues (as
in Habsburg Vienna) and grand spacious vistas of distant pros-
pects, as well as his need for parade avenues and large squares.[41]
The new city could become as orderly as Madame de Stael had
found old Berlin, but much more magnificent; its growth would
be structured.[42]

This penchant for rigidly schematic city-planning was re-

[40] See Speer, *Erinnerungen*, pp. 171–175; *Inside*, pp. 156–160; and the photographs of models following p. 160 in the *Erinnerungen*; after p. 286, *Inside*.

[41] He dreamed of a "magnificent perspective stretching from the South Station to the Triumphal Arch with the cupola of the People's Palace (*Volk* hall) in
the distance." (*S.C.*, p. 621, August 28, 1942.)

[42] Wolters, *Albert Speer*, p. 52. No attention was paid to Schultze-Naumburg
who had early written that "a well laid out street must be constructed in
curves . . . Any dead straight street will have a boring effect." (*Städtebau*, p.
55.)

flected in Schüller's praise for Mussolini's construction of wide avenues in Rome. The new Via dell'Impero (which runs through the capital), for example, or the Via della Conziliazione (which runs from the Tiber up to St. Peter's), were considered proof that Rome and Italy enjoyed a government which provided "a new order and a new form" for Rome, and, presumably, for Italian culture, too.[43] Both of these streets are straight and wide, terminating in imposing vistas of monuments, and were to be copied in Berlin.

One of the longest business streets in the world, the north-south axis, like the east-west, would be wider than the already impressive Unter den Linden.[44] The official and social life of the metropolis would flow along it. At each end would arise new railroad stations. This avenue was never built, but the east-west axis was nearly completed, its construction being easier since already existing streets were used. Today it is still possible to stand on the site of the Schloss and to have a relatively unobstructed view down Unter den Linden, Charlottenburger Chaussee, Bismarckstrasse, Kaiserdamm, to Heerstrasse, over seven kilometers to the west. Speer planned to extend it to the east along Kaiser Wilhelm Strasse. The older Victory Column was moved from its "ignoble" position in front of the burned-out Reichstag and placed on the axis elevated by seven meters on a drum, at the Great Star. South of the junction of the axes, Hitler's triumphal arch would be erected. At the crossing of the north-south axis and Potsdamerstrasse was planned the Round Platz, a circular plaza with four fountains and several statuary groups (by Breker). This would have a diameter of 210 meters, and would be surrounded by monumental buildings in neo-classical style.[45] Such was the scheme,

[43] Schüller, *Das Rom Mussolinis*, p. 96.
[44] See the description in Speer, *Erinnerungen*, pp. 148–150; *Inside*, pp. 134–137. As with much of the government's building program, this plan (the North-South Axis) was not new or revolutionary. Martin Mächler (1881–   ) had conceived a similar development in the twenties. (See Alfred Schinz, *Berlin: Stadtschicksal und Städtebau*, Braunschweig, Westermann, 1964, p. 168.
[45] See illustrations in Troost, *Bauen*, I, 76–77.

similar to Mussolini's Roman avenues, to be imposed on the heart of Berlin.[46]

Of the new buildings added to Berlin, the new Reich Chancellery and the Olympic Grounds were the most impressive, as the commentators duly noted. Others were erected and many more planned, all under the supervision of Speer, who saw to it that they were unified in style and general appearance. These were also given the critics' attention. Although their commentary was usually limited to illustrations, photographs, and plans, their approval was implicit. The Nordstern Building and the Reich Grain Offices curve in a quarter circle around the Fehrbelliner-platz.[47] Five storeys high and decorated with reliefs, they are in the same rectilinear style as the Chancellery, but in grey stone. In similar style and stone are the Exhibition Buildings on the Kaiser-damm, designed by Richard Ermisch. A huge new airport complex, designed by Ernst Sagebiel, was constructed at Tempelhof, in time to receive the many foreign visitors to the 1936 Olympics.[48] It consists of a large reception hall flanked by four wings, two of which, on the street side, curve half-way round another plaza, and the other two of which curve partly about the landing and service areas. The style is the same as the above-noted buildings, although the stone is of a golden hue.

Even buildings representing foreign powers took on the mood of their surroundings. Several new embassies, designed by different men, but under Speer's supervision, were constructed. Although the Italian embassy boasts maroon-colored walls, and although the beige façade of the Japanese embassy is surmounted by a large rising sun in gold, and has an entrance flanked by lions, both these and the new Yugoslavian embassy are similar in style; pillars in the Japanese embassy take the place of columns in the

[46] Many private *Grossbauten* were planned for the east-west axis, such as an office building for I. G. Farben; see Rittich, *Architektur und Bauplastik*, p. 104.

[47] The architects were Otto Firle and Ludwig Moshamer, respectively. See the photographs in Rittich, *Architektur und Bauplastik*, p. 102 and p. 111.

[48] See Troost, *Bauen*, I, 117 (photograph).

Italian, and a loggia decorates the side of Mussolini's embassy, but both are in the neo-classical vein Speer favored. These buildings strengthened the image of a "National-Socialist style," a stark classicism which is still to be seen in Berlin. This was the urban face with which Hitler wished to greet the world, and shortly (in the seven peacetime years of the Nazi regime) Berlin received much of its new countenance.[49]

After Berlin, the urban center most favored in reform plans was Munich, the city where the movement had begun, and where so much important party history still occurred. It was a city of art and music, and also the city where the neo-classicism of von Klenze and other early nineteenth-century architects provided a truly "German" atmosphere. For these reasons, it was highly regarded by Hitler himself. The revamping of the Königsplatz and the construction of the *Führer* and Administration buildings was only the start of a far-reaching program.[50] Hitler announced the reform of Munich on January 30, 1937; the plans were drawn up by May 30, 1938, and on December 21, 1939, a general consultant on buildings, Hermann Giessler, was appointed.

A monumental east-west axis was envisaged, 120 meters wide and 6,640 meters long, the longest and widest in the Reich, running from the new railroad station in the west through the Karlsplatz and Stachus and across the Isar to the east. A second great axis would run from the new south station and planned exhibition halls through the Theresienwiese to the new opera house in the north. (Of this, only Riemerstrasse, connecting with the Auto-

[49] Some other planned structures included: Speer's own *Volk* hall ("it will provide a symbol and a crown for the city and the Reich of the new spirit of our time, as once did the acropolis . . . or medieval cathedrals . . ."; Stephan, *Baukunst im Dritten Reich*, p. 18); a tower of over twenty-two storeys as a clinic for the university (Brenner, *Kunstpolitik*, ill. no. 48); and the buildings on the Round Platz, including the German Tourists' Center, "in a unified style and with unified proportions" (Rittich, *Architektur und Bauplastik*, p. 107).

[50] See Dehlinger, *Architektur der Superlative*, pp. 75ff; and Karl Fiehler, *München baut auf: Ein Tatsachen- und Bildbericht über den nationalsozialistischen Aufbau in der Hauptstadt der Bewegung*, München, Eher, n.d. Fiehler was then *Oberbürgermeister*.

bahn, was completed.) A replanned Schwabing district, and new
north and south cities were also envisaged; the latter would be
ideal Nazi communities, each centered on a party forum (with
Volk hall, etc.).[51] Much of the old town of Munich would be destroyed in this reconstruction, but the "artistically valuable"[52]
buildings of Ludwig I (1825–1848) who had expanded the city,
would be preserved.

The most important building in Munich was the House of
German Art, a large neo-classical structure, designed by Paul Ludwig Troost, and still to be seen on Prinzregentenstrasse. (Troost
died before it was completed, and the work was executed under
the supervision of his widow Gerdy, and Leonhard Gall.) The
cornerstone was laid on October 15, 1933, and the structure
opened on July 18, 1937.[53] Here were held exhibitions of good
"German" art. Hitler, with his interest in both painting and architecture, created an endowment to raise money for this museum,
and had promised Troost the job of designing it in the fall of
1930. Originally Hitler planned to build the new gallery in a large
party forum with a museum of contemporary history and the local
party offices, an undertaking which would have destroyed much
of the English Garden. Troost, who wanted to preserve the park,
protested, and there were "arguments for weeks," after which
Ziegler maintains that Hitler gave in to Troost's plan for a single
building on Prinzregentenstrasse with its rear facing the park.[54]

Because the House of German Art was one of the first large
buildings to be built in the Third Reich, much was written about
it. As a monumental, representative, and neo-classical "com-

[51] Dehlinger, Architektur der Superlative, pp. 110, 113, and 120 (plans for
these new settlements, rigidly symmetrical and rectilinear).

[52] Troost, Bauen, I, 58–60.

[53] Plans for the House of German Art were announced in the Völkischer
Beobachter in the July 16–17, 1933 northern edition, 2nd supplement.

[54] Ziegler, Adolf Hitler, pp. 189–190. In fact, Hitler claimed that he envisaged a new gallery for Munich before 1918. (Baynes, Speeches, p. 588, July 18,
1937.)

munity" building, it seemed to embody many of the architectural ideals of the period.

The gallery resembles a heavier, starker version of Schinkel's Old Museum (1822–1830) on the former Lustgarten in Berlin. (See illustration nos. 10 and 78.) Built of the same cream-colored limestone as the Königsplatz buildings, it has two storeys and its street front is long and low, with a colonnade of columns defined at each end by a pylon and a pillar. Heavy cornices above the doors echo the long heavy cornice and architrave at roof level. Its rectangular building stones are each stressed by recessed mortar. Eight steps along the entire length of the façade lead from pavement level up to the porch, stressing the horizontal. The blank walls are broken only by small barred windows. Originally a tablet on the front wall bore a saying of Hitler's: "art is a noble and fanatical mission." Two large braziers stood on the pylons at each end of the façade. (Like the tablet, they have since been removed but still to be seen is the stylized swastika pattern in red and green tile on the ceiling of the porch.)[55]

Hitler probably derived more personal pleasure from contemplation of this building than from any structure other than the Chancellery in Berlin. The latter edifice celebrated the *Führer*-statesman; the new Munich gallery reflected the *Führer*-artist. When he opened it in July 1937, he called it "truly great and artistic," an original structure, "unique and impressive." Although "large in its beauty," it was "functional" in its layout and equipment. It was a "temple of art."[56]

The commentators would have their readers believe that the new Germany would give a predominant place to the arts. National Socialism, after all, stood for the spirit, not solely for political power. Thus, the House of German Art was not only a

[55] Troost, *Bauen*, I, 21–23 (photographs). A swastika pattern was also in the glass roof of the Hall of Honor. (See Schulte-Frohlinde, *Bauten der Bewegung*, p. 89.)

[56] Domarus, *Reden*, p. 707 (July 19, 1937).

"community building," but also a "shrine."[57] Obviously art was something sacred to the "Aryan" race. For other writers, the museum showed that after the liberal and Marxist errors of the past, German architecture was returning to clarity and beauty again. One writer, describing it as "classicism without imitation Hellenism," found a "wonderful clarity" in its plan. Outwardly, with the "musical harmony" created by the contrast of pillars and columns with "severe horizontal lines," this new "temple of German art" would be "remote from engineer architecture executed coldly in iron, concrete, and glass."[58] Fritz Todt also approved the "clear, convincing plan," which indicated a move from "the style of unrest" towards "peace and greatness."[59] For these men, although not perhaps for Hitler, the completion of the House of German Art was a sign that German traditions and values were secure and safe against the intrusions of disturbing foreign ideas. In a time of unsettling changes, this gallery stood for the permanence of what they cherished.[60]

Much more was planned for the Capital of the Movement, but aside from the House of German Art and the Königsplatz buildings, little else of monumental proportions was constructed.[61]

[57] Troost, Bauen, I, 24. Rittich also called it a "temple." (Architektur und Bauplastik, p. 39.) Todt called it "a community structure," because public taxes had helped to build it. (Cited in Fritz, Bauten und Strassen, p. 10.)

[58] Franz Hofmann, "Der Markstein," Völkischer Beobachter, Berlin, 1933, cited in Teut, Architektur, p. 182. Hofmann was artistic advisor and critic for this newspaper, and later helped in the purge of German art galleries of "decadent" works.

[59] Todt, Bauschaffen, p. 227.

[60] As with other "buildings of the community," community reaction was not always favourable. The House of German Art was variously labelled "Palazzo Kitschi" and "Weisswurstbahnhof." (See Rave, Kunstdiktatur, p. 54, and Lehmann-Haupt, Art, p. 114.)

[61] Bavarian government offices were built on Ludwigstrasse, and like Bestelmeyer's Luftwaffe center, they successfully blended with their early nineteenth-century surroundings. (See the photograph in Troost, Bauen, I, 82.) Also very traditional in their design were the House of German Medecine, on Briennerstrasse, the House of German Law, on Ludwigstrasse (Rittich, Architektur und Bauplastik, pp. 117 and 114), and the offices of the Munich Department of Finance (Troost, Bauen, II, 135).

Nevertheless, with his desire for impressive representative buildings in this German metropolis, Hitler planned suitable structures
to impress both natives and foreigners. Across the street from tne
House of German Art would be built an even larger House of
German Architecture, designed by Troost. Woldemar Brinkmann's
Opera House would seat 3000 people, and would be three times
as big as the Paris or Vienna operas. Its curving façade formed the
usual colonnaded portico. It would be less stark, but even more
impressive than the House of German Art. This was one of Hitler's
favorite projects and doubtlessly something that had occupied
his mind since he left Vienna and came to Munich in 1913. In the
early thirties, he solicited funds from wealthy sympathizers for
this new theater.[62] Typically, its size was very important to him,
for, as he said in a speech in the House of German Art in 1938,
"We want the *Volk* in their thousands to be able to participate in
the works of German art."[63] (Grandiose dimensions had, for Hitler, a political significance.)

To impress the arriving visitor, whether German or foreign, a
new railroad station was planned, which the well-known Bonatz
was commissioned to design.[64] Hitler personally insisted on a
dome form for the reception hall, although the Reichsbahn authorities themselves were opposed to this shape. The tracks would
be underground, recalling Hitler's plans for a railway station for
Linz, made before he had even left for Vienna in 1907 — another
example of the *Führer*'s adherence to his adolescent dreams.

Moreover, just as Berlin received a new airport, so was
Munich to have one in the Riem district, also to be designed by
Sagebiel. The plans followed those for Tempelhof quite closely;

[62] Heiden, *Der Fuehrer*, p. 357. Ziegler says that Hitler discussed his plans
with him in 1932. (Ziegler, *Adolf Hitler*, p. 188.)

[63] Domarus, *Reden*, p. 984 (December 10, 1938). See the model in Troost,
Bauen, I, 84.

[64] To be 136 meters high, its steel cupola would tower above Munich's land-
mark, the Church of Our Lady (1468–1488), which was only 99 meters high;
see Dehlinger, *Architektur der Superlative*, pp. 94–101; the plan is on pp. 103ff.
On the technical problems involved, see pp. 157–62.

the reception rooms, hangars, and workshops were similarly laid out in a long wide curve.[65] A subway was also planned for the city. Thus Germany's two capitals were to be provided with the latest of technologically modern structures in the field of transportation, combining representation with efficiency.[66]

The plans for two other cities important to Hitler, Nuremberg and Weimar, are also good examples of Nazi city reform.[67] Aside from having the great rally grounds, Nuremberg itself was to expand into large radial sections. Lotz explained that the rally grounds were wedge shaped so that they, too, could be incorporated into a "natural and organic," but orderly growth of the city.[68] Plans for Weimar dealt less with organic growth. Hitler overrode suggestions from the city architecture office to develop the town to the west because he wanted his *Führer* buildings in a parklike valley elsewhere.[69] As was typical with much of Hitler's building policy, especially when he intervened personally, acres of granite were to replace greenery.[70]

These cities are examples of the stages upon which Hitler's

[65] See Troost, *Bauen*, II, 133.

[66] As well as the giant party memorial and the reconstruction of the German pavilion at the Paris Exhibition as a theater museum, Munich was to have a "Hall of Heroes," planned by Speer for the Court Garden. (Dehlinger, *Architektur der Superlative*, sketch after p. 112.) There was to be a large exhibition building on the Theresienwiese, over the size of which Hitler and the Munich Board of Works quarreled; Hitler, favoring monumentality, won. A giant civic swimming pool, a Labor Front hotel, and two office towers for the party publishing house were also planned. (See Dehlinger, *Architektur*, pp. 81–96 for sketches and descriptions.) The classical style prevailed here, although Dehlinger suggests that one of the new ceremonial halls looked "Persian." (See the sketches after p. 117.)

[67] There were plans for redesigning twenty-seven German cities (other than Berlin, Munich, Nuremberg, and Linz). The *Gauleiter* of these cities hoped to outdo each other in the magnificence of their towns.

[68] Wilhelm Lotz, "Das Reichsparteitaggelände in Nürnberg," p. 192.

[69] "I have a special love for Weimar," Hitler told Ziegler in 1928. "I need it like I need Bayreuth." "The day will come," he added, "when I shall give this city and its theater [the German National Theater] a great deal more assistance." (Ziegler, *Adolf Hitler*, p. 12.)

[70] See the plans, in Dehlinger, *Architektur der Superlative*, after p. 76.

monumental "community" architecture was to be constructed. They provide a stunning contrast to the more strictly *völkisch* architecture built elsewhere; yet they are symbolic of Hitler's paramount aims, and they faithfully represent his Germany. The romantic thatched cottages of the *völkisch* school, although ideologically accepted, would never really belong in this new "community," which was to be organized around the cold stone symbols of Hitler's power.

CHAPTER TWELVE

The "Word" Falls on Deaf Ears

THE ERA of the Third Reich witnessed the building and planning of large government structures, huge stadiums, great open squares, monuments, *Thing* places, military buildings, Hitler Youth centers, schools, and highways. Whole cities, too, were to be redesigned. Some authors of the literature which preceded or accompanied this architecture were propagandists for the Nazi party's political aims. Others were devoted to specific social or even personal ends. But political propaganda and private hobbyhorses merge in these writings, so that it would be misleading to label any one writer "sincere" or another "cynical." Nearly all commentators reacted to the sudden modernization of society with fear that their traditional Germany was in danger of extinction. Even before 1933, the party's ideology seemed to promise regeneration of the national community, partially through architecture. Some writers were possibly influenced by the radical architects of the early Weimar period who sought a new approach to social problems; unlike the radicals, however, they wanted to preserve rather than to create, and to do so within a national, not a European framework. To be sure, Hitler, with his drive for political power, cannot be described as simply a German patriot; nor can men like the technocrat Albert Speer, with his single-minded youthful ambitions, be described as motivated solely by love of Germany. However, a reading of this literature shows that, in its architecture program, the National Socialist government seemed, to many intellectuals and architects, to be defending German tradition and German values. For most of these nationalists although the ideology denoted anti-Semitism or revision of the Versailles Treaty, it primarily meant the salvation of German *Kultur* in a world which threatened to destroy it. Fundamentally reactionary, it seemed to promise a return to a better, more stable time before foreign ideas started to erode German values and to disrupt the German community.[1] This dislike of the modern environment was exemplified in the first German Art Exhibition in Munich, 1937–1938, which showed photographs of approved architecture and of old villages, but none of modern urban life. For the writers, then, the new architecture expressed a hope for a more stable, strong community. They were pleased to see the new representative government buildings threatening foreigners with a statement of German strength and reminding doubters living in the Reich that a new patriotic ideology had triumphed. They called the styles of these buildings and of the new settlements "German," and derived a sense of security from their connotations of the "good old days."

Because the party's architectural program was so appealing, it did not need to be coercive. Obviously, there was no architectural revolution in 1933 — nor was one desired. With the exception of the *Thingplatz* idea, the architecture of the Third Reich was not new in any way.[2] For most commentators, the new buildings were a comfortable and proud reminder that the Reich government was strong and that old values were again secure. In

[1] Peter Gay writes of the "hunger for wholeness," the "fear of modernity," and the "desperate need for roots and for community," which he finds in the culture of Weimar period. (*Weimar Culture: the Outsider as Insider,* New York, Harper and Row, 1968, p. 96.) Rosenberg shared this attitude, as did many of the commentators on architecture.

[2] For example, the editor of the government publication on the Reich Sport Field wrote that the building of the Olympic Grounds was "a conservative deed" which was based on traditional ideas. (Germany, Ministry of the Interior, *Das Reichssportfeld,* Berlin, Reichssport-Verlag, 1936, p. 5.)

the same way, because many intellectuals of the traditional and *völkisch* schools supported the party, Goebbels, Speer, and Hitler hardly needed to hire propagandists for the new architecture. Writers such as Gerdy Troost and the Munich circle believed in what they were doing. This sort of "grass-roots" support from a respectable intelligentsia meant that the building program had its own momentum, regardless of whether Hitler set deadlines or spent too much.

This is not to say that the *Führer* had no influence on this literature or on building itself. His own interest in monumental representative buildings as well as squares and stadiums meant that any building program would first include such structures. His lack of interest in public housing and in the *Thing* movement meant that little would be accomplished in these fields, yet did not prevent programs from including them. At the same time, his continued use of racial jargon inspired the Labor Front to erect buildings in the *völkisch* style and to publish books which explained how these structures expressed the ideology. Although, therefore, freedom existed to build any type of structure within widely placed limits, if the *Führer* was not interested, construction might cease, as with the *Thing* movement decline after 1937.

Hitler's concept of monumental architecture embodied a few simple principles, which the writers seem to have shared or adopted. He believed that architecture could be didactic and hence could be used as propaganda. Size was thus important to him; monumentality, above anything else, impressed the viewer, drew his attention to the "message" of the building, and also intimidated the little man. He rarely expressed his desire to control an unruly mob by ordering it in stadiums or squares, but he did declare that architecture could teach the crowd proper patriotic ideas. Publicly, too, he spoke of "the Word in stone," both reflecting and influencing those who propagandized symbolic and didactic architecture. Most of the writers agreed with Hitler, who claimed that his buildings would give the Germans, with their supposed inferiority complex, a sense of pride in German architectural achievements, while also teaching them that it was through him and his party that the Volk accomplished these "community" monuments.

Hitler called his monumental representative buildings "community" architecture, meaning that they expressed the strength of the united German people and that they were edifices which could give all Germans a sense of pride. But after reading these books and articles, and seeing the term "community" interpreted in so many different ways, one begins to wonder if it retained any real meaning. Some felt that good "German" architecture would express the patriotic unity of the Volk, and would hence be "community" architecture. Others, considering the country as a psychological whole, wrote that Nazi buildings would encourage group thinking and communal responses, helping to suppress selfish individualism. Some writers tried to show how the large new buildings were somehow created by the whole community through exercise of its "will." Obviously, Hitler's use of a term usually associated with socialist or public-housing projects was confusing; yet its vagueness was also encouraging, for it seemed to include all forms of architecture, and even more important, was patriotic. At all events, the Führer was often echoed in this literature because the concept of "community" architecture appealed to the widespread desire for conservative change in nationalist intellectuals reacting against modernity. These men were glad to see a government which maintained it was doing something for the German community and which could show as proof magnificent buildings. Thus the Nazi building program was successful with these writers because of its stress on the national community and its well being.

It was illogical to create buildings in order to stimulate community feelings, while at the same time repeatedly stating that community feeling had died out in Germany and that only communal unity could create great architecture. However, the kind

of community spirit, which the writers wished to see reborn, was
dead in Germany and would never revive. Thus the aim of these
writers was hopelessly utopian; they fell into the same fallacy as
did the historicist architects of the "age of decadence" which they
themselves condemned. Yet they did not seem to notice this lapse
in logic. Even where political propaganda colored their writing,
they seemed to be afflicted with wishful thinking.

There is a fundamental illogicality in the nationalist concept
of architecture as witness to national greatness. Whereas the Middle Ages might have created impressive buildings because the
German people then possessed a unified world view, the construction of large buildings in modern Germany did not necessarily indicate that such a situation existed in the Third Reich. How many
Germans were dedicated Nazis? Or, to narrow the range, how
many had the same hopes for Germany as did the Nazi party?
Surely not the vast majority of the population. The writers tacitly
admitted this when they hoped that architecture would teach.
Moreover, the great medieval cities which these writers loved
were produced at the end of a thousand-year development, in the
high Middle Ages. Yet the writers expected that, three or four
years after its inception, the "thousand-year Reich" would be able
to produce something akin to medieval glories. The cart came
before the horse.[3]

[3] Another instance of the diversity and illogicality of thinking on patriotic
architecture is found in the writing on Italian fascist architecture. The monumental neo-classicism of fascist Rome (the Foro Mussolini, for example) was seen as
embodying similar characteristics as German monumental buildings. Schüller
found the new Italian architecture "a clear and living mirror of a *Volk* molded
into a new unity," and a symbol of "the Italian *Volk*'s will to build." (*Das Rom
Mussolinis*, pp. 9 and 110.) The architect Hans Henniger noted that Italy's newer
buildings reflected "national characteristics." ("Die Baukunst des Faschismus,"
Deutsche Bauzeitung, LXXII (1938), 194–195.) Neither writer explained how
the Germans and the Italians could have the same national traits, but no doubt
the monumental traditionalism of the approved style and the "collapse of the
liberal epoch" (Schüller, *Das Rom Mussolinis*, p. 101) was appealing to antimodern architects. After the Rome-Berlin Axis was formed in 1936, articles and
books stressing links between these two dissimilar peoples were pleasing to the
government.

Moreover, not only was this view of architecture illogical, but the writers' knowledge of history was incorrect. Although the German-speaking parts of medieval Europe shared a common religious faith and were part of an empire, there was no such thing as a national community in the sense implied in this literature. In fact, not only did the German towns (usually cited as examples of corporate unity) soon become dominated by selfish oligarchies, but they also fought the German princes as well as each other, and resisted the attempts of the German emperor to increase his "national" power.

Another problem which the writers admitted only obliquely was that most styles in European architecture originated outside the linguistic area of Germany. Gothic was French, for example, and baroque was Italian. Probably only the Romanesque and — ironically — the *avant-garde* could be called German, but even in these two instances an argument could be made for their international origins. Faced with the creative sterility of German architecture, one writer claimed that nearly all styles prevalent in Germany were German: "The German style lives in the Romanesque . . . in the late Gothic, in the late Renaissance . . . in the late baroque of the rococo, in the *Jugendstil,* in folk art, etc., with such unmistakable vigor that one can almost speak of an 'eternal Gothic' as a way of describing the Faustian-German."[4] This comfortable vagueness was analogous to the manner in which the ideology was all things to all men.

These lapses, however, were not noticed because of the irrationalism of the whole intellectual mood of the time. The appeal to community feelings and to nationalism which suffused this literature suggests that for most writers, the National Socialist ideology was primarily a set of comfortable German patriotic principles, rather than a political doctrine or a philosophy of life. Moreover, the architecture which the government built after 1933 seems to bear this out. There was no one "Nazi" style, but Gerdy

---

[4] Eberlein, *Was ist deutsch in der deutschen Kunst?* p. 50.

Troost could comment that "in no other field of artistic creativity
has the ideological experience been so fruitful as in architecture."[5]
Desperately needing to feel proud of Germany, the commentators
made everything that was built seem "German" and thus a product
of the new national ideology. Also every style in the Third Reich
reflects an aspect of the multifarious ideology; thus, in a way that
Frau Troost probably did not intend, her statement was validated.
At the same time, these different styles were not necessarily contradictory. Some writers found a unity between the neo-classical
and the *völkisch* styles, a unity based on the supposedly identical
racial roots of each. Indeed, this racial consciousness was the basis
of the most right-wing nationalist thinking on architecture. The
architect's racial origin determined his building concepts. As so
many wrote, it was the "idea" or the "spirit" (which was always
based on "blood") that produced a structure. Thus it was not
the outward appearance of a building which really mattered, but
rather the ideology which created the impulse to build. Hence
if the ideology is considered as a form of extreme nationalism,
the architecture it produced did have a uniformity, spurious perhaps to the unbeliever, but real to many nationalist and right-wing
Germans, who saw the ideology as a set of German truths. Their
faith could accept structures which resembled the "worst" of
the "Bolshevik-Jewish" trend, provided the "ideas" which created
them included the improved health of the *Volk* or increased industrial production. Particular aspects of the ideology, such as
reverence for the soil, affected thinking on rural architecture,
and the stress on natural materials drawn from the "German"
earth gave a special "German" value to any structure, even the
Berlin Chancellery. Every kind of building and every style fitted
into this theory of architecture, although, because the monumental
or neo-classical style was more important to Hitler than any
völkisch or peasant style, the most "German" aspect of thinking
on architecture (the *völkisch*) was less well represented than

[5] Troost, *Bauen*, I, 10.

the most European aspect (the neo-classical). All traditional styles, except the Gothic, were to be found in the new buildings, and all traditional styles, even occasionally the Gothic, were described as "German." Because they were "German," they were good.

The dispute over the *avant-garde* was obscured in these writings, because a "German" definition of functionalism developed. For most of the writers, functionalism meant that each building should be designed to best fulfill its function. This did not mean the application of abstract rules to every building (as allegedly with the *Bauhaus* architects), but rather that a government building should express power and authority, while a peasant's home should express the peasant's values, such as love for the soil and the landscape. Through a lean, stark appearance, a factory could express ideals of efficiency and sobriety.

The "new" architecture and its commentary reflected well the unsettled state of right-wing German nationalists, newly thrust into the modern urban industrial society with their patriotism outraged and given, in 1918, a political jolt as well. The new buildings expressed facets of the eclectic and pragmatic ideology, particularly xenophobic patriotism. Thus the task of the commentators was a relatively easy one. Every new building, whatever its function, or style — because it was an object of national pride — became a manifestation of "the Word in stone."

The fate of "Nazi" architecture in postwar Germany is interesting. Much of it has survived, because its sturdy construction defied bomb damage. Much of it is also in use, as Germans were compelled to use any buildings left standing, regardless of their history or connotations. Moreover, structures such as the *Führer* and Administration buildings in Munich are technically modern edifices, for Nazi architects, despite their dislike of certain aspects of technological society, did not scorn up-to-date lighting or heating devices. Thus, the Munich buildings continue to serve the community (as an art gallery, music academy, and civic

archive), but not in the ideological sense which Werner Rittich
or Gerdy Troost desired. The many hostels also serve the youth
of Germany, and the Berlin Olympic Stadium serves the athletic
needs of the community, but, in both cases, without the racist
overtones of the Third Reich. The House of German Art in
Munich (now called the House of Art), exhibits paintings for
the community, but without the attempt to teach what "Aryan"
art is, or what "decadent" art is. Some structures, such as the
Thing places or the Nuremberg Zeppelin Field, cannot be used
for their original purpose, but they serve occasionally as outdoor
concert sites and multipurpose sport fields. A structure like the
Nuremberg Congress Hall, never completed, looms grotesquely
over the Dutzend Lake, but the floor of its vast interior has been
used as a tennis court, and the two adjacent halls are used by a
recording studio. Hence, in ways the writers did not intend, Nazi
"community" architecture still serves the German community.

Aesthetically, most of the above structures are not appealing
to contemporary taste. The House of German Art and the Olympic
Stadium, for example, although admittedly imposing buildings,
seem unduly severe and heavy. Yet they are probably not much
different than buildings architects in the rest of Europe designed
in the thirties, forties, and fifties. Many of these designers shed
the over-decoration of the later nineteenth century, yet lacked
the boldness to use confidently the new architecture of glass, steel,
or concrete, and produced noncommittal, blank stone walls and
boringly empty façades. Many a city in North America and
Europe possesses a town hall or court house in this transitional
style, vaguely traditional, but not yet modern. Of all the deliberately ideological structures of the Third Reich, only the youth
hostels are still attractive, and exude an admirable respect for
local architectural tradition and landscape.

As for the "decadent" architecture of the twenties, it suffered
little during the peaceful years of the Third Reich, although, as
has been noted, flat-roofed structures were sometimes "improved"

by being given peaked roofs. Less was built in this style than earlier, of course. During the war, aerial bombardment and house-to-house fighting did not discriminate among buildings, and some of the finest examples of the modern style, such as Mendelsohn's Columbushaus (1931–1932) in Berlin, were destroyed along with the architecture of earlier centuries. When Germany began to rebuild, many architects chose to work in the styles pioneered by the "decadent" architects. As a result, the architectural sights of modern German cities are often strikingly modern buildings such as the Philharmonic Hall (Scharoun) or the new National Gallery (Mies van der Rohe) in Berlin. Although careful restoration has been made on medieval buildings in old towns like Nuremberg, there has been no widespread attempt to continue the "healthy" "Doric" classicism of the Nazi years. Of course, the architecture of the Third Reich was by no means totally worthless. In technical buildings, there was some stylistic continuity between the twenties and the thirties. The youth hostels contributed to the rural German scene. The highways and their bridges were also a notable achievement.

Nevertheless, the nationalist theory of architecture seems to have had little profound or lasting influence. Architecture, because of the limits that practical necessity place on it, and because of its relatively limited range of expressiveness, as compared to painting or sculpture, is not an art that easily lends itself to an ideological purpose.[6] Consequently, "National Socialist" or "German" architecture, particularly in its monumental form, remained to a large extent a creature of the imagination of the writers. An interesting study could be made of the impression this architecture actually had on people; there are many instances of its failing to impress at all, and many witty nicknames were coined for certain Nazi buildings. Domarus doubts that the Germans learned anything from this didactic architecture. "The passion of the Third Reich for representation," he writes, "found little response

[6] Lehmann-Haupt discusses this well. (*Art*, p. 25.)

with the German people. Their attitude was cautious, even dis-
trustful."[7] The nationalists' efforts suggest that buildings probably
cannot function as propaganda. Perhaps, too, the monumental
architecture of the Third Reich was simply too ugly to elicit an
ideological reaction, whereas the *völkisch* buildings were too
familiar and acceptable to elicit any political reaction at all. At
all events, even the most emphatically "Nazi" buildings seem to
have failed in the long run to carry the message expected of
them. The Königsplatz in Munich, or the House of German Art
in the same city, do not seem to speak to Germans today of
"Aryan" values. The Air Ministry in communist East Berlin, where
one might expect a decidedly negative reaction to "Nazi" architecture, still stands and is in use. Because nearly every German
city has some such structure which could carry the ideological
torch, then (given the Nazis' architectural theory) surely the
neo-Nazi movements of the fifties and the sixties might have been
stronger. Indeed, considering the relative weakness of these movements, as well as the public skepticism toward these buildings, it
is evident that the "Word in stone" never reached and is still not
reaching the majority of the German *Volk*.

[7] *Reden*, pp. 1035–1036.

Bibliography

Prefatory note

As THIS book was primarily based on a study of books printed in the Third Reich, articles in newspapers and periodicals do not appear in the bibliography. Neither does a reference to the long invaluable exchange of letters with Albert Speer; the reader will find precise references to this correspondence and to journal articles in the footnotes.

The Nazi party directly administered the Knorr und Hirth, the Albert Langen-Georg Müller, and the Deutsche publishing houses. Any mention of the Zentralverlag der NSDAP (or Franz Eher Nachf.), the Verlag der Deutschen Arbeitsfront, the Reichssport-Verlag, or a Gauverlag refers to publishing firms of the party itself or the government. The Nordland and Hoheneichen presses worked for individual branches of the party, while the Volk und Reich, Hanseatische, Lehmann, Schlieffen, and Stalling publishing houses were favorable to the Nazis. (See Dietrich Strothmann, *Nationalsozialistische Literaturpolitik. Ein Beitrag zur Publizistik im dritten Reich*, Bonn, Bouvier 1968, section C; and Oron J. Hale, *The Captive Press in the Third Reich*, Princeton, N. J., Princeton University Press, 1964.) Although all publishers had to toe the government line and although the Gestapo was prepared to seize editions of books considered undesirable, deviations from the party line (which was not consistent at the best of times) were tolerated, if the subject was not considered too dangerous. (See Lehmann-Haupt, *Art under a Dictatorship*, p. 104; and Paul Otto Rave, *Kunstdiktatur im dritten Reich*, Hamburg, Mann, 1949, p. 73.) After forbidding the publishing of specifically *avant-garde* works, it seems the government may have had little need to create a literature on "German" architecture, so great was the national interest.

282   THE WORD IN STONE

Bibliographies

Bauen im nationalsozialistischen Deutschland: ein Schrifttumsverzeichnis. Munich, Zentralverlag der NSDAP, Eher, 1940.

Heinz, Greta and Agnes F. Peterson, eds. *NSDAP Hauptarchiv: Guide to the Hoover Institution Microfilm Collection.* Stanford, Hoover Institution on War, Revolution, and Peace, 1964.

Jürgens, Adolf, ed. *Ergebnisse deutscher Wissenschaft: eine bibliographische Auswahl aus der deutschen wissenschaftlichen Literatur der Jahre 1933–35.* Berlin, Essener Verlagsanstalt, 1939.

Collections of Articles, Readings, Documents

International Military Tribunal. *Trial of the Major War Criminals before the International Military Tribunal, Nuremberg, 14 November 1945 – 1 October 1946,* Nuremberg, 1947–1949.

Mosse, George L., ed. *Nazi Culture: Intellectual, Cultural and Social Life in the Third Reich.* New York, Grosset and Dunlap, 1966.

Teut, Anna, ed. *Architektur im Dritten Reich 1933–45.* Berlin, Ullstein, 1967.

Volz, Hans, ed. *Von der Grossmacht zur Weltmacht 1937.* Berlin, Junker und Dünnhaupt, 1939.

Wulf, Joseph, ed. *Die bildenden Künste im dritten Reich: Eine Dokumentation.* Gütersloh, Sigbert Mohn, 1964.

Wulf, Joseph, ed. *Theater und Film im dritten Reich: Eine Dokumentation.* Gütersloh, Sigbert Mohn, 1964.

National Socialist, Völkisch, and Other Contemporary Literature on Architecture and Politics

Anheisser, Roland. *Das mittelalterliche Wohnhaus in deutschstämmigen Landen: Seine Schönheit im Stadtbild in Aufbau und Einzelheit.* Stuttgart, Strecker und Schroeder, 1935.

Böckler, Erich. *Landschaftsgemäss bauen? Eine Antwort durch Wort und Bild.* Munich, Callwey, 1943.

Braumüller, Wolf. *Freilicht- und Thingspiel: Rückschau und Forderungen.* Berlin, Volksschaft-Verlag für Buch, Bühne, und Film, 1935.

Darré, Walther R. *Neuadel aus Blut und Boden.* Munich, Lehmann, 1935.

Decker, Will. *Kreuze am Wege zur Freiheit: Ein Ehren- und Gedächtnisbuch.* Leipzig, Koehler, 1935.

Dresler, Adolf. *Das Braune Haus und das Verwaltungsgebäude der Reichsleitung der NSDAP.* 3rd ed. Munich, Zentralverlag der NSDAP, Eher, 1939.

Dreyer, Ernst Adolf, ed. *Deutsche Kultur im neuen Reich.* Berlin, Schlieffen, 1935.

Eberlein, Kurt Karl. *Was ist deutsch in der deutschen Kunst?* Leipzig, Seemann, 1934.

Eilemann, Johannes. *Deutsche Seele, deutscher Mensch, deutsche Kultur, und Nationalsozialismus.* Leipzig, Quelle und Meyer, 1933.

Emmel, Felix. *Theater aus deutschem Wesen.* Berlin, Georg Stilke, 1937.

Erffa, Wolfram Freiherr von. *Das Dorfkirche als Wehrbau.* Stuttgart, Kohlhammer, 1937.

Erste deutsche Architektur- und Kunsthandwerkaustellung, im Haus der deutschen Kunst zu München, 22. Januar bis 27. März 1938. Munich, Knorr und Hirth, 1938.

Feder, Gottfried. *Die neue Stadt.* Berlin, Springer, 1939.

Feistel-Rohmeder, Bettina. *Im Terror des Kunstbolschewismus.* Karlsruhe, Müller, 1938.

Fritz, Georg. *Strassen und Bauten Adolf Hitlers,* Berlin, Verlag der Deutschen Arbeitsfront, 1939.

Germany. Ministry of the Interior. *Das Reichssportfeld,* Berlin, Reichssport-Verlag, 1936.

Goebbels, Joseph. *Vom Kaiserhof zur Reichskanzlei, eine historische Darstellung in Tagebuchblättern.* Munich, Zentralverlag der NSDAP, Eher, 1934.

Goering, Hermann. "Die Bauten des 3. Reiches," *Reden und Aufsätze.* Munich, Eher, 1938.

Günther, Hans F. K. *Rasse und Stil,* Munich, Lehmann, 1926.

Günther, Hans F. K., *Die Verstädterung.* 3rd ed. Leipzig-Berlin, Teubner, 1938.

Hager, Werner. *Die Bauten des deutschen Barocks 1690–1770.* Jena, Eugen Diederichs, 1942.

Hansen, Walter. *Judenkunst in Deutschland.* Berlin, Nordland-Verlag, 1942.

Harth, Philip. "Die Bedeutung des Dreidimensionalen in der Architektur," *Aufsätze über Bildhauerische Gestaltung.* Berlin, Riemerschmidt, 1939.

Hartmann, Heinrich. *Werkhefte für den Heimbau der Hitler-Jugend.* Ed. by the Reichsjugendführung der NSDAP. Leipzig, Skacel, 1937, Vol. I.

Haupt, Albrecht. *Die älteste Kunst insbesondere die Baukunst der Germanen von der Völkerwanderungen bis zu Karl dem Grossen.* Leipzig, Degener, 1909.

Hoffmann, Heinrich. *Deutschland in Paris: Ein Bilderbuch von Heinrich Hoffmann.* Munich, Heinrich Hoffmann Verlag, 1937.

Labouchère, G. C. "Der Anteil der Niederlande an der Entwicklung der nordische Baukunst," *Die Niederlande im Umbruch der Zeiten.* Ed. by Max Freiherr du Prel. Würzburg, Konrad Triltsch, 1941.

Lindner, W., and Erich Böckler. *Die Stadt: Ihre Pflege und Gestaltung.* Munich, Callwey, 1939.

Lindner, W., and Erich Kulke et al. *Das Dorf: Seine Pflege und Gestaltung.* Munich, Callwey, n. d.

Lotz, Wilhelm. "So baut Europa," *Europa: Handbuch der politischen, wirtschaftlichen und kulturellen Entwicklung des neuen Europa.* Ed. by the Deutsches Institut für aussenpolitische Forschung. Leipzig, Helingsche Verlagsanstalt, 1943, pp. 173–183.

March, Werner. *Bauwerk Reichssportfeld.* Illustrated by Charlotte Rohrbach. Berlin, Deutscher Kunstverlag, 1936.

Moeller van den Bruck, Arthur. *Der preussische Stil.* 5th ed. Breslau, Korn, 1931.

Müseler, Wilhelm. *Europäische Kunst: Völker und Zeiten.* Berlin, Safari, 1942.

Wolters, Rudolf. *Neue Deutsche Baukunst.* (Edited by Albert Speer.) Berlin, Volk und Reich, 1943.

Oncken, Alste. *Friedrich Gilly, 1772–1800.* Berlin, Deutscher Verein für Kunstwissenschaft, 1935.

Pfister, Rudolf, ed. *Bauten Schultze-Naumburgs.* Weimar, Alexander Duncker, n.d.

Pinder, W. "Architektur als Moral," *Gesammelte Aufsätze aus den Jahren 1907–1935.* Leipzig, Seemann, 1938.

Reichsheimstättenamt der Deutschen Arbeitsfront. Planungsabteilung. *Städtebild und Landschaft.* Berlin, Verlag der Deutschen Arbeitsfront, 1939.

Rietdorf, Alfred. *Gilly: Wiedergeburt der Architektur.* Berlin, Hans von Hugo, 1943.

Rittich, Werner. *Architektur und Bauplastik der Gegenwart,* 3rd ed Berlin, Rembrandt, n.d.

Rosenberg, Alfred. *Der deutsche Ordensstaat: Ein neuer Abschitt in der Entwicklung des nationalsozialistischen Staatsgedankens.* Munich, Zentralverlag der NSDAP, Eher, 1934.

Rosenberg, Alfred. *Gestaltung der Idee: Blut und Ehre.* Vol. II: *Reden und Aufsätze von 1933–35.* Munich, Zentralverlag der NSDAP, Eher, 1942.

Rosenberg, Alfred. *Der Mythus des 20. Jahrhunderts: Eine Wertung der seelischgeistigen Gestaltenkämpfe unserer Zeit.* Munich, Hoheneichen, 1936.

Rosenberg, Alfred. *Das politische Tagebuch aus den Jahren 1934, 1935, und 1939.* Munich, Deutscher Taschenbuch Verlag, 1964.

Rosenberg, Alfred. *Portrait eines Menschheitsverbrechers: Nach dem hinterlassenen Memoiren des ehemaligen Reichsministers.* Ed. by Serge Land and Ernst von Schenck. St. Gallen, Zollikofer, 1947.

Rosenberg, Alfred. *Revolution in der bildenden Kunst.* Munich, Zentralverlag der NSDAP, Eher, 1934.

Schäfer, Carl. *Deutsche Holzbaukunst: die Grundlagen der deutschen Holzbauweisen in ihrer konstruktiven und formalen Lage.* Dresden, Jess, 1937.

Schirach, Baldur von. *Revolution der Erziehung: Reden aus den Jahren des Aufbaus.* Munich, Zentralverlag der NSDAP, Eher, 1942.

Schlösser, Rainer. *Das Volk und seine Bühne: Bemerkungen zum Aufbau des deutschen Theaters.* Berlin, Langen Müller, 1935.

Schmitthenner, Paul. *Die Baukunst im neuen Reich,* Munich, Callwey, 1934.

Schönleben, Eduard. *Fritz Todt, der Mensch, der Ingenieur, der Nationalsozialist: Ein Bericht über Leben und Werk.* Oldenburg, Stalling, 1943.

Schrade, Hubert. *Bauten des dritten Reiches.* Leipzig, Bibliographisches Institut, 1937.

Schrade, Hubert. *Das deutsche Nationaldenkmal.* Munich, Langen Müller, 1934.

Schramm, Wilhelm von. *Neubau des deutschen Theaters: Ergebnisse und Forderungen.* Berlin, Schlieffen, 1934.

Schüller, Sepp. *Das Rom Mussolinis: Rom als moderne Hauptstadt.* Düsseldorf, Mosella, 1943.

Schulte-Frohlinde, Julius, ed. *Die landschaftlichen Grundlagen des deutschen Bauschaffens: Der Osten.* Munich, Callwey, n.d.

Schultze-Naumburg, Paul. *Die Kunst der Deutschen: Ihr Wesen und ihre Werke.* Stuttgart, Deutsche Verlags-Anstalt, 1934.

Schultze-Naumburg, Paul. *Kunst und Rasse*. Munich-Berlin, Lehmann, 1938.

Schultze-Naumberg, Paul. *Städtebau*. Vol. IV of *Kulturarbeiten*, Munich, Callwey, 1909.

Senger, Alexander von. *Krisis der Architektur*. Zürich, Rascher, 1928.

Speer, Albert, ed. *Die neue Reichskanzlei*, 3rd ed. Munich, Zentralverlag der NSDAP, Eher, 1940.

Stephan, Hans. *Die Baukunst im dritten Reich: Insbesondere die Umgestaltung der Reichshauptstadt*. Berlin, Junker und Dünnhaupt, 1939.

Stephan, Hans. *Wilhelm Kreis*. Oldenburg, Stalling, 1944.

Straub, Karl Willy. *Architektur im Dritten Reich*. Stuttgart, Akademischer Verlag Dr. Fritz Wedekind, 1932.

Tamms, Friedrich, ed. *Paul Bonatz: Arbeiten aus den Jahren 1907 bis 1937*. Stuttgart, Hoffmann, 1937.

Thiede, Klaus. *Das Erbe germanischer Baukunst im bäuerlichen Hausbau*. Hamburg, Hanseatische Verlagsanstalt, 1936.

Todt, Fritz, ed. *Die Strassen Adolf Hitlers*. Berlin, Hermann Hillger, 1938.

Troost, Gerdy, ed. *Das Bauen im neuen Reich*, Vol. I, 1938; Vol. II, 1943. Bayreuth, Gauverlag Bayrische Ostmark.

Wendland, Winfried. *Kunst und Nation: Ziel und Wege der Kunst im Neuen Deutschland*. Berlin, Reimar Hobbing, 1934.

Willrich, Wolfgang. *Säuberung des Kunsttempels: Eine Kunstpolitische Kampfschrift zur Gesundung deutscher Kunst im Geiste nordischer Art*. 2nd ed. Munich, Lehmanns, 1938.

Wolters, Rudolf. *Albert Speer*. Oldenburg, Stalling, 1943.

Wolters, Rudolf. *Vom Beruf des Baumeisters*. Berlin, Volk und Reich, 1944.

Ziegler, Hans Severus. *Wende und Weg: Kulturpolitische Reden und Aufsätze*. Weimar, Fritz Fink Verlag, 1937.

The Works, Speeches and Conversations of Hitler:

Baynes, Norman H., ed. *The Speeches of Adolf Hitler, April 1927–August 1939*. London, Oxford, 1942. 2 vols.

Die deutsche Kunst als stolzeste Verteidigung des deutschen Volkes: Rede, gehalten auf der Kulturtagung des Parteitages 1933. Munich, Zentralverlag der NSDAP, Eher, 1939.

Domarus, Max, ed. *Reden und Proklamationen, 1932–45.* Munich, Süddeutscher Verlag, 1965.

Hitler's Secret Conversations, 1941–44. New York, Signet Books, 1961.

Hoffman, Heinrich, ed. *Sieben Aquarelle.* Munich, Heinrich Hoffman, Reichsbildberichterstatter der NSDAP, 1938.

Mein Kampf. Boston, Houghton Mifflin, 1962.

Picker, Henry. *Hitlers Tischgespräche im Führerhauptquartier, 1941–1942.* Ed. by Percy Ernst Schramm, with Andreas Hillgruber and Martin Vogt, Stuttgart, Seewald, 1963.

Reden des Führers am Parteitag Grossdeutschland 1938. Munich, Zentralverlag der NSDAP, Franz Eher, 1939.

Index

Note: major buildings constructed during the Third Reich and discussed at any length in this book are given a separate entry below. Other buildings are listed under their location, usually a city.